THE LOST GOLD
OF ROME

To Italy, for granting me political asylum in 1984 and to my Italian-Canadian wife Maria

THE LOST GOLD
OF ROME

THE HUNT FOR
ALARIC'S TREASURE

DANIEL COSTA

SUTTON PUBLISHING

First published in the United Kingdom in 2007 by
Sutton Publishing Limited · Phoenix Mill
Thrupp · Stroud · Gloucestershire · GL5 2BU

British Library Cataloguing in Publication Data
A catalogue record for this book is available from the British Library.

Hardback ISBN 978-0-7509-4397-0
Paperback ISBN 978-0-7509-4398-7

Typeset in Sabon.
Typesetting and origination by
Sutton Publishing Limited.
Printed and bound in England.

Contents

List of Plates

Acknowledgements

The late Giovanni Paganini, a Roman and a dear friend, sent me valuable books about the archaeology and history of Rome. To Luigi di Girolamo from Rome I owe thanks for help in contacting the Italian authorities in charge of granting permission for reproduction and photographic rights, and for the books he kindly gave me. I also wish to register my appreciation of the expert help provided by Roberto Piperno, also of Rome, both in person and through his superb website (www.romeartlover.it), in locating old prints depicting Roman sites of interest to this investigation. My sincere thanks go to the Ministerio per i Beni e le Attività Culturali for allowing me to include in this book photographs of buildings' exteriors in Rome.

I am grateful too to Nicolino Noce, retired lawyer of Siderno, Calabria, for infusing me with his enthusiasm for the history of Calabria and Cosenza and for encouraging me to persist in the writing of this book. My sincere thanks go to Franco Noce from Cosenza for guiding me through the fascinating old quarter of the town and for his other contributions. I am grateful too to Dr Michele Noce of Rome for his suggestions. To Giovanni de Marco from Celico, the province of Cosenza, I am indebted for the pictures of Busento and Cosenza. Finally, I would like to acknowledge the help of Ursula and Axel Stuck (Mississauga, Ontario, Canada) with the translation of von Platen's poem.

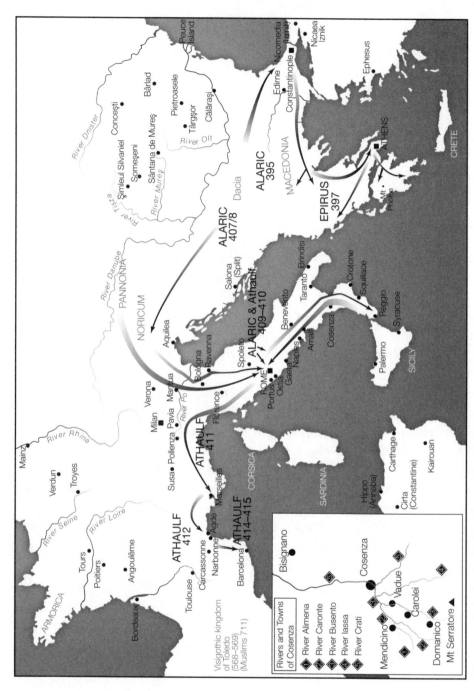

The Visigoths before and after the death of Alaric in 410.

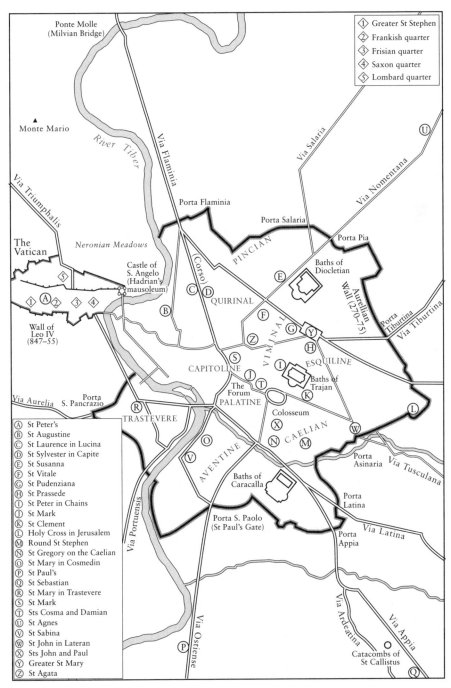

1	Greater St Stephen	
2	Frankish quarter	
3	Frisian quarter	
4	Saxon quarter	
5	Lombard quarter	

Ponte Molle
(Milvian Bridge)

Monte Mario

River Tiber

Via Flaminia

Via Triumphalis

Via Salaria

Via Nomentana

U

The
Vatican

Neronian Meadows

Porta Flaminia

Porta Salaria

Porta Pia

PINCIAN

Castle of
S. Angelo
(Hadrian's
mausoleum)

(Corso)

Baths of
Diocletian

E

Aurelian Wall (270–75)

5
1 A 2 3 4

C D

QUIRINAL

Wall of
Leo IV
(847–55)

B

F

G

Y

Porta
Tiburtina

Via Tiburtina

Z

VIMINAL

H

CAPITOLINE

S

ESQUILINE

Via Aurelia

Porta
S. Pancrazio

R

J

I

Baths of
Trajan

L

T

K

TRASTEVERE

The
Forum
PALATINE

Colosseum

Holy Cross in Jerusalem

W

X

O

N

CAELIAN

M

Porta
Asinaria

Via Tusculana

V

AVENTINE

Baths of
Caracalla

Porta
Latina

Via Portuensis

Porta S. Paolo
(St Paul's Gate)

Porta
Appia

Via Latina

Ⓐ St Peter's
Ⓑ St Augustine
Ⓒ St Laurence in Lucina
Ⓓ St Sylvester in Capite
Ⓔ St Susanna
Ⓕ St Vitale
Ⓖ St Pudenziana
Ⓗ St Prassede
Ⓘ St Peter in Chains
Ⓙ St Mark
Ⓚ St Clement
Ⓛ Holy Cross in Jerusalem
Ⓜ Round St Stephen
Ⓝ St Gregory on the Caelian
Ⓞ St Mary in Cosmedin
Ⓟ St Paul's
Ⓠ St Sebastian
Ⓡ St Mary in Trastevere
Ⓢ St Mark
Ⓣ Sts Cosma and Damian
Ⓤ St Agnes
Ⓥ St Sabina
Ⓦ St John in Lateran
Ⓧ Sts John and Paul
Ⓨ Greater St Mary
Ⓩ St Agata

Via Ostiense

P

Via Ardeatina

Via Appia

Catacombs of
St Callistus

Q

Plan of late ancient and medieval Rome (after Shepherd). *(Courtesy of The General
Libraries, University of Texas at Austin)*

Preface

To date, only seven books about the Visigothic king Alaric have been published, two of them novels. *Alarich: Roman aus der Volkerwanderung* (Alaric: A Novel of the Migration of the Peoples) by Woldemar Urban, was issued in 1889 by Reissner Verlag, Leipzig. *Alarich* by Franz Spunda, published in 1937 by Bischoff Verlag, Vienna, was also a historical novel. *La vie d'Alaric* (The Life of Alaric) by Marcel Brion of the French Academy, published in 1930 by Gallimard, Paris, was a romanticised biography. It covers Alaric's burial in six pages. *Alarico: Nell'inerte Impero* (Alaric: Inside the Inert Empire) by Aldo Mazzolai, published in 1996 by Le Lettere in Italy, covers Alaric's life, but allots only four pages to a discussion of the mystery of his burial. *Alarico. Re dei Visigoti* (Alaric. King of the Visigoths), published in 2000 by Le Nuvole in Italy, is a collection of articles by five different contributors. This work was presented in Milan on the occasion of the participation of the city of Cosenza in the Borsa Internazionale del Turismo (BIT) in February 2000. The book discusses the role of the historical and mythical accounts of Alaric's burial in the development of Cosentine identity. I have not been able to find *Alarico* by Coriolano Martirano, published by Periferia in Cosenza in 1999. Finally, there is the epic poem 'Alaric ou Rome Vaincu' (Alaric or Rome Vanquished) by Georges de Scudery, published in The Hague in 1685.

I believe I am the first author of non-fiction to examine systematically various aspects of the fascinating search for Alaric's grave and treasure in the context of his deeds and the crucial events of his era. There are many limitations to the historical and archaeological evidence available for such an early period. As a result, much of what we know about the Visigothic king derives from a mixture of ancient literary sources, archaeological evidence for life in late antiquity and a bit of knowledgeable guesswork.

In the preparation of this book, I have examined the culture of the Goths as far as the sources available permit. I have consulted both ancient and modern works of history. Fully aware of the impact the press has on the general public, I have also researched the archives of major newspapers from many countries. I have, too, examined various academic sources. I have made every effort to be as precise as possible. The figures are intended to help the reader locate many of the important sites and events mentioned in the book.

Most readers are unlikely to go digging to find Alaric's tomb and treasure. However, there are many other wonderful intellectual and emotional experiences to be found in the search for Alaric's grave, not least the excitement of discovery when previously disparate facts suddenly come together. I hope every reader finds this type of treasure.

Daniel Costa
Toronto, Ontario

Introduction: Alaric Alive

O Romans, be it your care to rule the nations with imperial sway; these shall be your arts: to impose the rule of peace, to spare the humble and to crush the proud.

Virgil, *Aeneid*, Book 6, ll. 851–3

This book is an investigation into the search for the treasure of Alaric I, king of the migrant Visigoths, who between 24 and 27 August AD 410 sacked the wealthy city of Rome and died shortly thereafter.[1] In 551 or 552, Jordanes, a Germanic Christian who lived in the Eastern Roman Empire in the time of Emperor Justinian, wrote in his *Getica (The Origins and Deeds of the Goths)* that Alaric was secretly buried 'with many treasures' under the River Busento near Cosenza, southern Italy.[2]

The hunt for this treasure is hundreds of years old and stretches from the fourteenth to the eighteenth centuries and to the Third Reich and beyond. Over the years, many amateur archaeologists thought they had found the tomb of the Visigothic king, but expert examinations never confirmed their claims. Alaric's grave is still being sought by academic and amateur archaeologists and antiquarians.[3] It also ranks high among the undiscovered finds of interest to treasure hunters.[4] The quest for Alaric's treasure goes on even now.

But this story encompasses more than just Alaric and more than just one treasure. It is the story of an age – the story of the fall of the Roman Empire, the survival of Christian Rome, the rise of the Catholic Church, and the making of the Middle Ages.

Why should we awaken the ancient king Alaric I from his long and deep sleep? Why should we once more resurrect the spectre of the barbarian who sacked Rome in AD 410? Perhaps today few are interested in the deeds of a man who was king of a people that vanished from history in AD 711, but this may change in the future.

In the story of the treasure of Alaric I, king of the Visigoths, we see the story of a world on the edge, a dying civilisation plagued by the brutal forces marching on its cities and breaking through its gates. We see, however dimly and however distorted, a dark mirror of our own world poised on the brink of catastrophe.

It seems that the search for Alaric occurs in times of trouble, when major transformations are threatened. It is most remarkable that, with few exceptions, public interest in the story of Alaric's death and burial seems to increase when the world goes through such major changes, as if people, worried about anticipated or ongoing military, political, economic, social and personal disasters, hope to find formulas for their own survival in the story of his troubled times.

PART ONE

Sacking Rome

ONE

The Gothic Peoples

Our investigation into Rome's lost gold will begin with the migration of the Goths and their occasionally horrifying customs. We will then explore the emergence of the Gothic tribes on the borders of the once-mighty Roman Empire and the threat they posed to classical civilisation. As background to the description of Alaric's sack of Rome, we will examine the situation of the magnificent city before the invasion of the Goths. Then our enquiry will follow the rise of the mysterious Gothic king Alaric, examine his sack of Rome and go on to consider the consequences of his actions for Rome, for the Empire, and for the lost treasure his followers may have hidden at his death. And, in an attempt to separate the booty of Alaric from other riches stolen from the city in late antiquity and the early Middle Ages, we will also look at the fate of Rome's remaining ancient treasures during the four centuries that followed the sack by Alaric and the crucial events that took place in Rome in that period.

En route, we will discover what may well be one of the best-kept secrets of Islam, a deed that has great significance for the religious unrest of our times. Finally, we will review the efforts of the treasure hunters who, starting in the Middle Ages, have tried to locate the mythical tomb of Alaric. Of course, we will examine the increasingly numerous contemporary attempts at finding it. But before we can join the search for the fabulous gold plundered 1,600 years ago, we must begin where Alaric himself began, in the marshy delta of the Danube.

THE GOTHIC TRIBES

While exploring its innumerable inland lakes and waterways the modern traveller to the extraordinarily peaceful Danube Delta will notice little disturbing other than the peculiar smell of the slow and stagnant waters.

Today, many tourists visit the Danube Delta to admire the waterfowl, enjoy the cooked freshwater fish and seafood and get merry on the local wines. However, only a few of them know that Alaric was born in this area in about AD 370, reportedly on what the ancients called the island of Peuce (Fir),[1] an unidentified place situated between the lower and middle arm of the Danube Delta in today's Romania.[2] As Wolfram explains, Alaric was a member of the nobility of the Tervingi Gothic tribe and belonged to the respected clan of the Balthi (the Bold).[3]

According to Heather, the Tervingi lived between the Lower Danube and the River Dnister (Nistru in Romanian) in modern eastern Romania and Moldavia. Further north-east, another Gothic tribe, the Greuthungi or Ostrogoths, was located between the Dnister and Dnipro rivers in today's Ukraine.[4] Both Tervingi and Greuthungi Goths were Germanic peoples.

There are scholars who believe that in the last centuries BC, the forefathers of the Goths migrated from southern Sweden to the southern Baltic shore between the Rivers Oder and Vistula, the starting point of their great drive to the Black Sea and the Danube, accompanied by the Vandals and Gepidae, who were Germans as well. In this very old academic debate, some scholars disagree.[5] The Goths were largely unable to read and write in the first three centuries of the Christian era.[6] Alaric spoke the western dialect of Gothic, a now extinct East Germanic language.[7]

One of the most important topics when discussing the customs of these Goths concerns their burial practices. As the elusive tomb of Alaric is said to contain fabulous treasures, we must ask ourselves the following question: did the Gothic nobles really inter their dead with riches?

THE GOTHIC PRINCELY BURIALS

As a warrior people, the Goths were very familiar with untimely death. Though the youthful Alaric had his life and his glory still ahead of him, he knew from an early age what to expect when his death came, as it could at any moment and almost did more than once. The Goths had centuries of tradition associated with death, and sacred pre-Christian rites defined what would occur.

In his description of the early German funerals written in the first century AD, Tacitus emphasised their austerity. The Germans simply burnt the deceased with their weapons. On occasion, the horse of the departed was also incinerated. Tacitus reported that the Germans did not erect sumptuous monuments for the dead; instead, men kept alive the memory of the deceased in their minds. It was left to the women to bewail and lament the loss of the departed.[8] We will see that the funeral practices of the Goths differed significantly.

Archaeologists call the remains of Gothic civilisations by many different names. One of these, the northern Wielbark culture, flourished in what is now Poland during the first decades AD, the time Tacitus describes. Their culture differed from those found in the neighbouring lands in north central Europe in two main respects. First, in the Wielbark cemeteries, both interment and incineration of the dead were practised, while in the adjacent cultures cemeteries contained only the remnants of incineration. Second, in the Wielbark cemeteries the men were not laid to rest with arms. As archaeologists note, the Wielbark interment and incineration cemetery pattern and the weapon-free male grave pattern persisted into the later Cherniakhov-Sântana de Mureş culture, thus providing evidence for the spread of funeral customs (Cherniakhov is near Kiev, Ukraine; Sântana de Mureş is near Târgu Mureş, Romania). Other typical Wielbark features persisted into the Cherniakhov-Sântana de Mureş culture too, such as those relating to the style of earthenware, decorative pins, women's clothing and domestic building practices.[9]

Heather draws attention to the fact that the Germans in northern and central Europe, particularly after the first century AD, practised princely burials (*Fürstengräber*) in which the clans attempted to demonstrate their privileged status by depositing considerable riches in the graves in order to astonish the less well off with the amount they could part with.[10]

It would, then, not be surprising at all if King Alaric, a member of a much-respected and powerful clan belonging to a Germanic tribe, was buried with precious items, for there was a centuries-old precedent for such burials, and Alaric was heir to that tradition.

In the Wielbark burial grounds, the presence of interment and its expansion at the expense of incineration, and especially the appearance of more massive graves, reflect social division. In the more recent Cherniakhov cemeteries, social standing is indicated mainly by the dimensions of the grave. Moreover, many of these burial sites were robbed in ancient times of whatever treasures they once held.[11]

THE GOTHS IN COMBAT

From their first contact, the early German warriors shocked the Romans with their recklessness in battle. Their behaviour during combat seemed driven by a death wish. The Roman historian Ammianus Marcellinus, himself a former soldier, vividly described how the taller and stronger German Alamanni put their lives on the line in the hope of facilitating a victory in the battle of Strasbourg, and came forward to try and lure the Romans into breaking ranks.[12] As the disciplined Romans were slaughtering these reckless warriors, countless other Germans kept on coming. In the end, the fallen Germans were dying or lying wounded and in agony in such large numbers that a hellish chorus of moans and blood-curdling screams dominated the battlefield. Only at that point were the Germans overwhelmed by fear and began to run for their lives.

Wolfram observes that the recklessness of the Goths was particularly evident during the great invasions of the third century, when they perished in large numbers after penetrating too deep into Roman territory without adequate logistical support.[13]

Ammianus Marcellinus tells us that before engaging in combat the Goths sang savage tributes to their ancestors, while the Romans responded with the *barritus*, an initially low-pitched, then booming rallying cry.[14]

After their defeat in the third century, there were Goths who ended up living in the Roman Empire and amazed the locals with the sheer size of their bodies and their fighting qualities. There were also Goths who became Roman soldiers. From this frequent warfare and contact, the Goths came to learn about Roman life and Roman culture, including the strange Christian religion that would eventually replace their own polytheistic faith.

CULT AND RELIGION AMONG THE GOTHS

When, in 376, the Goths crossed the Danube into the territories of the Roman Empire, each Gothic tribal division carried a statue or a wooden post. These articles may have been used by the Goths to venerate the forefathers of their chieftains, seen by them as noble and partly divine. These were the Anses mentioned by Jordanes, and priests and priestesses escorted these images. The Goths also worshipped the god of war, whose

Gothic designation may have been replaced by the Greek Ares or the Roman Mars by the fourth century. In addition, they might have venerated rivers, as suggested by the unpublished findings of Shishkin. Indeed, the Tervingi Goths martyred St Saba in the River Museus (Buzău in Romanian), an act which, according to Schwarcz, 'may be interpreted as sacrifice to the river god'. While various contemporary authors have implied the practice of shamanistic rituals, borrowed from the Finnish, Sarmatian and Dacian peoples, the extent to which these rituals were actually practised by the Tervingi Goths has, however, not been established.[15]

Christianity arrived among the Goths with the Roman captives from the great Gothic raids of the third century.[16] In 348 the Christian bishop Ulfilas and his Gothic flock had to seek asylum in the Roman Empire because of maltreatment by the Tervingi Goths, but not all Christian Goths accompanied him, as indicated by the resumption of the anti-Christian persecution in the time of Athanaric (*c.* AD 360–81).[17] Schwarcz proposed that the proportion of Christians among Alaric's followers may have reflected the spread of Christianity among the Balkan peoples of the Roman Empire.[18]

The same Arian bishop Eusebius of Nicomedia (Turkish Kocaeli/Izmit near the Sea of Marmara) who had baptised the Emperor Constantine before his death in 337 consecrated Ulfilas in 341 as bishop of the Goths living in what is today Romania. As a result, Alaric and his Visigoths were Arians and the Visigoths and Ostrogoths remained Arians after they overran the West. The Lombards, a Germanic tribe that invaded parts of Italy in the second half of the sixth century after the Byzantines crushed the Italian kingdom of the Arian Ostrogoths, were part Arian and part pagan.[19] The Arianism of several of the invading barbarian tribes delayed the unification of the western Christians under the leadership of the Catholic popes of Rome until the age of Charlemagne.[20]

Alaric was himself an Arian Christian.[21] It would be very difficult to gauge the depth, intensity and authenticity of his Christian beliefs. The Christian Catholics loosely labelled the Balkan Goths as Arians. Arianism, initially promoted by the presbyter Arius from Alexandria, proposed that the Son was not equivalent to the Father and his existence had not paralleled the eternality of the Father. For Arians, the Son was only the primary and the highest of all finite beings created by God. He was divine but not completely so,[22] a belief that contradicted the recently promulgated

Nicene Creed. It was a crucial debate at the beginnings of Christianity, which provided a monotheistic faith universally available, but differentiated itself from Judaism by ascribing divine attributes to Jesus Christ.[23]

At the time of Alaric, such debates were for the power brokers to squabble over. For the ordinary people, the ancient rites still held some sway, even under the tutelage of the Christians. These rites included human sacrifice, perhaps even the sacrifice of gravediggers, who Jordanes said were killed to hide forever the burial place of the Gothic leader Alaric.

HUMAN SACRIFICE AMONG THE GOTHS

Even though the murder of Alaric's prisoners on the occasion of his burial might not have been a true sacrifice, the practice of human sacrifice probably did exist among the Teutonic peoples. In his *Germania* Tacitus related that the Germans were permitted to perform such sacrifices to one of their gods on certain days.[24]

Jordanes, himself of Germanic stock, referred specifically to the practice of human sacrifice by the Goths. Indeed, he mentioned that the Goths expressed their adoration for Mars with brutal ceremonies and the sacrifice of prisoners, because they believed that the god of war had to be placated with offerings of human blood.[25] Presumably, as they became more christianised, such practices died off among Alaric's followers.

As we have seen, while still north of the Danube, the Tervingi Goths had martyred St Saba in the River Museus, an act that has tentatively been interpreted as human sacrifice to the river god.[26]

Regarding the Ostrogoth chieftain Radagaisus, Orosius had this to say: 'Radagaisus, the most savage by far of all former and present enemies, in a sudden attack spread over all Italy. For it is said that among his people there were more than two hundred thousand Goths. This man, in addition to his incredible number of followers and his indomitable courage, was a pagan and a Scythian, who, as is customary with such barbarian peoples, had vowed to offer to his gods the blood of the entire Roman race.'[27] Of course, the Romans often reported only the worst rumours about peoples outside the empire; nevertheless, the consistency of such reports would seem to indicate that human sacrifice did occur.

The Roman general Stilicho surrounded, captured, and executed Radagaisus.[28] (Regarding Orosius' designation of Radagaisus as 'Scythian', many ancient authors used the term to describe any tribespeople originating from the northern hinterland of the Black Sea.)

Such sacrifices continued into the Dark Ages. In 539, the Franks led by King Theudebert unexpectedly invaded northern Italy. Procopius noted at the time that on the arrival of the Franks at a Roman bridge over the River Po, the local Goths allowed them to cross in peace, but once the Franks had taken control of the bridge, the latter apprehended Gothic children and women, sacrificed them to the river god and hurled their remains into the waters 'as the first-fruits of the war'. Procopius observed that the Franks, although formally Christians at that time, continued to practise their old religion, including human and other sacrifice 'of an unholy nature' in order to foretell the future.[29]

CHRISTIANITY AND THE CONTINUATION OF SACRIFICE

Like the sixth-century Franks, the Christian supporters of Alaric were also relatively new to their faith at the beginning of the fifth century. Among them, there were Christians belonging to the Tervingi of the two leaders, Fritigern and Alaviv. Following them, these Christian Goths had crossed the Danube in 376. Most likely, Alaviv was a pagan.[30]

Of course, not everyone in Alaric's army was a Christian.[31] In fact, Alaric's forces included many former adherents of Radagaisus, the pagan Goth who had vowed to sacrifice all the Romans to his gods. In all probability, these people were not Christians. Moreover, the army of Alaric included non-Germanic warriors such as Huns and Alans, people not likely to have been Christian either.[32]

For those among the followers of Alaric who were Christians, the sacrifice of the captives might have been a solemn return to religious rituals that were part of their tradition. In fact, the example of the Franks, also Germanic, indicates that even 129 years after the death of Alaric there were Germans who were nominally Christian but who were prepared to resume the practice of human religious sacrifice should the occasion arise.

In addition, as Heather explains, Alaric's army included former non-Roman imperial soldiers whose families had been slaughtered by Romans in 408.[33] Their loathing of Romans and desire to avenge the deaths of their loved ones may have been a decisive element in the potent mix of religious precedent and hatred that could lead to the sacrifice of captives. Thus, there are reports of human sacrifices performed by the Germans in both early and late antiquity, and in particular by the Goths.

Though Alaric probably spent little time dwelling on the pageantry of his death, surely he would have recalled the Goths' long migration through Europe and now to Rome; present events could not but resurrect memories of their ancestors, whom the Goths honoured in their prayers and sacrifices. Nevertheless, as the Goths prepared to enter Roman territory, they must have paused to remember too the legends and stories of how they came so far from their ancestral home, and then they must have stood in mute awe of the great empire that lay spread before them, an empire of turmoil and tumult, of gold and glory, of faith and fear. As we move with the Goths towards Rome, we must turn our attention to the history of the imperial city to understand the origins of the fantastic fortune the Goths would come to call their own.

TWO

The Grandeur that was Rome

At its height, the Roman Empire stretched across much of Europe and North Africa and part of the Middle East, but it was rarely completely at peace. As it passed its peak, between 254 and 259 the Romans had had to engage in five successive campaigns to repulse the Germanic tribesmen who flooded northern Italy, the very heart of the empire. In the wake of these dangerous barbarian attacks, the Romans decided to build a wall around Rome.

According to Coarelli, the original Aurelian Wall had been built by the emperor Aurelian between 271 and 275; and Probus, his successor, completed the project. The wall hugged hills and any larger buildings that might have been used by the enemy as offensive fortifications. As well, the path it followed was chosen to take account of strategic, topographical and economic points of significance.[1] The Aurelian Wall had sixteen imposing gates for egress by the major roads leaving the city and smaller gates, *posterulae*, reserved for local traffic.[2] The perimeter of the wall measured 11.41 miles (18.837km) and it protected 3,390.16 acres (1,372 hectares) of the total 4,447.73 acres (1,800 hectares) of the city.[3]

The northern portion of the wall is the one best preserved, in the area of Porta Flaminia (today's Porta del Popolo) and Porta Pinciana, and especially east of Porta Pinciana, where there are eighteen towers in good condition and parts of the wall are used as living quarters. On the southern side of the city, the wall jumped the Tiber and surrounded a good part of the Trastevere district. The Gate of St Paul (Porta San Paolo), which is the ancient Porta Ostiensis (The Gate of Ostia) remains one of the best-preserved of the wall's gates. Next to it is the Pyramid of Cestius, which the builders incorporated into the Aurelian Wall, as they did other structures they encountered in its path. This pyramid is in fact a tomb from the early imperial period.[4]

It seemed that the gradually increasing height of the wall reflected the mounting anxiety of the Romans in the face of the anticipated barbarian invasion. At the top, the wall had a covered passage with narrow slits for archers. Above the covered passage, there was a roofless walkway with battlements that could accommodate *ballistae* and onagers, projectile-throwing war machines. Some of the gates of the Aurelian Wall were transformed into veritable fortresses by various changes and additions. The Wall of Rome was reported to have 383 towers, 7,020 battlements, 116 latrines, and 2,066 great external windows. The ancients considered the Aurelian Wall a colossal achievement matched only by the Wall of Constantinople built under Theodosius II (408–50).[5]

The Aurelian Wall was immense and, by the standards of antiquity, so was the city it protected. To manage an urban settlement of this size must have been quite a task.

RUNNING THE CITY

The chief administrator of Rome was the prefect of the city (urban prefect), who chaired Senate meetings and coordinated public services.[6] His jurisdiction extended over the 87 miles (140km) around Rome, including the maritime ports of Ostia and Portus.[7]

As Wallace-Hadrill points out, the pagan historian Ammianus Marcellinus' respectful description of the deeds of the urban prefects of Rome in the fourth century reveals the provincial nature of their business.[8] The urban prefect and the security prefect were in charge of the urban police. The prefect of the watch was chief of the firefighters.[9]

The prefect for grain and agricultural produce, Gatto tells us, was in charge of a unified and complex service that included the bakers, as well as the sailors and boatmen who transported the foodstuffs from the mouth of the Tiber to the port of Rome and the warehouses there. As in earlier times, in the late imperial age the provinces paid tax in kind, thus providing grain, oil, wine and pork that were used by the public system of *annona* to feed the huge population of the former capital. Rome had around three hundred storehouses with markets for grain and other foodstuffs, which tended to be located in the 13th region, situated in the angle formed by the Tiber and the southernmost portion of the Aurelian Wall.[10] However, a very long siege could empty these storehouses.[11]

Rome had around two hundred and fifty public bakeries manned by millers and bakers recruited from the ranks of slaves and convicted felons.

Flour was obtained from millstones powered by donkeys or ground in the watermills located on the Janiculum Hill by the aqueduct of Trajan. By law, the job of master-baker was hereditary. The citizens of Rome loved pork, which was more difficult to obtain. Romans with money could buy bread, meat and other foodstuffs at independent markets.[12]

According to Lançon, from the early fourth century, the maritime port of Ostia was gradually superseded by Portus, located a bit farther north. The reason for Ostia's decline as a port for goods for Rome is not entirely clear, but it is believed that by the sixth century the Ostian branch of the Tiber had become difficult to navigate. In Portus, as previously in Ostia, specially appointed clerks checked the amount and quality of the merchandise included in the *annona* brought by the Roman fleet. Afterwards, the foodstuffs were loaded onto riverboats, which were then pulled for some 19 miles (30km) to the quays of Rome.[13]

The superintendent of the maritime port of Rome oversaw the navigation thence to the city. The superintendent of the aqueducts coordinated the maintenance of the aqueducts. The superintendent of the waters was responsible for the distribution of the water.[14]

Aside from the inhabitants' requirements for sustenance, their health needs were also addressed. Surprisingly, Rome had fewer public physicians than other Roman cities. Up to the time of Valentinian I (364–75), only three public doctors were active in Rome. These physicians were remunerated in kind from the public *annona*. In 386, Valentinian I ordered the urban prefect Praetextatus to assign one physician to each of the fourteen regions of Rome. These doctors were to provide care to the indigent free of charge. Nor were the public doctors allowed to charge wealthy Romans for their services.[15] Rome also had private doctors who catered for affluent citizens. In the third and fourth centuries, the average age in Rome was 35 years, and it remained so in the fifth and sixth centuries.[16]

The most affluent citizens, the patricians and senators, inhabited the north-eastern areas between Via Salaria and Via Nomentana. The areas located inside the old Servian Wall were home to people of the middle class and those of modest means. The Servian Wall, made obsolete by the expansion of the city, was first built by the sixth king of Rome, Servius Tullius, but the surviving portions date back to the fourth century BC. (An impressive remnant of the Servian Wall can be seen in Piazza dei Cinquecento near Stazione Termini, Rome's main railway station.)[17] Many of the poor lived in the quarter of ill repute named Suburra, where brothels and wretched hovels stood cheek by jowl.[18] The memory of this ancient Roman neighbourhood seems to be preserved in the name of Piazza della Suburra, which is immediately west of the Cavour Metropolitan Station.

After the Severan dynasty (193–235), no more large tenement buildings (*insulae*) were erected in Rome and the population gradually took to living in individual residences, the *domus*, which varied in size from a small house to a luxurious palace. As a result, by the fourth century many such buildings had been erected on empty land or on land made available by the demolition of old structures.[19] The geographic indexes of fourth-century Rome listed, among others, 28 libraries; 6 obelisks; 11 fora; 10 basilicas; 9 circuses and theatres, the latter including two for mock naval battles; 15 enormous fountains; 22 equestrian statues; 80 gold statues; 74 ivory statues; 36 triumphal arches; 856 private baths; 11 public baths; 46 brothels. As today in the older sections of Rome, property was costly and only the affluent could afford the comfort of seclusion. In many parts of Rome, apartment buildings, houses of the rich, filthy slums in narrow streets and monumental public edifices could be found side by side.[20]

There were public bathing facilities in each region of Rome, and the great baths of Diocletian, Caracalla and Constantine on the Quirinal Hill attracted large crowds.[21] The basilica of St Mary of the Angels (Piazza della Repubblica), located in the *frigidarium* (a covered pool of unheated water) of the Baths of Diocletian, is a miraculously surviving example of an urban attraction and central meeting place dating from the years immediately before the sack of Rome by Alaric.[22] The reign of Diocletian, the emperor after whom these baths were named, was an important period in the run-up to Alaric's assault on the city.

THE EMPEROR ABANDONS ROME

In the century and a half before Alaric, Rome faced unprecedented upheaval that left it vulnerable to the Gothic hordes. When the great emperor Diocletian (284–305) came to power the Roman economy was in shambles after repeated usurpations, widespread corruption, rampant inflation[23] and the devastating Gothic invasions of the third century.[24] Diocletian attempted to stem the tide of decay by reorganising the empire. Recognising that Rome's territories, which stretched from Spain to Syria and from Britain to Egypt, were too vast for one man to govern, he divided the empire into eastern and western halves. He and a co-emperor, Maximianus, would have the title *Augustus* and would reign in half the empire and each would have a vice-emperor, or *Caesar*.[25] In his efforts to restore order, Diocletian implemented a harsh economic policy, instituting a ruthlessly imposed system of taxation and attempts at price control. Even prostitutes had to pay the heavy business tax.[26] At the local level, town magistrates or councillors were responsible for tax collection, in the process of which they acquired a significant portion of their riches.[27]

The foodstuffs collected through the tax on agricultural labour known as *annona* were used to pay soldiers and, later in the fourth century, imperial bureaucrats. The imperial estates, the personal properties of the emperors, and the domains of the Church in the late Empire, were all legally responsible for the general *annona* or land tax. The practice of paying the army in kind began before Diocletian came to the throne because the coinage was worthless and there was a shortage of precious metal. Worried citizens concealed gold or used it to buy goods from the East.[28] Thus, the Roman state had already begun losing its fabled gold.

Diocletian spent most of his time away from Rome, the historic capital, as did his co-emperor Maximianus. The departure of the imperial government from Rome resulted in the loss of many lucrative contracts, a decrease in population, relative impoverishment and social and political decline.[29]

At the end of his reign, Diocletian was weakened by disease, disillusioned by the failure of his efforts to restore the empire, and burdened by his responsibility in the last great persecution of the Christians. Frustrated by the intransigence of the monotheistic Christians, which seemed an act of defiance to his authoritarian, regional approach to governing, Diocletian unleashed a persecution that lasted for a decade and claimed numerous victims in many cities of the empire and especially in Rome.[30] Galerius, Diocletian's son-in-law and his deputy in the East, has been blamed for inciting this persecution. Hardly surprisingly, the pagan authorities did not keep records of those massacred, so in some of the pious traditions the real historical events of the persecution[31] have become entangled with legend.[32]

In 305, Diocletian retired along with his co-emperor Maximianus. Constantius in the West and Galerius in the East were promoted to *Augustus* and replaced them. Diocletian also announced that Maximinus Daia (305–13) in the East and Severus (305–6) in the West, were promoted to *Caesar*.

Many were shocked to learn that the ambitious Constantine, the son of the benevolent Constantius, had not been made a junior emperor.[33] The machinations of Galerius had succeeded.[34] The 20-year-old Constantine had for a number of years been a member of Galerius's staff.[35] Galerius saw himself as the sole ruler of the empire.[36]

Diocletian travelled quietly to his villa in Salona (Split in modern Croatia). He left behind an empire that, although bleeding profusely, was more or less intact. But it was an empire ripe for a transformation that echoes down the centuries to this day.

CONSTANTINE CUTS ACROSS EUROPE

In a letter to Galerius, the ailing Constantius expressed the wish to see his son Constantine. After some procrastination, Galerius finally told Constantine that the young man was to leave the following morning.[37]

Constantine, wary of Galerius's intentions, did not wait until morning but left in secret immediately after dinner. At each staging post of the road, he removed the horses kept there by the state. This way, he prevented Galerius from apprehending him or sending orders hostile to him. Constantine galloped and galloped, until finally he met his father in Gaul (France). Reunited, father and son campaigned in Britain against the savage Picts and thus Constantine had the opportunity to develop a good relationship with the soldiers. On 25 July 306 Constantius died at Eboracum (York)[38] and the legions immediately proclaimed his son the new *Augustus*. There is a majestic statue of Constantine in the immediate vicinity of York Minster where a special service was held at midday on 25 July 2006 to mark this significant moment in history.[39]

Resentful, Galerius limited the elevation of Constantine to the lesser position of *Caesar* and promoted Severus, the previous *Caesar*, as *Augustus* in the West.[40] Then a large number of citizens unexpectedly proclaimed Maxentius emperor in Rome.[41] He was the son of Maximianus, Diocletian's old friend and co-emperor. Unfortunately for Maxentius, the African provinces rebelled and his son Romulus died in 309. Taking advantage of his troubles, Constantine took over Spain. With his tax-collecting base reduced, Maxentius was forced to resort to much disliked financial and administrative measures. As a result, his popularity plummeted.[42]

Though Maxentius reportedly humiliated Pope Marcellus and banished Pope Eusebius shortly after his election, later in his reign, desperate to recruit some much-needed support, Maxentius undertook to return to the Christians the property confiscated from them by Diocletian and to stop interfering with the election of the bishops of Rome. The disillusioned Christians rejected his overtures.[43]

The battle for supremacy in the empire continued for some years, between Maxentius and Constantine in the West and Licinius and Maximinus Daia in the East. Constantine, who aspired to become sole ruler, forged an alliance with Licinius.

In 311, the dying pagan Galerius, tormented by remorse, published an edict that was to put an end to the persecutions. In this document, a stunning volte-face, he ordered the Christians to pray to their God for his welfare.[44]

CONSTANTINE TAKES ROME

In 312, Constantine made his decisive move against Maxentius and crossed the Alps. After three victories, he arrived in the vicinity of Rome.[45] Maxentius had been waiting in the city during the previous battles, having taken the counsel of his fortune-tellers who had predicted certain death for him, if he ventured outside of Rome.[46]

Lactantius narrates how, in October 312, the armies of Constantine pitched camp not far from the Milvian Bridge. Maxentius' soldiers built a bridge of boats to cross their large army. According to Lactantius, Maxentius was attending a public spectacle in celebration of his fifth year on the throne while his army crossed the bridge and began its collision course against Constantine whose forces were deployed north of the river. During the entertainment, the crowds began chanting 'Constantine cannot be overcome'. Maxentius, encouraged by a statement from the prophetic Sibylline Books, 'On the same day the enemy of the Romans should perish', decided to join battle.[47]

Constantine himself led his cavalry charge, which attacked on both flanks. The shields of Constantine's legionnaires displayed a never-before-seen monogram made from the Greek letters *chi* X and *rho* P. Only the Praetorian Guard, loyal to Maxentius, put up a fierce resistance.[48] Then, disaster struck: the bridge of boats collapsed. Maxentius, who was fleeing the battlefield, drowned with many of his cavalrymen, soldiers and horses. Constantine had won a resounding victory.[49]

THE ROMAN MYSTERIES OF CONSTANTINE

In Rome, the Arch of Constantine (Piazza e via del Colosseo) is located immediately south-west of the Colosseum, the modern symbol of ancient Rome. The arch was erected to celebrate the victory of Constantine over Maxentius, and it was inaugurated on 25 July 315. This monument is a mirror of pre-Alaric Rome and it displays an enigma related to a crucial moment in the history of humanity.

At first there seems to be no obvious reference to Christianity on the arch, while several pagan deities are clearly represented, including the Sun god in the medallion on the narrow side facing the Colosseum. But let us examine this arch more carefully, with the help of Coarelli.[50]

The attics on the northern and southern sides feature the same lengthy inscription, but the southern one is much more legible. The inscription includes two baffling words: *instinctu divinitatis* (inspired by the deity). They have stirred debate for at least two hundred years: Do they openly proclaim Constantine's Christian faith and recognise its role in his victory over Maxentius? According to Eusebius (not the Eusebius who baptised Constantine) and Lactantius, Constantine's father had encouraged him to embrace Christianity.[51] His mother, St Helena, also inspired his enthusiasm for Christianity.

In no uncertain terms, Eusebius wrote that Constantine had revealed to him that he converted to Christianity after having a vision in the early afternoon sky some time before his decisive battle with Maxentius, and that his entire army had witnessed the wonder. Not far from the sun he had observed a glowing cross on which he was able to read the words 'Conquer by This [Sign]'.

The following night, Constantine had a dream in which Christ told him to make a replica of the heavenly vision and use it for protection during all his battles. Constantine did just that. His Standard of the Cross – *Labarum*, consisted of a cross formed from a golden lance and a transverse rod, on which was superimposed a golden, gem-encrusted garland at the top. In the centre of the garland, the Greek letters *chi* X and *rho* P, crossed one another, just as they appeared on the shields of the victorious soldiers at the

Milvian Bridge. Those were the first letters of the name of Christ in Greek. In addition, the transverse rod carried a tetragonal standard, it too lavishly decorated with gold and gems. Just a bit higher than this standard, there was a golden likeness of Constantine and his children. Eusebius then relates that after hearing more about the meaning of the miracle from learned Christians, Constantine dedicated himself to the study of the scriptures and surrounded himself with Christian advisers.[52]

All this would seem to indicate that Constantine's conversion happened before the battle of the Milvian Bridge. Initially, however, Constantine worshipped Mithras, also known among Romans as *Sol invictus* (The Invincible Sun).[53]

The fact that X was also the symbol of the Sun[54] and that Constantine's vision of the heavenly cross was located near the Sun may point to his earlier worship of the Sun God (Mithras), a deity of oriental origin revered by many of his soldiers. Perhaps in the days of high tension during Constantine's offensive on Rome, the symbols of the two religions somehow fused in his mind. In this regard, Constantine was probably not very different from many other Christians of his time. Even a century and a half later, Pope Leo the Great complained bitterly that the Christians still knelt to salute the Sun before entering the basilica of St Peter.[55]

In fact, archaeologists have found early Christian places of worship located near Mithraic shrines, a circumstance that suggests that these religions enjoyed a mysterious relationship in this period. Mithras, god of light, considered similar to the Sol Invictus of Constantine and to the Greek deity Apollo, opposed the forces of darkness.[56]

Thus, Mithraism offered Romans a dualistic framework new to them. The Mithraic shrines were tiny, like the one in the church of St Clement (Piazza di San Clemente), an ancient basilica filled with priceless works of art and famous relics, including those of St Cyril, the Apostle of the Slavs. In Mithraism, the ceremonies performed and the sacred vestments worn were characterised by moderation. Initiation involved seven degrees with seven matching titles. The supreme title was that of Father of Fathers. The purpose of the Mithraic shared meals and initiation rites was to make amends for wrongs and to achieve purification. Adherents of Mithraism had a strong sense of religious community.[57]

Linda Jones Hall has concluded that the most likely origin of the Arch of Constantine's famous *instinctu divinitatis* appears to be Cicero's idea of *instinctu divino* as presented in his *De Divinatione*, a work used to foretell the future. The nuance of the expression *instinctu divino* persisted among the late ancient Romans through the works of famous Roman authors. In a discourse delivered in 324, Constantine himself proved he was familiar with Cicero's formulation. In the opinion of Hall, the presence of *instinctu divinitatis* on the Arch of Constantine suggests that the pagan Senate may have acknowledged the significance of Constantine's famous vision before the dedication of the Arch in 315.[58] It is an interpretation that confirms the views expressed by Rossi and Lanciani[59] more than a century earlier.

The victorious Constantine, mindful of the feelings of the more numerous pagans, also approved a medallion ascribing his conquest of Rome to Sol Invictus (Mithras)[60] and accepted the title *Pontifex Maximus*, the role of leading high priest of the old Roman cult of the state. In fact, all Roman emperors from Constantine the Great up to Gratian (375–83), the first to decline the title, accepted the honour in spite of being Christian, though Julian the Apostate (360–3) openly returned to paganism and tried to restore it throughout the empire.[61]

Further down the Arch of Constantine, the decorative sculptures on the pedestals of the columns and those at a level located immediately above the lateral smaller arches, are the creations of workers contemporary to Constantine. Alas, these sculptures lack the perspective and the spatial authenticity of classical Greek and Roman sculpture.[62] Instead, the subjects are represented frontally and in ranks. This is strikingly different from what we see at the level of the attics, especially the attic of the western narrow side of the arch, which displays the most magnificent surviving sample of Roman official historical sculpture, stolen from the Forum of Trajan. The impressive Dacians standing on the top of each column were also appropriated from Trajan's forum.[63]

The inferior production of Constantine's sculptors foreshadowed the comparative regression in art of the Middle Ages. The terrible violence of the third century had seen the disappearance of the highly specialised sculptors who had previously thrived on lucrative imperial commissions in Rome.[64]

Perhaps Constantine himself, a learned and observant man, noticed the decay in the skills of the workers and the fact that they had tried to immortalise his victory by disfiguring monuments meant to commemorate the victories of previous emperors. Perhaps what he saw made him think even more about an alternative route to immortality.

To please the God from whom he expected everlasting life, and for his own political reasons, Constantine engaged in an extensive and swift campaign of church building and endowment in Rome. He wanted to give the young faith of Christianity the necessary tools to propagate its teachings, to show everyone the power of the Christian God and to demonstrate his own imperial might.[65]

CONSTANTINE'S GIFTS FOR ALARIC

In his devout generosity, Constantine gave rich gifts to the new Christian churches, thus becoming the unwitting provider of a significant part of Alaric's future treasure.

Many believe that Constantine's prudence in dealing with the pagans is shown by the location of the churches he built in Rome. Of these, only the church of the Holy Cross in Jerusalem and St John in Lateran are inside the city's Aurelian Wall, in the most peripheral position possible. However, according to Bertrand Lançon, Constantine was forced to build churches at the edge of the city because of the high concentration of buildings in the historical centre of Rome.[66]

What Constantine gave Pope Sylvester (314–35)[67] and his churches was to make Alaric very happy less than a century later. Constantine provided to the Church of the Holy Cross in Jerusalem (Piazza Santa Croce in Gerusalemme, n. 12), as listed in the Book of Pontiffs: 4 silver candelabra, 80lb each; 50 silver chandeliers, 15lb each; a 10lb *scyphus* (a drinking bowl) of finest gold; 5 gold service chalices (cups for the smaller amounts of wine used for mass) 1lb each; 3 silver *scyphi*, 8lb each; 10 silver service chalices, 2lb each; a 50lb silver paten (plate for eucharistic bread) chased with gold and jewels; a 250lb silver altar; 3 silver *amae* (an *ama* was a vessel to receive the wine presented by the participants at mass), 20lb each. Constantine also assigned many properties and their substantial revenues to the new church.[68]

The *Liber Pontificalis* (Book of Pontiffs) is the name commonly used for the set of accounts relating to the lives of the popes of Rome up to 891.[69] The Book of Pontiffs provides precious information on treasures donated to churches, starting with the time of Constantine the Great.[70]

The Church of the Holy Cross in Jerusalem is also home to the famous relic that gives this church its name. According to tradition, the fragment of the True Cross was brought to Rome by St Helena, Constantine's mother. Whether this is historically accurate or not, it seems that the fragment of the Cross was already in this church by the time Alaric besieged and sacked Rome.[71] The relic has survived Alaric and countless other plunderers.

The sumptuous Basilica of St John in Lateran, the Cathedral of Rome to this day and the first church ever erected by Constantine,[72] built in monumental dimensions to impress both pagans and Christians, retains to a large extent the original design. It was erected on the site of the barracks of the Imperial Cavalry Guards, which Constantine broke up after they fought for Maxentius. By the late 200s, the Roman emperors began admitting barbarians into the Roman army. Constantine himself showed a strong preference for German soldiers. Constantine endowed the new Christian shrine with astonishing riches. He also assigned the revenues of various properties to provide 'for the lights' of this basilica. The latter was called The Golden Basilica because of its large areas decorated with yellow marble.[73]

Not long afterwards Constantine built the adjoining Lateran Palace, the residence of the popes throughout the Middle Ages. The existing one dates back to 1585–90 and was completed after the demolition of the original building.[74]

Constantine also erected with his own money the nearby Baptistery (Font), which defies the passage of the centuries in Piazza di San Giovanni in Laterano. He built it in porphyry and decorated it lavishly. The Book of Pontiffs is wrong in stating that Constantine was baptised in the Holy Font. The champion of Christianity was in fact baptised in Nicomedia in 337, once he realised he was about to die and no longer had time to fulfil his dream of being baptised in the River Jordan, like Jesus Christ.[75]

Constantine also founded old St Peter's Basilica. He built it in record time. It was conceived mainly as a roofed graveyard for the interment of notable Christians who wanted to be buried near St Peter. According to Cecchelli, it was also used as a funeral banquet hall.[76]

Christian veneration of relics dates back to the Apostle Paul – things that had come into contact with him were reputed to have healing powers. The tradition of erecting places of worship above martyrs' tombs and burying relics under their altars started in Rome in the time of Constantine the Great.[77]

In the cult of holy relics, not seen in Judaism or Islam, the martyrs were believed to be 'companions' of God and so were considered able to obtain divine protection for supplicants.[78] This cult already had momentum in the time of Constantine, to the dismay of the pagans, who were disgusted by the Christians' adoration of dead bodies. The mighty Constantine himself, realising that his death was at hand, implored God for mercy in a basilica dedicated to Christian martyrs.[79]

As narrated by Rendina, there is a legend that tells how Amalasuntha, the learned daughter of the Ostrogoth Theodoric the Great, king of Italy (490–526), possessed the following relics: the jaw of St Biagio; a piece of St Marta's skull; three teeth of St Mary Magdalene; a stone used to kill St Stephen; the cubitus of St John the Baptist; the finger used by St John the Baptist to point out Jesus to his disciples; three coals used to burn Emperor Julian the Apostate.[80]

Like the Arch of Constantine, old St Peter's Basilica was a patchwork. Lanciani explains that access was through five doors. The columns came from various parts of the empire and their bases and capitals were diverse in the extreme. The apse and the arches were built with bricks stamped with Constantine's name, but the hotchpotch of architraves and friezes bore the names of Titus, Trajan, Gallienus and other emperors.[81]

This basilica was a perfect example of the liberal assimilation of pagan elements into early Christian architecture. Supported by ninety-two columns, it had a kingpost roof, in which a vertical piece of wood stands in the middle of a horizontal tie beam, the latter being supported by columns at each end. The king post reaches the apex of the roof where it props an edge.[82] Because it was deemed unsafe (the enormous roof beams marked with the name of Constantine were full of holes sheltering countless rats), old St Peter's was demolished in the sixteenth century and replaced with the extant structure.[83]

The list of gifts and estates bestowed on St Peter's Basilica is equally astonishing. One of its most impressive items was the famous 150lb (68kg) cross of gold, placed on a 5ft copper cube containing the tomb of St Peter. The inscription on it included the names of Constantine Augustus and Helena Augusta, which would date the cross to between 325 and 327–8. Spiral columns of porphyry also decorated the tomb of St Peter. In addition to these riches, Constantine endowed St Peter's Basilica with many properties.[84]

Other churches built by Constantine included the Basilica of St Paul without the walls,[85] enlarged successively by Valentinian II, Theodosius,

Arcadius and Honorius. St Paul's was severely damaged by fire in 1823. The existing basilica was rebuilt incorporating the ruins of the old one.[86]

In the time of Constantine, Rome also witnessed the completion of many pagan projects, including the Baths of Constantine near the Temple of the Sun on the Quirinal Hill and the Temple of Cybele on the Vatican Hill.[87]

But the great emperor made one more fateful decision.

CONSTANTINE LEAVES ROME FOR BYZANTIUM

In 324, Constantine vanquished the eastern emperor Licinius (308–24) with whom he had legalised Christianity by the Edict of Milan in 313, and became the sole emperor of the Romans. In 325, Constantine played a major role in orchestrating the consensus attained by the Council of Nicaea, but the defeated Arians continued even after that to oppose the Nicaean belief that the Father and the Son are identical in substance and the Son must be fully God to be able to overcome wickedness and redeem sinners.[88]

In 326, the empire celebrated Constantine's twentieth year on the throne, but the emperor was filled with revulsion by the pagan sacrifices performed in Rome to mark the occasion. That same year, Constantine left Rome for Byzantium, determined to make it his new, completely Christian capital. Byzantium was surrounded by water on three of its sides and it was easier to defend than old Rome. It was also located at the meeting point of major commercial routes and less vulnerable to barbarian attack.[89]

The West and Rome lost considerable income and other resources as a result. Many rich senators moved to the newly renamed city of Constantinople. With their departure, Rome became even more exposed to danger.[90]

THE STILL UNBLEMISHED URBAN GLORY OF ROME

The city of Rome was still the richest urban centre in the West. The historian Edward Gibbon described in impressive detail the opulence of the former imperial capital. In the time of Theodosius in the late fourth century, it contained within its walls no less than 1,780 homes of the affluent. A large number of these palatial edifices were nearly equivalent to cities within the city.[91]

At the time of the sieges of Alaric, some of the wealthiest among Rome's senators, collected from their domains 4,000lb of gold a year. These earnings were in excess of £160,000 sterling, according to Gibbon writing in the eighteenth century.[92] (They would be roughly equivalent to £18.86 million at 2005 rates or US $34.12 million at 2005 rates.) Add to this the customary amount of grain and wine, which, if sold, might have yielded the equivalent of some £5.89 million at 2005 rates or US $11.37 million at 2005 rates more for the fortunate senator.[93] In the time of Honorius, there were aristocrats who marked their year in office as praetor with a week-long feast resulting in expenditure exceeding £100,000 sterling of Gibbon's time (roughly UK £11.79 million at 2005 rates or US $21.71 million at 2005 rates).[94]

As Coarelli narrates, the historic centre of the city[95] included the Capitoline Hill, the focal point of the old Roman state religion;[96] the Roman Forum; the imperial forums; and the Palatine Hill, the location of the Imperial Palaces. In Rome, where today we see old bricks and broken stones, the Romans of the early fifth century beheld splendid travertine (a porous rock consisting of calcium carbonate), coloured stucco, or marble of glorious hues.[97] The fine marbles included antique red, antique yellow, purple porphyry, oily green serpentine, Egyptian red and grey granite, and fiery-red African.[98] The imposing and ornate Roman buildings and the many gilded statues contributed to the magnificence of the city. Countless bronze roofs glistened in the sun. The glitter of the metallic ornaments and the large amounts of gold spread throughout the city fascinated the traveller of the early fifth century.

The Capitoline Hill was the main centre of political life in ancient Rome and continued to be the seat of the government of the city of Rome in the early 400s. The Palazzo Senatorio, which can be quickly identified because of its characteristic belfry, was built in 1143 atop the Tabularium, which stored the public archives of the Roman state, and became the home of the new Roman Senate.[99] In our time, the Palazzo Senatorio houses the offices of the Mayor of Rome.

Still on the Capitoline Hill and south-west of the Palazzo Senatorio, the Romans of the early 400s saw the intact Temple of Jupiter,[100] now replaced by Palazzo Caffarelli.[101] This temple must have had a somewhat neglected look following the prohibition on pagan temple rites imposed by Theodosius in 391.[102] However, its shining roof of gilded bronze tiles could probably still be seen from a great distance. This famous shrine was the oldest temple of Rome. Immediately north-east of the Palazzo Senatorio, the Romans could see the Arx, the fortified rock of the Capitoline Hill, a spot occupied now by the Church of Aracoeli.[103] This mysterious church, through its location a symbol of Christianity's victory over paganism, is home to the relics of St Helena, mother of Constantine the Great. St Helena's stupendous porphyry sarcophagus, which was previously in the now ruined mausoleum known to locals as Tor Pignattara, is currently in the Vatican Museum. The chief treasure of St Mary in Aracoeli is Il Santo Bambino (The Holy Child), the most famous sacred object in Rome, and believed to work healing miracles. On 1 February 1994, somebody stole the statuette and what is on show today is probably a copy. Il Santo Bambino remains popular among children in various countries of the world, as shown by the many letters they send him. At Christmas the Bambino becomes part of a spectacular Nativity scene.

Until the early twentieth century the wide and steep flight of steps leading to the church of St Mary in Aracoeli was also credited with working miracles. To find out the winning lottery numbers, one had to climb the steps on one's knees at night, reciting the Ave Maria and Psalm 129 over and over and asking the three Magi to help.

In the Middle Ages the Roman Forum was used as a pasture for cattle. On the eve of the invasion of Alaric, the Roman Forum, the heart of Roman history, preserved its imperial image and very old buildings from the Republican era.[104] Having descended into it from the Capitoline Hill by way of the Capitoline Slope (*Clivus Capitolinus*), if we face the Palazzo Senatorio with its belfry, we will see under it the stern façade of the Tabularium.[105]

Attached to the south-western end of the Tabularium, we see to our left the colonnade of the *Dei Consentes*, which sheltered six statues each of gods and goddesses grouped in pairs, a Roman adaptation of the Greek Pantheon. This temple must have been virtually intact in the early 400s because Praetextatus, the pagan prefect of Rome in 367 and a man known for his dislike of Christianity, had defiantly refurbished the *Dei Consentes* in one of the last attempts at pagan revival in the increasingly Christian Rome.[106]

As Lançon notes, Praetextatus' priestly titles, included in his epitaph, illustrate clearly the two layers of late ancient Roman paganism. First, in the Greek-influenced ancient Roman religion, the Romans venerated the old gods of Rome associated with the Roman state. The second layer of Roman paganism was that which incorporated the oriental religions (e.g. the cult of Cybele – the Great Mother, and the cult of Mithras), brought to Rome by soldiers, administrators and merchants from the late third century on. They offered solace to those preoccupied with their end – death, the final judgement and the like – and were popular in the years when Christianity was still a marginal faith.[107]

North-east of the colonnade of the *Dei Consentes*, the Romans beheld the still-standing Arch of Septimius Severus and, as we do today, noticed with puzzlement the signs of alteration in the inscription. It was Emperor Caracalla who erased the name of his brother Geta after he murdered him in 211.

Similar changes can be seen on the Arch of the Moneychangers and Bankers (Arco degli Argentarii), erected in 204 by the moneychangers, bankers and merchants of the Velabro area. This arch is attached to the left external wall of St George in Velabro, a church probably founded in the sixth century and rebuilt by Pope Leo II in 682. This very old and tranquil church, unique because of its symbolic union with an ancient Roman arch, shelters a legendary relic: half the skull of St George, the patron saint of England.

Near the Arch of Septimius Severus there was and still is the legendary Curia (Senate), with seats for three hundred senators.[108] Such was the reputation of the Senate that as late as the fourth century, there were emperors who desired to become senators.[109] Gatto tells us that traditionally the senators were great landowners from around Rome and southern Italy. The patrician families, senators and emperors maintained political and/or financial connections, a nexus that was a forerunner of the modern system of political patronage.[110]

By the time of Constantine the Great, the Senate had grown to 600 members. During his reign, Constantine introduced into the Senate many equestrians (Roman knights) from the West, raising the total number of senators to 2,000. This meant the end of the equestrian order, a social class ranking below senators but above ordinary citizens.[111] Obviously, the old Senate building was too small to accommodate such numbers.

The powers of the Senate remained significant until Rome was the capital, albeit they had decreased substantially after the end of the Republic in 27 BC. Eventually, the jurisdiction of the Senate shrank to the limits of

Rome itself and the Senate ended up functioning more like an esteemed municipal council. Because its city was Rome, the emperors tried to stay on good terms with the Senate and preserved some of its dignities. In 402, the majority of the senators were pagan; by 408–9, the Senate had become completely Christian.[112]

The Basilica Aemilia, which the Romans could see immediately south-east of the Curia, was a superb meeting hall with magnificent columns of African marble and a floor covered with yellow, *cipollino* (green and white marble with black streaks), and Porta Santa (Holy Gate) marble.[113]

In the rest of the Roman Forum, the Romans could admire many other venerable and impressive monuments, including the still standing Arch of Titus, which narrated the triumph of Vespasian and Titus in 71 while imperfectly depicting the legendary treasures of the Jerusalem Temple. The Roman Forum continued to display its old grandeur in the early 400s.[114]

The imperial palaces on the Palatine Hill dominated the Roman Forum and the Circus Maximus. Since the time of Maxentius (306–12), no emperors made these palaces their home. But on occasion, the emperors and members of their families rested there during visits to the city.[115]

When in 357 Constantius II came to Rome to celebrate his twentieth year on the throne, he was very impressed with the city his father Constantine the Great had left behind three decades earlier. From Ammianus Marcellinus we know that in 357 the Imperial Rostra, the Temple of Jupiter on the Capitoline Hill, the Temple of Rome, the Theatre of Pompey, the Circus Maximus and many other buildings and monuments were still standing, as resplendent as ever. In the Forum of Trajan, Constantius II stood in awe. The Forum of Peace, a common appellation for the Temple of Peace in the Late Empire,[116] where Vespasian had deposited the Jerusalem Temple treasure in 71, was among the monuments listed by Ammianus Marcellinus as part of the urban scenery during Emperor Constantius' visit to Rome in 357.[117] Modern archaeologists also believe this temple was extant at the end of the fourth century.[118]

Though it was no longer the centre of the Roman world, Rome maintained the religious treasures centuries of pagan and Christian worship had bestowed on it. For its symbolic importance and its still-great wealth, Rome was a tempting target.

THREE

Rome in the Age of Alaric

In the early fifth century, the Roman Empire's declining fortunes saw it much changed since the glorious days of the Early Empire. So, too, was Rome changed, a change perhaps foretold even in the myths of its beginning. According to tradition, Rome's foundation involved Romulus killing his brother Remus, the admission of outlaws into the new city and the seizure of the neighbouring Sabine women.[1] Through the years of glory, this mythical foundation did not seem so dark, but in the early fifth century, Rome could see in its past a bleak reflection of its war-torn future.

Rome had lost its political importance to the eastern capital of Constantinople and the western cities of Milan and Ravenna where the western emperors held court. The Senate wielded no significant influence in the affairs of state. However, the venerable city remained the symbol of the empire to which it had given its name, and it kept its title *caput mundi* (Head of the World). Rome continued to be a stunning city that dazzled travellers with its architecture, urban facilities, wealth, sophistication and decadence.[2] But was it ready to face the hordes of Alaric?

ROME'S PREPAREDNESS FOR WAR

While Alaric planned his attack on the magnificent city, the Romans found some encouragement in the knowledge that no outside invader had breached her defences in eight centuries. Little did they suspect that the organisation and infrastructure of their metropolis would leave it vulnerable to a devastating attack.

The empire's efficient road system was a great boon to travellers and merchants, bringing people and goods efficiently from all over the empire to the great walls surrounding Rome (to which all roads led), but few realised that it could also help invading foreign armies.[3]

In the time of Honorius, his master of soldiers and father-in-law, the powerful general Stilicho had doubled the height of the Aurelian Wall (401–2), which had already been doubled by Maxentius, in an effort to prepare the city for an attack by the Goths. The addition of Maxentius is noticeable because it is made of horizontal layers of bricks and tufa parallelepipeds. Stilicho included in the wall the Mausoleum of Hadrian, today's Castel Sant'Angelo.[4] As a mausoleum, this building contained the remains of Hadrian and several emperors of the Antonine and Severan houses. The last emperor to be laid to rest there was Caracalla.

Eight bridges traversed the Tiber of late ancient Rome, two of which were erected in the century preceding the sack by Alaric. One of them is considered the project of Emperor Gratian; the other was built under Theodosius the Great. The bridge identified as Ponte Sisto in our times was renovated by Valentinian I (364–75).[5]

The oldest surviving bridge of Rome is Ponte Quattro Capi (Via di Ponte Quattro Capi) built in 62 BC by Lucius Fabricius, *curator viarum* (superintendent of the roads), as evidenced by the inscription still visible on its arches. This venerable bridge joins the Isola Tiberina with the left bank of the Tiber.[6]

With Coarelli as our guide, we find the site of the ancient commercial Port of Rome (Portus Tiberinus) on the Tiber. It was located between today's Church of San Nicola in Carcere (Via del Teatro di Marcello n. 46), erected on the remains of three pagan temples of the old Forum Holitorium (the vegetable market), and the Temple of Portunus, god of harbours. The Temple of Portunus and, just south of it, the round Temple of Victorious Hercules, still stand in the green space between St Mary in Cosmedin and the left bank of the Tiber. The egress into the Tiber of the *Cloaca Maxima*, the great sewer of Rome, is located between these two ancient temples.[7]

How important was the control of the maritime harbour of Rome, Portus, would become evident during the sieges of Rome by Alaric.

The inhabitants of Rome obtained water from the Tiber, which was probably unclean, as well as from freshwater wells and springs.[8] Also, Rome had superb aqueducts, which transported large amounts of water into the city, but their extramural sections were exposed to the risk of destruction by invaders.[9] Including those in the city itself, there were nineteen aqueducts.[10]

Nero added a long limb to the Claudia aqueduct. Modern Romans know his addition as Aquedotto Neroniano. A landscaped portion of this ancient marvel still stands inside the British Embassy in Rome, located in Villa Wolkonsky. An even longer tract of this impressive aqueduct runs from the Church of the Holy Cross in Jerusalem to the Basilica of St John in Lateran.[11]

The nine oldest aqueducts brought into the city around 992,200 cubic metres of water daily. According to some estimates, in the time of Trajan, the population of Rome was 1 million. That meant 1,000 litres of water per inhabitant, which compares favourably with 1,475 litres per day expected by a Roman citizen in 1968.[12] It has been suggested that before Alaric's sack of the city in 410, Rome had about eight hundred thousand inhabitants.

The population estimates for ancient and early medieval Rome are the subject of academic debate. Recently, Gatto has suggested that the estimates for the Early Empire are too high.[13] If he is correct, then the volume of water per inhabitant in early imperial Rome was even greater than 1,000 litres. Most or all of the aqueducts of Rome were probably working in the early 400s.

Being outside the walls, the cemeteries, catacombs, as well as the churches of the emerging Christian Rome would be defenceless in the face of a barbarian invasion. According to the law, there were no burial grounds inside the city, and this promised to be a major problem in case of siege.

The buildings and infrastructure of late ancient Rome are fascinating, but what of the people who lived in the Eternal City before the sack of Alaric?

SOCIAL INSTABILITY IN ROME

The picture of Roman society in this era painted by Ammianus Marcellinus, who is considered a reliable source, is one of moral decline and social discord bound to work to the advantage of the besieging Visigoths. To Ammianus aristocrats were conceited, hedonistic, dishonest and vain, flaunting their many coats and slaves; and lazy plebeians were given to a variety of dissipations from drinking and gambling, to visiting prostitutes and idling away their time at public shows, chariot races and other amusements.[14] Ammianus' view of the plebeians is obviously unsympathetic. The plebeians made their living at various occupations and some of them collected money from one or more patrons. They also benefited from having access to free or cheap food.[15]

Ammianus relates that a few professors of classical studies were banished from Rome during the food shortage of 384 because they were not born in the city. He was furious that three thousand dancers with their choruses and an equal number of dance teachers were permitted to stay with no questions asked. Historians suspect that his resentment stemmed from the fact that he himself may have been among those kicked out of Rome.[16]

Gatto explains that at the top of the social hierarchy in late imperial Rome were the toga-wearing senators. Chief among them were the illustrious men (*viri illustri*), whose ranks provided the urban prefect and the prefect of the grain and who came from the patrician families of the city, such as the Decii and the Anicii; the lower-ranking senators known as the distinguished men (*viri clarissimi*) and the notable men (*viri spectabiles*), who participated in Senate meetings but were not allowed to sit or make speeches.[17]

The middle classes included the bankers, merchants, craftsmen and workers. The honourable men (*viri honesti*) included imperial and municipal employees, physicians, architects, lawyers and diverse intellectuals. The teachers, physicians and public speakers were considered public employees, were paid in kind from the *annona*, did not pay taxes and were highly regarded by the government.[18] Then there were the soldiers and, finally, the humble, the poor, the servants and the homeless, who together made up the picturesque and legendary crowd populating the public areas of Rome.[19]

As to the magistracies of the republican era, the aedileship and the tribunate of the plebeians had vanished by the year 300. In the Late Empire, Rome had quaestors, praetors and consuls chosen on a yearly basis. Although these were mostly nominal dignities, as the real power was in the hands of the emperor and urban prefect, they were highly valued in spite of the huge spending involved (holding public shows and making donations of money) because they opened the door to the highest ranks of the social and political civilian pecking order.[20]

The trades were organised in corporations operating according to state laws under the patronage of distinguished citizens. Those corporations, which were working for Rome itself, had certain advantages. In the case of corporations considered essential for the well-being of the community as a whole, the positions had to remain in the family by law and the tradesmen had to keep their belongings as collaterals to the execution of the jobs expected of them. The wholesalers were important to the economy of the city. The Roman retailers loathed the Greek wholesale traders, who were expelled from the city in the first decades of the fifth century but in 440 Valentinian III allowed them to operate again in Rome.[21]

Rome had many craftsmen involved in the construction of both private and public buildings. Skilled artisans such as mosaicists, painters, sculptors and goldsmiths embellished public edifices, the houses of the nobility and Christian places of worship.[22]

The charioteers, pimps, prostitutes, innkeepers and actors were kept under close observation by the urban prefect. After conversion to Christianity, they were not allowed to resume their previous work since these occupations were considered dishonourable.[23]

In general, the great city had come to rely less on the power of slaves when compared to previous centuries, because since the time of Trajan's Dacian campaigns, there were no more Roman invasions for the purpose of annexing distant territories. However, even in the Christian era, the use of slaves remained widespread, and the Christians did not agitate for the abolition of slavery. All the clergy did was to urge the owners to be kind to their slaves.[24]

In 316, Constantine forbade the branding of slaves on the face with a red-hot iron. After that, slaves had to wear chokers indicating the name and address of their owner. The owner who killed a slave by beating was liable to retribution according to a law of 319, except when the beating came as punishment for some recognised offence. In 321, Constantine permitted the freeing of a slave in church (in addition to the customary procedures for freeing slaves), in the presence of the local bishop. Runaway slaves risked ending up doing time in the mines or having a foot amputated.[25]

Many of the slaves in Rome on the eve of Alaric's invasion were Goths captured after the defeat of Radagaisus by Stilicho in 405–6. These slaves were burning with the desire to extract revenge from their masters. In fact, the Goths taken prisoner as a result of the defeat of Radagaisus were so numerous that they were sold for one *aureus* each, a price usually paid for inexpensive livestock.[26] (The *aureus* was the typical gold coinage from Julius Caesar to Constantine. The *solidus* issued by Constantine gradually superseded it.)[27]

TURMOIL IN THE RUN-UP TO THE SACK BY ALARIC

Tension continued to threaten the Roman state in the years before the sack of 410. Discord within the Roman government, an increasing divide between the city's Roman and non-Roman populations, Christian–pagan confrontations, Arian Christian–Nicaean Christian clashes, conflict within the emerging Christian hierarchy and between the Church and emperor also helped to weaken Rome.

On the death of Constantine the Great in 337, his sons Constantine II (337–40), Constantius II (337–61) and Constans (340–50) divided the empire in three. The soldiers, probably not of their own volition, slaughtered all the other relatives of Constantine the Great apart from Gallus and Julian, the sons of Julius Constantius, Constantine's half-brother.[28] Julian was to be the last pagan emperor (361–3), also known as Julian the Apostate.

After the death of his brothers, Constantius II became sole ruler of the empire in 353. In the spirit of his father, Constantius II wanted to use Christianity to enhance the cohesion of the Empire. He attempted to achieve this by embracing Arianism and eliminating all backing for Athanasius and the formula of Nicaea.[29]

Pope Julius I (337–52) erected St Mary in Trastevere (Piazza Santa Maria in Trastevere), the first church in Rome dedicated to the Virgin Mary.[30] In 339 he openly gave communion to Athanasius, the exiled champion of the Nicene Creed and former bishop of Alexandria, and challenged his Arian opponents then meeting at Antioch (Antakya in modern Turkey) in the East to participate in a council at Rome to tackle the controversy, which had continued to rage unabated after the death of Constantine.[31]

In a hostile letter, the eastern bishops disputed Julius' authority to give communion to someone denounced by one of their councils. The letter emphasised that the founders of Rome's sacred power, the Apostles Peter and Paul, first taught in the East before travelling to Rome. Moreover, the eastern letter stated, all bishops of the empire were equal in status.[32] This first major challenge to the supremacy of Rome foreshadowed the future East–West division of Christianity that continues to this day. Julius died in 352.

Liberius (352–66), the new pope, firmly withstood Constantius's pressures on him to join the Arian camp, but gave in during his banishment to Thrace (roughly, today's Bulgaria) and was permitted to travel to Rome in 358. Evidently, his lapse far away from home did not stop the people of Rome rallying in the streets to demand his reinstatement. Somehow Liberius managed to rehabilitate himself and resumed his anti-Arian stance.[33] His confrontation with the emperor prefigured the bitter conflicts of the papacy with the emperors of the Middle Ages.

Pope Damasus (366–84) followed Liberius and continued his anti-Arian line. In his engaging style, Rendina narrates that the election of Damasus was accompanied by a vicious confrontation between his supporters and the supporters of Ursinus (366–7), who had himself been elected by another faction in St Mary in Trastevere. In those years, the populace participated directly in the elections of the Roman bishops.[34]

Ammianus Marcellinus relates that the fighting in the streets was so intense, that the urban prefect Viventius was forced to leave for the relative safety of the outer reaches of Rome.[35] When order was finally restored, 137 corpses were discovered in the Christian basilica of Sicininus.[36] The gangs of Damasus included the *fossores* (the tough and ruffianly catacomb diggers), gladiators and charioteers.[37] The brutality of the competition between Damasus (known as the 'ladies' ear tickler' for his ability to flatter wealthy women into donating large sums to the Church) and Ursinus suggests that the office of the Roman bishop was already prestigious.

Ammianus Marcellinus expresses himself with supreme sarcasm when he denounces the worldly motives of those aspiring to be elected pope. In an implicit acknowledgement of such abuse of office, an imperial ruling issued in 370 expressly prohibited the clergy from entering the residences of wealthy widows and heiresses. St Jerome, who cannot be suspected of pagan bias, also wrote scathing lines about those who entered the priesthood only to follow their secret materialistic desires.[38]

In those years, the farsighted among the popes sought to convert the pagan attachment to the Eternal City into an attachment to the Roman Church. The Christians led by Pope Damasus ran a tenacious campaign for the removal of the Statue of Victory from the Senate,[39] an initiative opposed by the still-existing pagan faction of the Senate led by Symmachus, perhaps one of the last Romans to wear the ancient toga.[40] The pedestal of this famous statue can still be seen between the two doors at the back of the Senate in the Roman Forum.[41] In the end the Christians won.

Damasus was a strong defender of the Nicene Creed. He must have been delighted when Theodosius (379–95), a zealous Catholic, became emperor in the East. In February 380, Theodosius issued his famous decree ordering all Romans to follow the Christian religion 'as the Pontiff Damasus manifestly observes it'.[42]

In 381, Theodosius organised a council at Constantinople, the first after Nicaea. No bishops or delegates from the West attended. This second council put together a creed that included the Nicene formula and at the same time offered an acceptable way out of the Arian controversy. The new creed is known as the Constantinopolitan-Nicene Creed and is still part of the Catholic and Anglican liturgy.[43]

Theodosius also prohibited Christians from worshipping in non-orthodox churches and transferred the properties of the latter to the orthodox ones. Those who nevertheless adhered to branches of the faith deemed heretical such as the Arians and the Donatists were subjected to persecution and often slaughtered.[44]

Duffy relates that the emboldened popes began imitating the manners of the Roman emperors. Pope Siricius' (384–99) first epistle sounded like a list of imperial answers formulated to create legal precedents. Pope Innocent I (401–17) emphasised in his letter to the African bishops that 'it has been decreed by a divine, not a human authority' that every resolution made in the provinces of the empire, even those located far away, had to be confirmed by the Holy See.[45]

The clergy were well organised. Gatto tells us that Pope Fabian (236–50) divided the city into seven districts, each under a deacon who was in charge of administering the material aspects of their community life, helping the poor and writing and preserving the archives. While still numerically inferior to the pagans, the Christians of those years were so numerous that they had to give up the organisation centred on the catacombs.[46] It has been estimated that there were some eighty thousand Christians in Rome in the time of Pope Damasus.[47] The popes, surrounded by the Roman clerical bureaucracy, saw themselves as lawgivers,[48] but they were still excluded from the politics of the city and the empire. However, this was beginning to change.

Emperors Gratian (375–83) and Theodosius were the first to refuse the designation of Pontifex Maximus, which the popes later adopted.[49] We do not know when exactly the popes began using this title, which is still in use today.

Emperor Theodosius announced to the senators of Rome in 389 that public funding of pagan sacrifices was to be terminated.[50] In 391 Theodosius prohibited both public and private pagan worship[51] in a decree that directly affected the pagans of Rome and the pagan temples of the city.[52] However, the authorities generally tended to protect the disused pagan temples adorning the city. Large, openly pagan enclaves persisted in Rome until the intolerant Theodosius administered the final blow to paganism in 391.[53]

Only in the fifth century were the pagan temples no longer renovated used as a source of building materials in the construction of new Christian churches.[54] Already in the fourth century, the furnishings and objects associated with the pagan cults were being recycled on a large scale for use in Christian worship. For example, statues of Juno or Minerva became St Mary the Mother of God. Furnishings such as plates, bowls, cups, censers, patens, chandeliers and basins were easily transferred from use in the pagan rites to use in Christian ritual.[55] The church of St Susanna was erected during the century before the sack of Alaric and was built above the two houses belonging to Susanna's father and uncle. In 295, the men of Emperor Diocletian beheaded Susanna in front of her home for refusing to marry a pagan selected by him. Today's charming St Susanna is the home of the American Catholic Church in Rome.

Many aristocrats living in Rome converted to Christianity and donated their worldly possessions to the poor, like the famous St Marcella. Disgusted by the decadence of Roman society, the Christians lost all confidence in the corrupt state and dedicated themselves to mystic meditation in seclusion. Their sense of belonging to the Roman community and interest in its politics evaporated and was replaced by withdrawal into an ascetic life. However, during these years when Christianity was attracting so many converts and leaving the catacombs behind, some of its previous egalitarian teachings, aimed at clearly differentiating Christian from pagan morals, were abandoned.[56]

EMPERORS AND THE CITY

But, as Wallace-Hadrill tells us, emperors rarely visited Rome in those years.[57] The Arian Constantius II saw Rome in 357. In 389, Theodosius the Great came to Rome, thus making the first imperial visit after that of

Constantius. Initially, Theodosius attempted to appease the pagans by appointing two notables, Nichomachus Flavianus and Symmachus, to important positions. However, under the influence of the radical Ambrose, bishop of Milan, in 391 Theodosius ordered Flavianus, the prefect of Italy, to put into effect his decree prohibiting all pagan sacrifices and cults.

In reaction to this hostile volte-face, the pagans gave the Western crown to Eugenius (392–4), a philo-pagan, after the death of Valentinian II in 392 in dubious circumstances. Eugenius ruled from Milan and many distinguished pagans, among them Flavianus, joined his camp. Theodosius, with the Gothic army commanded by the Arian Alaric on his side, defeated Eugenius in 394 in the battle of the River Frigidus (Vipava, Slovenia).[58]

There was one last happier imperial visit to Rome before the invasion of Alaric, that of Honorius in 403–4. During the fourth century the Romans had witnessed the impressive growth of the Roman Church and of the authority of its popes. However, this had not been enough to restore to the city the prosperity it had enjoyed in the past due to the presence of the imperial court in Rome, or to alleviate the constantly escalating fears of barbarian invasion.[59]

At the beginning of the fifth century, the Romans eagerly asked Honorius to return to Rome. And return he did in 403, accompanied by his master of soldiers and father-in-law Stilicho, who, as we shall see, was still basking in the glory of his partial victory over Alaric at Pollentia in 402 and was finishing the works of improvement on the Aurelian Wall, aimed at preparing the city for a Gothic attack. Claudian described in grand terms the Roman sojourn of Honorius, complete with triumphs, pageantry, long-forgotten ceremonies enacted at Rome's famous sites and a delighted citizenry.[60] The emperor resided in the imperial palaces on the Palatine, rarely used in the previous century. The imperial faction was trying hard to alleviate Rome's rising anxiety.[61]

Thus, Honorius treated the populace to chariot races, hunting shows (*venationes*) and exotic dancers. The deadly gladiatorial combats had been banned by Constantine and, after him, by Theodosius, Honorius' father. Honorius, for some reason, did not restate the prohibition.[62]

In the Colosseum, the gladiators resumed their traditionally violent confrontations, taking Honorius' silence as tacit authorisation. When the Christian monk Telemachus realised that one of the gladiators was going to die, he jumped into the arena and struggled to separate the combatants in a daring attempt to prevent the useless loss of life. The enraged spectators, still yearning to see the loser die, stoned the poor monk to death. Honorius was compelled to intervene and banned the games.[63] The hunting shows vanished during the sixth century, in both the East and West.[64]

Towards the end of 404, upon learning that hordes of Ostrogoths under Radagaisus had invaded Italy, Honorius left Rome. It was not the first Gothic invasion of Italy, but Honorius must have been troubled by the increasing reports of barbarians battering the gates of his empire.[65] He decamped to safer terrain, leaving the great city to fend for itself.

Indeed, a more famous Goth named Alaric had shown up in the Italian peninsula only three years earlier. As it was he who eventually stole from Rome the treasure of interest to us, we will now discuss in more detail his wanderings through the Roman realm.

FOUR

Alaric Invades the Empire

In 401 Alaric and his mainly Gothic followers invaded northern Italy for the first time. The local Romans, unused to the presence of invading armies after centuries of safety and peace, witnessed to their horror the march of the entire Gothic people along the Roman roads. Their fantastic convoy included good-looking, tall, fair-skinned, blond, long-haired horsemen and foot soldiers covered in all sorts of wild animal skins; wagons and carts loaded with their belongings, provisions and heaps of gold, silver, jewellery and other precious objects; sturdy blonde women wearing linen embroidered with purple; and the children and elderly, too.[1] The arms of the women were completely bare, but their clothes concealed their breasts.[2] The men sported big moustaches and short to medium beards. In contrast to the toga-clad Romans, they wore trousers.[3]

Italy and Rome were in great danger. Where had Alaric and his fierce people come from and how had they accumulated their astounding treasures?

ENTERING ROMAN TERRITORY

A quarter of a century earlier, in the summer of AD 376, the northern shore of the Danube in the flatlands of modern south-eastern Romania, perhaps in the area of Călăraşi (opposite Bulgarian Silistra),[4] was crowded with tens of thousands of wretched Gothic men and women of all ages. After two battles with the Huns, the Goths had come to the conclusion that they simply did not know how to fight them. Many Goths became refugees.[5] On arriving at the Danube, they frantically sought permission to enter the Roman Empire, their traditional enemy, to save themselves from annihilation by the Huns.[6]

The Goths were waiting anxiously inside a gigantic circle formed by bulky, cumbersome carts and wagons. They were waiting for the return of their representatives, who had crossed the river on rafts to talk to the Roman soldiers manning the watchtowers and fortresses on the southern bank. Inside the circle were thousands of foot warriors carrying round shields and spears. Their swords were hidden in scabbards that hung on additional belts attached to their rather wide main belts or to baldrics (belts worn diagonally from shoulder to hip). Some of the men sported showy buckles decorated with gold, silver, or precious stones that were sparkling in the sun. The warriors carried clasp-type helmets (*Spangehelm*) that, when worn, completely covered their foreheads and gave them a stern and menacing look. These helmets were made of four to six plates connected by strengthening strips and had neck, cheek and nose guards.[7] That day the weather was too hot for helmets, and there was no indication that a battle was imminent.

There were many wounded among the warriors, their families helping them.[8] Hundreds of horsemen stood by their steeds. Some would gallop north at the request of their worried companions only to return after a while covered in dust, their lips parched, to tell the crowds sitting or wandering inside the circle to relax because they had seen no enemy fighters moving towards the camp. The horsemen and the foot warriors were not in a belligerent mood. On the contrary, they looked tired and concerned.

Another large group of Goths[9] crossed the Danube at a different point, but still on the territory of today's Romania, an area that had once been a Roman province. Desperately seeking safety, many of these people on the run were going to become followers of a mysterious chieftain named Alaric, a man who changed the course of history.

THE GOTHS AND ALARIC IN THE EASTERN ROMAN LANDS

When Alaric was about 6 years old, his princely family must have sought refuge in the Roman Empire with the thousands of Goths who were fleeing the unbeatable Huns. The Romans, weak and divided politically into Eastern and Western halves, consented to let in the Goths,[10] and the barbarian tribes crossed the Danube into the empire. But, it is alleged, before the Romans brought them across the river, the Goths took an oath to continue to fight the Roman Empire in any manner accessible to them.[11] The Romans had good reason to be suspicious of the fearful new tide of refugees clawing their way into the empire, but according to the ancient writer Eunapius, there were Romans who saw in the difficult situation of the Goths an opportunity to acquire their fabulous riches. The Romans did not disarm the Goths as they crossed,[12] perhaps intending that the tribes should serve in Rome's army. This would prove to be a mistake.

After the crossing, the leaders of the Tervingi Goths admitted into the empire, including Prince Alaviv, attended a dinner given by the Romans with the purpose of discussing contentious matters. The Romans were totally unprepared to deal with so many refugees, and many things went wrong (for example, there were food shortages and instances of exploitation of the Goths by rapacious Romans), causing deep resentment among the Goths. Violence broke out at the dinner.[13] After this episode, the name of Alaviv no longer appears in the reports of Ammianus Marcellinus.[14] It has been suggested that the Romans killed him. Heather[15] and Schwarz[16] agree that Prince Alaviv of the Tervingi and Alaric were perhaps related and note that, according to Claudian, Alaric was left fatherless as a child.

In 378, when Alaric was about eight, the Tervingi Goths rebelled and, in alliance with horsemen from other tribes, inflicted a historic defeat on the Roman army at Adrianople (Turkish Edirne). As reported by Wolfram, they killed in combat the majority of the Roman generals and thirty-five high-ranking officers.[17] Valens also perished. He was the second Roman emperor the Goths killed in battle, after Decius in 251; and the Goths captured Valens' imperial treasure.[18]

The following year, in 379, Emperor Theodosius the Great (379–95) succeeded Valens as emperor in the East. Three years later, in 382 he concluded a treaty with the Goths. By means of this treaty, Theodosius settled the Gothic tribes between the Danube and the Balkan Mountains as autonomous peoples federated to Rome. Under the treaty the tribes were obliged to go to war under Roman command if ordered to do so by the emperor.[19]

Prince Alaric was probably twenty-one in 391. Only a few rudimentary images of him survive, including a stone seal, which is housed in Berlin's Bildarchiv Preussischer Kulturbesitz,[20] and a coin.[21] While von Platen's poetic Alaric in 'Das Grab im Busento' had shoulder-length hair, both the coin and the seal show him with rather short hair, more like a Roman. We have seen that according to the ancient writers, the Goths were tall, blond and handsome; and Alaric was probably no exception.[22] Whatever his looks, as a Gothic prince Alaric was already in a position to command men in battle, and he was intent on wresting for himself the leadership of all the Gothic people and turning them against the empire that sheltered them.

In 391, Alaric made his first appearance on the scene in grand fashion: he broke the treaty of 382. Under his leadership, multitudes of Goths and other tribesmen crossed the Balkan Mountains and began moving towards the fields of Thrace and the capital, Constantinople. Theodosius lost the ensuing battle and was very close to becoming the third Roman emperor killed in combat with the Goths, but General Promotus rescued him. For this act of bravery, Theodosius made Promotus commander-in-chief of his anti-Gothic operations. Promotus lost his life in battle that same year.[23]

Theodosius replaced Promotus with a highly able general, the half-Roman, half-Vandal Stilicho. Stilicho was married to Serena, a niece of Theodosius. The new commander defeated and encircled Alaric in 392 but, amazingly, Theodosius ordered Stilicho to release him. Historians tell us that Theodosius no longer had the choice of wiping out an army of imperial federates, however rebellious they showed themselves to be, because the weakened empire no longer had the power or resources to do so. Theodosius decided on a policy of expediency: he would co-opt Alaric and the Goths into the Roman forces.[24]

This was the starting point of a perplexing series of four battles between Stilicho and Alaric over the next ten years (392–402), a sequence of battles which is counted among the most puzzling military rivalries in history.[25]

As we have seen, in 394, the supporters of paganism in the West rallied around the usurper Eugenius against Theodosius. In the battle that followed, the Goths led by Alaric were placed on the front line and sustained severe losses (some 50 per cent of their forces perished). They began to suspect that the Romans were trying to get rid of them by attrition.[26]

After brutally bringing to an end the brief pagan revival of Rome, Theodosius died in 395 and his sons Honorius (395–423) and Arcadius (395–408) became rulers of the West and East respectively. The Roman prefecture of Illyricum, which corresponds roughly to modern Greece and the former Yugoslavia, was divided between East and West along the Drinus (Drina) River. In the time of Alaric, the governments of Arcadius and Honorius quarrelled extensively about this province.[27]

Because of the new emperor's youth, in the first half of the child Honorius' reign, the actual ruler was his master of soldiers, Stilicho, his future father-in-law. Intermarriage with the offspring of prominent Germans was already acceptable to the Roman imperials. For example, the future wife of Arcadius, Eudoxia, was the daughter of the Frankish general Bauto, Master of Soldiers under the Western emperor Gratian. It should not escape our attention that both Alaric and Stilicho (on his father's side) were of German descent, details that reflect the slow but steady Germanisation of the Roman Empire. The ultimate effects of this process were going to be ruinous.[28]

After the death of Theodosius in 395, it seems that the payments the imperial government had made to keep the Goths loyal dried up. Angered, Alaric resigned his position in the Roman army and was elected king. Alaric did not waste much time. He publicly accused the Romans of not paying the promised subventions[29] and rebelled again.[30] He marched towards the capital, Constantinople, but changed course after Rufinus, the imperial counsellor and an enemy of Stilicho, held a confidential meeting with him.[31]

Alaric's followers during these years were mainly but not exclusively Goths.[32] (Cassiodorus coined the term by which we know them, Visigoth, or Western Goth, only in the sixth century.[33]) When finally in the field of Thessaly, not far from Larissa, Alaric's people quickly made a defensive circle of their carts and wagons to protect their families and goods and awaited the Romans.[34]

The whole Roman army, Eastern and Western, arrived under the command of Stilicho. Indeed, the entire Roman army had been in the West since the campaign of 394, in which Alaric also participated. Stilicho's troops positioned themselves in a way that prevented any further Gothic movements.[35]

Then the impossible happened. When Stilicho was close to initiating an attack, which was almost certain to succeed because of the numerical superiority of his army, Arcadius, counselled by Rufinus, commanded him to send the Roman troops contributed by the Eastern Empire back to Constantinople. Arcadius also instructed Stilicho to return to the West.[36] Stilicho complied and sent the Eastern troops to the great city, and Arcadius and his entourage came out to greet them. The soldiers, led by the fierce Gainas, a tribesman of Alaric, suddenly cut off Rufinus' arms and decapitated him.[37] It is thought that Stilicho was behind this gruesome assassination.[38]

After the lack of unity between the two heirs of Theodosius caused the break-up of the Roman army, the Goths engaged in plundering the defenceless citizens, cities and temples of Greece for about a year, when they were encircled, starved and dehydrated by Stilicho at Pholoe in the north-western mountains of the Peloponnese. Instead of destroying the warriors and seizing their enormous booty, Stilicho reached some secret agreement with Alaric and departed without attacking.[39]

Stilicho's perplexing decision has been blamed variously on the unruliness of his Germanic soldiers, on the discord between East and West, or on Stilicho's preferred strategy of using Alaric to achieve his own political goals.[40]

In 397, the government of Arcadius gave in to Alaric's demands and allowed the Goths to settle in the centre of Macedonia, in the disputed Illyricum. Alaric, who had just finished looting and burning Greece, was promoted to master of soldiers in Illyricum (subordinate only to the praetorian prefect) and was also given imperial authority to oversee the public services of these lands, arms, shops, storage facilities and the like.[41]

Then something decisive happened. Emboldened by the successes of Alaric's Goths, the Greuthungian Goths, who served in the Roman army in Asia Minor (Turkey), rebelled and the ethnically non-Roman armies sent to restore order fraternised with them. Even the Arian Gainas, a tribesman of Alaric's and leader of the Roman army in the East, defected to them in 399–400.[42]

Gainas proved so inept a ruler that in the summer of 400 the infuriated citizens of Constantinople took up arms. The populace killed thousands of Goths. It was clear that the Eastern Romans were no longer willing to tolerate the unruly Goths. The Huns, in control of the lands north of the Danube in today's Romania, captured the fleeing Gainas and sent his head to Constantinople. Arcadius responded with gifts and made a treaty with them. Caught between hostile Romans and hostile Huns,[43] the Goths were intimidated. Alaric understood that there was no longer a future for him and his people in the East.[44]

Still relatively stable and strong, the Eastern Roman Empire had a thousand years ahead of it. A more tempting field of conflict was the Western Empire. That was where Alaric would find his new hope and new target – and his treasure.

THE END OF ALARIC'S FIRST INVASION OF ITALY

We are now ready to return to Alaric's first invasion of Italy, which, as we have seen, commenced in 401. On 6 April 402, at Pollentia (modern Pollenzo near Turin in northern Italy), the Roman army caught unawares the Goths of Alaric, who were not anticipating an attack because it was Easter Day.[45] The ensuing battle ended in stalemate, but not before Stilicho had managed to capture the entire treasure of the Goths, including the scarlet-dyed robes of Valens which the Goths had seized at Adrianople in 378.[46]

Given the ancestral gold lust of the Visigoths, the loss of their treasure at Pollentia must have made them extremely angry and highly motivated to plunder the wealthy urban centres of imperial Italy.

As surprising as it seems, Stilicho let Alaric escape again. The contemporary poet Claudian, a protégé of Stilicho, tells us that Stilicho spared Alaric's life for political reasons.[47]

That same year, Alaric stopped at Verona in northern Italy. In the manoeuvres that followed, Stilicho's troops surrounded the Gothic king on a hill, a strange replay of his situation at Pholoe in Greece. Alaric's warriors abandoned him in large numbers, Visigoths included. Amazingly, Stilicho let him escape yet again.[48]

Amid the feverish activity of his machinations against the East and his efforts to oppose Alaric's repeated onslaughts at the heart of the empire, Stilicho did not pay enough attention to the increasing risk posed by the restless barbarian tribes on its Western borders.[49] And so began the lengthy and painful process of the disintegration of the Roman Empire.

WEAKNESS OF THE ROMAN EMPIRE IN THE WEST

Alaric and his people settled in eastern Illyricum without the permission of Constantinople.[50] In 404–5, Stilicho forged a treaty with Alaric and, in a flagrant intrusion into the affairs of the Eastern Empire, appointed him master of soldiers in Illyricum.[51]

But before trying to install Alaric in his new position, Stilicho had to deal with a massive Ostrogoth invasion from the north in 405–6, led by the ferocious pagan Goth Radagaisus, the same who had vowed to sacrifice all the Romans to his gods.[52] Stilicho succeeded in stopping it. There was also a usurpation of imperial power by a man named Constantine in Britain (407–11). The situation was further complicated by the untrue reports of Alaric's death received by Stilicho.[53]

But the worst was what happened at the end of 406, not long after the defeat and execution of Radagaisus. In the West, on 31 December 406, and for reasons still unclear, large groups of Vandals, Suevians and Alans crossed the Rhine at Mainz (Germany). The Western Romans were no longer able to drive them out of Gaul as their resources had been drained by the attacks of Alaric and Radagaisus on the core of the empire.[54] The invasion of 406 started the slow but steady dismemberment of the Roman Empire in the West, which cleared the map for the eventual rise of the modern nation-states of Europe.[55]

By 408, Stilicho was forced to come to terms with the East, and he no longer needed Alaric. The Visigothic king, however, marched towards Italy but stopped before advancing into it and demanded 4,000lb of gold, and we have seen that this was roughly the yearly income of a rich senator (equivalent to some £18.86 million or US $34.12 million in 2005 terms). Honorius, who was again in Rome between November 407 and May 408,[56] convened the Senate in the imperial palace.[57] Stilicho barely managed to persuade the Senate to agree to these terms and appointed Alaric master of soldiers in Gaul, where the Goth was to lead the Roman army and his tribesmen in a campaign against the usurper Constantine. The payment and the appointment never materialised.[58]

In an attempt to halt the expansion of the barbarian authority at the imperial court, the Roman anti-German faction convinced the pitiable Honorius that Stilicho was plotting with Alaric to seize the throne.[59] Honorius agreed to bring down his own father-in-law, one of the last capable Roman generals of the West.[60] Stilicho was decapitated on 22 August 408.[61] The empire was deprived of its best general at the very moment when it needed him the most, a disaster that reflects the monumental incompetence of Honorius. Nor did the bungling anti-German party stop at this incredibly foolish move. They encouraged the Roman soldiers to massacre the families of their non-Roman comrades. As a result, these foreign soldiers defected *en masse* to Alaric.[62]

The Visigothic king could not believe what was happening: the Romans were emasculating themselves as if they wanted to make it easier for him to strike.

ALARIC LAYS SIEGE TO ROME

Alaric continued to demand 4,000lb of gold as recompense for his retreat, but Honorius did not agree. After marching into Venetia, Alaric unsuccessfully attacked Ravenna, which was protected by swamps.[63] The city of Rome was a tempting treasure, and Alaric knew it was all but his for the taking, so he marched on the heart of Italy.

The extraordinary Visigothic procession, now without the sparkling treasures captured by the Romans at Pollentia, began moving again on the roads of Italy.[64] Military units to match the army of Alaric did not protect the ill-fated Rome, whose hapless citizens were handed weapons and underwent some instruction in their use.[65] Though Rome had long ceased to be the capital of the empire, the old city retained great symbolic importance in the minds of Romans, all of whom shared citizenship in that city.

In October 408, Alaric approached the Eternal City for the first time and organised a cordon around it. He took over Portus and put an end to the flow of grain to the city, seizing a load recently shipped from Africa.[66] He began to starve Rome slowly, hoping that this kind of pressure was going to get him what he wanted. The Visigoths possessed neither the skills nor the technology to break through the very high, antique-gold-coloured brick walls that seemed to touch the pale blue October skies.[67]

Within the walls, the Romans made drastic cuts to their daily bread allowance. They attempted to eat things such as acorn flour.[68] Inevitably, the city gradually exhausted its provisions and endured starvation and epidemics. Everywhere there were rotting corpses and these had to be buried within the city, as the Visigoths would not allow the Romans to leave it for their traditional cemeteries and catacombs.[69]

The siege, and the ravages it wrought, was a disaster unprecedented in Rome's long history.

The city sent embassies to Alaric. After talking about an equitable peace, the Roman emissaries told the king that the inhabitants were also ready for battle, should the peace talks end in failure. Alaric erupted into laughter and said, 'The thickest grass is more easy to cut than the thinnest'. He made it clear that the siege would continue unless the Roman authorities handed over to him all the gold and silver in the city, as well as all the domestic wares and barbarian slaves. The ambassadors of Rome relayed the extremely harsh conditions to the populace, and most of those inside the walls were filled with despair.[70]

In these moments of hopelessness, some citizens recalled the old pagan gods who were associated with Rome's glorious past. Zosimus, a pagan author, claimed that Pope Innocent I approved the performance of private pagan rites in the hope that they might bring relief to the desperate city.[71] However, no one had the courage to perform publicly what the ancient pagan rites required, so the city leaders decided to do everything to meet Alaric's demands.[72]

The Christians must have feverishly implored God, using the tombs of saints or holy relics as intermediaries, to deliver them from the hands of the ferocious Visigoths.

A certain Palladius collected contributions from individual Roman denizens according to their wealth, but he failed to obtain the required sum. To the dismay of Zosimus, the Romans acquired the still-needed precious metals by stripping the statues of the pagan gods of their dazzling adornments and by melting a number of those made from gold or silver, including the statue of Virtus (Valor). Zosimus noted that those Romans knowledgeable in the old ways of worship were of the opinion that the stripping of the old statues of the pagan gods rendered them impotent.[73]

To save their skins, the Romans delivered up to Alaric 5,000lb of gold (2,200kg); 30,000lb of silver (13,000kg); 4,000 silken robes; 3,000 purple-dyed furs; and 3,000lb of pepper (1,300kg).[74]

Seemingly satisfied, Alaric permitted the Romans to spend three days in Portus to provide the starving city with grain, but marauding Visigoths ambushed the Roman convoys coming back to the city and captured their foodstuffs. Alaric intervened personally to make sure his part of the agreement was fulfilled. Around that time, large numbers of slaves abandoned their Roman masters and joined the forces of the Visigothic king.[75]

At that point Honorius sent to Rome 6,000 Dalmatian (Dalmatia corresponds to the Adriatic coastal region of today's Croatia) troops to try and break the barbarian stranglehold on the city, but the Visigoths prevailed. The discouraged urban prefect took two senators with him and travelled to Ravenna to appeal to Honorius and persuade him to try again to release Rome from the horrendous blockade, but the son of Theodosius refused Alaric's terms, particularly the demand for hostages.[76]

Alaric withdrew to Tuscany around the time of the arrival of winter in 408. The disruption caused by the Goths had destroyed the economy and, because of inflation, all their gold could not adequately feed them. Alaric realised they needed to settle lands with inhabitants who would work to feed his indolent warriors.[77] In January and February 409 he tightened the blockade.[78]

In reaction to it, a new Roman delegation arrived in Ravenna. Besides senators, this embassy included Pope Innocent I.[79] Rendina observed that it was the first time in history that a pope intervened in secular politics.[80] More than 1,500 years later Pope John Paul II would still recall the papacy's first incursion into the politics of Europe in a 1981 speech.[81] Honorius gave in and sent his praetorian prefect Jovius to negotiate with Alaric in Rimini, but the talks ended prematurely and Alaric renewed his torment of the dying city.[82]

As autumn was approaching, a third delegation, headed by Attalus, the urban prefect, and Pope Innocent I, travelled to Ravenna to convey Alaric's demands to Honorius: the payment of annual levies, regular supplies of grain, his own appointment as Master of Soldiers (formerly Stilicho's position), and the territories from northern Italy to the German frontier.[83] Because Count Heraclian of Africa had ordered the Roman sea-going ships transporting grain to remain in Carthage, the Visigoths were hungry, too. Again Honorius rejected Alaric's terms.[84]

Then the government of Honorius reportedly hired 10,000 Hun horsemen, at which Alaric promptly reduced the size of his territorial demands. He also withdrew demands for his military appointment and the annual levies, but Honorius' government did not budge.[85] The Romans seemed to hope that the myth of Rome's invincibility was going to save the city.

Alaric reacted by encircling Rome again. Under pressure, the Senate agreed in December 409 to proclaim the urban prefect Attalus emperor. Alaric had himself appointed supreme military commander and Athaulf leader of the cavalry. But Attalus, a true Roman at heart, did not really govern as a puppet of the Visigothic king. For instance, he made the two German chieftains share their positions with Romans who were openly anti-Gothic.[86]

In January 410, Alaric and Attalus marched on Ravenna, joined by Jovius, the praetorian prefect. It was a very strange situation: a barbarian king accompanied by the praetorian prefect and the former urban prefect proclaimed emperor by the Roman Senate were marching menacingly on the legitimate emperor. In the meantime, Honorius had received the African *annona* and taxes. His position had also been strengthened by the arrival of troops from the East.[87]

It was an incredible roller-coaster ride. Now it was Alaric's turn to be under pressure. His people were hungry again. Halfway through the year 410, Alaric deposed Attalus in an attempt to appease Honorius and eventually managed to hold talks with him in person. It has been reported that the Roman emperor and the Visigothic king were close to reaching an accord that would have included the creation of a Gothic realm on Italian territory.[88]

At that moment, at the head of a squadron of some three hundred warriors, a Goth by the name of Sarus, a rival of Alaric, launched a surprise attack on the Gothic army. Honorius gave Sarus a favourable reception. This was unacceptable to Alaric, who marched on Rome again,[89] this time resolved to break into the city.[90]

The Visigothic king was filled with rage and his actions were unmistakably those of an enemy.[91] Returning to his army encamped around Rome's protective wall, Alaric was determined to further tighten his grip on the already starving city and weaken it until it was ripe for the taking. Within the city walls, whispered prayers, holy Christian relics, wailing and lamentation could not save the Romans from the barbarians.

FIVE

The Sack of Rome

The prolonged siege had devastating effects on the inhabitants of Rome. Desperation mounted. St Jerome[1] and Procopius[2] reported that the besieged had resorted to cannibalism. Alaric had set up his command centre not far from the Salarian Gate[3] (Porta Salaria, which stood in the area of today's Piazza Fiume; this gate looked not very different from the surviving St Paul's Gate), where the terrain was more even and the wall seemed more vulnerable, but his long-haired warriors must have clustered at all the gates of the Aurelian Wall to make sure nobody escaped the doomed city.

Eventually Alaric managed to get inside Rome, possibly through treachery by Arians and pagans.[4] In the accounts of Procopius, he is said to have pretended to give up the siege and, in an insincere gesture of good will, sent into the city 300 youthful Goths to act as servants to the senators of Rome. Before letting them into the city, Alaric commanded these adolescents to gather at the Salarian Gate at noon on a certain day not long after that, overwhelm and kill the guards, then allow their barbarian kinsmen to enter the city. The Romans usually had their midday sleep at that time, which would have increased the chances of success for Alaric's secret agents.[5]

Purportedly with the help of this fifth column made up of virtual teenagers, the Visigoths broke through the Porta Salaria on 24 August 410, almost two years to the day after the execution of General Stilicho. The nineteenth-century historian Ferdinand Gregorovius thought this account was a myth.[6]

According to other reports mentioned by the ancient historian Procopius, it was Proba, a rich matron of senatorial rank, who ordered her slaves to open the Porta Salaria in the belief that this would put an end to the suffering of the Romans.[7] The problem with this version of events is that it implies that Proba did not anticipate the disaster that the Goths would unleash upon the city if they were allowed to enter or, worse, that she did not care. Moreover, while it is possible that the slaves who allegedly overwhelmed the guards at Porta Salaria came from the house of Proba, they may equally have been part of that large contingent of servants which Alaric is supposed to have sent into the city to act as a fifth column. Exactly who helped the fighters of Alaric to break through Porta Salaria is still a mystery.

THE VISIGOTHS IN ROME

For the first time in 800 years, an invading army entered the Eternal City.[8] The rapacious Visigoths plundered it for three long days. The Salarian Gate they broke through led directly to the angle between Via Salaria and Via Nomentana, the district that was home to the richest inhabitants of Rome, its patricians and senators.[9]

The Visigoths set fire to the splendid gardens and Palace of Sallust located not far from the Porta Salaria, to the magnificent Basilica Aemilia located in the Roman Forum, to the Temple of Peace, situated just north of the Roman Forum, and to the Bath of the Palatine. They destroyed the liturgical ornaments at St Mary in Trastevere.[10] Other buildings set alight by Alaric's men included aristocratic houses on the Celian and Aventine Hills and the Suran and Decian Baths.[11] They caused severe damage to the Bath of Diocletian.[12] They wrecked the Basilica of Sts John and Paul on the Celian Hill.[13] They even looted the ornaments of the synagogue in Trastevere.[14] Outside the Aurelian Wall,[15] they ravaged the Christian and Jewish catacombs.[16] The obelisk that used to decorate the ancient gardens of Sallust, a mistaken Roman imitation of an Egyptian obelisk (the hieroglyphs are upside down), is now in front of the French church of Santissima Trinità dei Monti, situated just above the flight of steps descending to the Piazza di Spagna (the Spanish Steps). Today, the Aventine Hill is an exclusive residential area, exactly as it was before the sack of Alaric.

The sources do not mention any armed civic militias opposing the barbarians on the streets of Rome.[17] We should not forget, though, that the Romans were weakened by starvation and that the circumstances were extremely unusual: a huge city was left with no extra- or intra-mural military protection to face 40,000 battle-hardened, ferocious and merciless barbarians,[18] many of them unforgiving former slaves and vengeful former soldiers in the Roman army who had seen their families slaughtered by the Romans.[19] For the hordes of Alaric, dealing with the citizens of Rome was an easy butcher's job.

But even if the Romans had been well fed, they no longer possessed the fighting spirit of their ancestors. There was no heroic leader to rally round. There was no universally held ideal to do battle for. The Christians prayed, some of them in the presence of holy relics, but many of them no longer believed in the earthly Roman state and were focused instead on the kingdom of God. The Visigoths, however, made no distinction; they destroyed symbols of both the heavenly kingdom and the empire.

In ancient Rome, basilicas served as courts of law and places for public meetings. In early Christian and medieval times, the basilica was a type of building erected to serve as a church. Alaric's fighters torched the Basilica Julia, located in the Roman Forum,[20] built by Caesar and Augustus and then rebuilt by Diocletian[21] after the fire of Carinus in 283.[22] As we have seen, they also burned the Basilica Aemilia, an ancient structure that served as a hall of justice and public gathering place. Its pavement shows stains that look like marks left by coins melted in the heat of the blaze. The Romans restored this basilica after the fire, but an earthquake destroyed it beyond repair in 847.[23]

Right behind the Basilica Aemilia and the Temple of Antoninus Faustina was the Temple of Peace.[24] As a result of a construction programme carried out in the 1930s it is now almost completely buried under the intersection of Via dei Fori Imperiali and Via Cavour.[25] Emperor Vespasian had built the Temple of Peace in AD 71–5 to celebrate the victory over the Jews, and it is known to have sheltered the sacred objects of the Temple of Jerusalem captured by Titus in 70. The southern angle of the Temple of Peace survives as the Church of St Cosmas and St Damian situated near the Roman Forum, entered from Via dei Fori Imperiali.[26]

Assuming that the sacred objects taken from the Jerusalem Temple were still in place just before the sack of Rome, if Alaric's men set the Temple of Peace on fire they probably plundered it first, based on their well-documented habit of seizing gold and treasure. It simply would not make sense to presume that they set this temple on fire without pillaging it first.

Following this line of argument, some historians have suggested that the Visigoths made off with the Jewish Temple treasures. As we noted earlier, the Temple of Peace had been destroyed by a fire in 192 in the time of Commodus and it is not known where the Jerusalem treasure was kept before this fire, during it or, indeed, after it. The Temple of Peace was renovated under Emperor Septimius Severus (193–211).[27] This relatively rapid restoration might suggest that the Temple of Peace was a public edifice deemed important for the maintenance of Roman national prestige. The same might hold true for the objects it used to shelter, so we might speculate that the Jerusalem Temple treasure remained in or was brought back into the Temple of Peace. We have seen earlier that the Temple of Peace was probably intact when the Visigoths stormed the city. On the other hand, one of the pre-Alaric Christian emperors might have transferred the treasure, in its entirety or divided up, to one or more Christian churches of Rome, or, indeed, somewhere else.

Authors of late antiquity such as Jordanes, Procopius and Gregory of Tours were interested in the Jerusalem Temple and its treasure, which were connected through their history and symbolism to both the Old and New Testaments. Their curiosity may have been the reflection of a more widespread Christian interest in those matters, but we do not know with certainty how accurate was their information on the source of particular plundered objects.

The early Christians were fascinated with the Holy Land and its legendary sites and relics.[28] Indeed, it might be that in the minds of the early Christian pre-Alaric emperors, the treasure of the Jerusalem Temple belonged more in a great Christian church than in a pagan temple. Almost all the practices and teachings of the early Christian Church had their roots in Judaism, with the obvious exception of belief in Christ and everything associated with Him.[29]

This is highly speculative, but the idea that the Jerusalem Temple treasure might have ended up in the Christian churches of Rome does not seem far-fetched if one looks at the mentality of the early Christians and their desire to appropriate at least some of the prestige that came with the venerable and long history of Judaism. This is in keeping with the Christian idea that the Christian Churches had replaced the Temple of Jerusalem in a new covenant with God.[30] The problem with this hypothesis is that in their inescapable and permanent engagement with the Judaism of Jerusalem, the Christians have always been of two minds: they simultaneously removed and took possession of its realities.[31]

THE VISIGOTHS RAPE AND PILLAGE

Orosius, a Christian who lived at the time of the sack of Rome, related that the Visigoths captured the beautiful Galla Placidia, Honorius' half-sister, during the invasion of Rome.[32]

Zosimus wrote that Galla Placidia was a hostage of Alaric. His history ends before the invasion of Rome, so Galla Placidia may already have been Alaric's prisoner when his men stormed the Porta Salaria.[33] Unfortunately for our investigation, the Roman historical tradition was dying out. Claudian, the last of the Roman classical poets, had died in 404 in Rome, so the demise of the ancient city was never commemorated in verse with the voice of a classical bard. Ammianus Marcellinus, the last of the Roman classical historians, too had passed away, in 395 in Rome, so a chronicler of the calibre of Tacitus never reported the fall of the city.

Jordanes, himself a Germanic Christian[34] with a thinly veiled pro-Gothic stance at a time when Justinian's Ostrogothic wars, commonly referred to as the Gothic Wars, were approaching an end, downplayed the tragedy of conquered Rome. He wrote that on special orders from Alaric, his men did not set alight the city but limited themselves to plundering it, without causing grave damage to its churches.[35]

Orosius relates the story of an Arian Christian Goth who, while running around Rome in search of treasures, chanced upon an elderly virgin in a place of worship and deferentially asked her to hand him the gold and silver he suspected was to be found there. The Goth was filled with awe at the sight of the treasures that the old woman let him see. When he heard that those riches belonged to the Apostle Peter, the Goth sent a messenger to Alaric with the news that the fabled treasure of St Peter had been found. According to Orosius, Alaric immediately sent his men to escort both sacred objects and elderly virgin to the Church of the Apostle, as well as any Christians who might want to seek refuge there.

Then Orosius narrates how increasing numbers of invaders escorted the team of people who carried the holy items, and the swelling multitude hoping to find salvation in the church of the Apostle Peter. Orosius also relates that as the Romans were singing a hymn to God, the barbarians spontaneously joined their voices to those of the Roman choir.[36] Interestingly, Orosius seems to assume that the barbarians were familiar with the Latin words of the hymn.

None of the ancient authors wrote that the Visigothic king, a Christian and a married man, prohibited rape. Did Pope Innocent forget to mention that issue to Alaric? Or, if he did ask Alaric to protect the Roman women, what did Alaric do about it? Sozomenus reports an episode during the sacking of Rome in which a young invader, an Arian Christian, attempted to rape a beautiful Catholic Christian married woman, but eventually gave up when he realised that the woman, who was already bleeding from a cut he had caused with his weapon, was determined to die rather than suffer dishonour at his hands. Perhaps ashamed of his actions, he escorted her to the Basilica of St Peter and handed six pieces of gold to the sentinels on duty at the holy place with the request that they protect her.[37]

This episode, meant by Sozomenus to illustrate the virtues of Christianity, instead calls attention to the prevalence of rape in ancient warfare. There is no doubt that many Roman women were raped during those three days in late August 410 and that, after Alaric's men left, few raped Roman women were willing to disclose what had happened to them. It is easy to understand why.

The British historian Edward Gibbon took due note of the background, motivations and emotional state of the invaders as factual elements determining their conduct. He stated clearly the obvious, namely that the few main churches could offer protection and shelter only to a limited number of inhabitants, and that numerous soldiers from Alaric's army were not Christian. The British historian doubted that, in the chaos and barbarism of the sacking, Christian teachings played a significant part in the conduct of the Gothic followers of Jesus.[38]

In Bethlehem, the birthplace of Jesus Christ, today's travellers can see the severely ascetic rooms, well below ground level, where St Jerome, who was also contemporary with the sack of Rome, lived and worked on the translation of the Bible. St Jerome was a giant of scholarship. He not only translated the Greek New Testament into Latin, but also the Old Testament, mostly from Hebrew. Roman Catholics used the resulting Bible, the Vulgate, until the 1900s.[39] The amount of work required by these projects was enormous.

St Jerome left touching accounts of the plight of the inhabitants of Rome who fell prey to Alaric:

Who would believe that Rome, built by the conquest of the whole world, had collapsed, that the mother of nations had become also their tomb; that the shores of the whole East, of Egypt, of Africa, which once belonged to the imperial city, were filled with the hosts of her man-servants and maid-servants, that we should every day be receiving in this holy Bethlehem men and women who once were noble and abounding in every kind of wealth but now are reduced to poverty? We cannot relieve these sufferers: all we can do is to sympathise with them, and unite our tears with theirs.[40]

In these lines wounded Roman pride reverberates down the centuries.

St Jerome also wrote about the fate of St Marcella in the city invaded by the Goths. The fact that his account is based on reports taken from eye-witnesses makes it of even greater interest. The story of Marcella, who was reportedly in her convent on the Aventine Hill when the barbarians found her,[41] is a microcosm of the countless individual human tragedies enacted during Alaric's sack of Rome.

St Marcella, who belonged to the famous family of the Marcelli, is considered by hagiographers to be 'the model of all Christian widows'.[42] Seven months after her marriage, St Marcella's husband died. Thus, her daughter Principia lost her father before she was born. St Marcella was an extremely attractive woman. An older man of consular rank by the name of Cerealis tried in vain to persuade her to marry him. So eager was he to secure her hand that he even promised he would put all his vast wealth in her name.[43]

At a very young age, St Marcella embarked upon an ascetic life, although still in Rome. She dedicated herself to the study of the Holy Scriptures and became an authority in matters of doctrine. St Jerome guided her in the study of the Bible. He noted that she fasted assiduously, rejoiced in the study of the Holy Scriptures, and would sing at length lines proclaiming her dedication to the Christian faith.

St Jerome learned with great sadness that St Marcella died during Alaric's sack of Rome. Here follows a fragment from his letter of 412 to Principia, St Marcella's daughter, which serves as a sort of eulogy:

When the soldiers entered she is said to have received them without any look of alarm; and when they asked for her gold she pointed to her coarse dress to show them that she had no buried treasure. However they would not believe in her self-chosen poverty, but scourged her and beat her with cudgels. She is said to have felt no pain but to have thrown herself at their feet. . . . She said she was thankful too that the taking of the city had found her poor, not made her so, that she was not in want of daily bread, that Christ satisfied her needs so that she no longer felt hunger, that she was able to say in word and deed: 'Naked came I out of my mother's womb, and naked shall I return thither: the Lord gave and the Lord has taken away; blessed be the name of the Lord.'[44]

To many people who hear for the first time about the catacombs of Rome, they are dark, deep and sinister underground tunnels that do not offer very much to the visitor. Yet Alaric, a man who has been dubbed by some the world's first tour operator,[45] did send his men to raid the catacombs. He must have known that there was something valuable in those tunnels.

In spite of the typically Jewish features, such as menorahs, that held prominent positions in the Roman Jewish catacombs, the similarities in appearance between the Jewish and Christian catacombs are striking. For example, they display wall paintings with identical or very similar spatial organisation, ornamental motifs, depictions of animals and rustic scenes.[46] Very likely, the Jews hired artisans from the same workshops as their Christian counterparts. Moreover, as numerous early Christians of Rome were of Jewish extraction,[47] they probably persisted in using their old ways of subterranean interment and the next generations of Christians simply continued with the same method.[48] This should explain at least in part the resemblance between the Roman Christian and Jewish catacombs.

The last interment in the Christian catacombs of Rome took place in 535,[49] but, as Lanciani notes, the burials in those Christian underground graveyards seem to have largely ceased after Alaric's hordes plundered them in 410.[50]

The most recent archaeological and epigraphic finds from the Roman Jewish catacombs date from the beginning of the fifth century.[51] This probably means that in 410, Alaric's men also raided the Jewish catacombs, not only the Christian ones. The Visigothic savagery ended forever the trade of the catacomb diggers (*fossores*) and a long tradition of Christian funerary inscriptions. It is not certain when precisely the practice of Christian burials within the city began, but they are definitely documented for the reign of Theodoric (493–526).[52] There seems to be no information on the fate of the Jews of Rome during the sack of Alaric.

Alaric's soldiers raided the convents, sexually assaulted the nuns and frantically searched for treasures. Some nuns committed suicide rather than experience defilement. The invaders slaughtered a large number of Romans and corpses were strewn all over the city. St Augustine, who was contemporary with the sack of Rome, lamented that the city had not enough gravediggers to bury the bodies.[53]

After being starved and forced into cannibalism, the citizens of Rome were then robbed, raped, massacred, or taken into captivity. This was the horrific end of a myth.

HONORIUS' RESPONSE

The emperor's reaction to the sacking of his empire's most important city was decidedly understated.

Procopius related that, according to a story he had come across, Emperor Honorius, who was in Ravenna at the time, had a large rooster named Rome. When a eunuch came to the emperor with the message that Rome had died, Honorius exclaimed, 'And yet it had just eaten from my hands!' When the eunuch explained that he had spoken about the city of Rome, Honorius gave a sigh of relief and indicated he had thought his bird had passed away. Procopius noted, 'So great, they say, was the folly with which this emperor was possessed.'[54]

So outlandish are some of the accounts that they raise the suspicion of mental illness in Honorius. The disastrous decisions made by him during his reign led Bury to conclude that he was a man of weak mental abilities.[55]

Mazzolai thought that the story of the imperial cockerel is consistent with the patterns of behaviour exhibited by Honorius.[56] Others have noted that Galla Placidia, whom we last encountered as Alaric's hostage, left Rome for Constantinople in 423 to escape the unsavoury advances of her half-brother, the emperor.[57] Honorius had been married to Maria, daughter of Stilicho and Serena. When she died in 408, ten years after the wedding, Maria was reputedly still a virgin. The same year, Honorius married Thermantia, the other daughter of Stilicho and Serena. When later that year he betrayed his father-in-law Stilicho and had him beheaded, he also repudiated Thermantia, who, it was claimed, was also still a virgin.[58]

THE MAGNIFICENCE OF THE VISIGOTHS' ROMAN BOOTY

As Honorius wasted valuable time fretting over his rooster, the Visigoths carried out one of the greatest looting operations in the history of the world.

Even a partial list of the unbelievable gifts of Constantine the Great to the Basilica of St John in Lateran, as provided by the Book of Pontiffs, shows just how rich the Visigothic booty must have been: a 2,025lb silver *fastigium* (a sort of canopy) of hammered burnished silver with a vault of the finest gold; at the front of the *fastigium*, a 5ft, 120lb figure of the Saviour seated on a chair and 12 Apostles, each 5ft high and weighing 90lb with crowns of the finest silver; at the back of the *fastigium*, a Saviour seated on a throne, 5ft high, of the finest silver weighing 140lb, and 4 spear-carrying angels, each 5ft tall and weighing 105lb, also of the finest silver, with Alabanda jewels in their eyes; hanging beneath the *fastigium*, a light of the finest gold embellished with 50 dolphins of the finest gold, 50lb each, with chains weighing 25lb each; 4 crowns of the finest gold with 20 dolphins, each weighing 15lb; the apse vault of the basilica, of gold foil in both directions, 500lb; 7 gold patens, 30lb each; 7 *scyphi* (drinking vessels or goblets) of the finest gold, 10lb each; a special *scyphus* of hard coral, adorned on all sides with prase (a light-green, translucent variety of chalcedony) and jacinth (an ancient gem believed to be amethyst or sapphire); jewels, inlaid with gold, total weight 20lb 3oz; 2 *amae* of the finest gold, 50lb each; 40 smaller chalices of the finest gold, 1lb each.[59]

The Book of Pontiffs provides evidence that the Visigoths looted the gold and silver furnishings of the Christian churches. Thus, it mentions that in the time of Pope Sixtus (Xystus) III (432–40), Emperor Valentinian replaced the heavy silver *fastigium* of the Lateran basilica that 'had been removed by the barbarians'. Earlier, Pope Celestine (422–32) is recorded as having endowed the Basilicas of Sts Peter and Paul with silver furnishings 'after the Gothic conflagration'.[60]

Of course, the Visigoths raided the neighbouring Baptistery (Battistero), in which the porphyry Holy Font was covered inside and out with 3,003lb of finest silver. At its centre, there was a porphyry column supporting a golden basin containing a 52lb golden candle in which 200lb of balsam were burnt at Eastertide. A 30lb gold lamb, from which water poured, stood on the rim of the font between a 170lb, 5ft silver Saviour and a

100lb, 5ft silver St John the Baptist. There were seven, 80lb silver stags pouring water. Finally, there was a 15lb gold censer (a container for burning incense) encrusted with 42 prase and jacinth jewels.[61] Such magnificent treasures were, undoubtedly, beyond the wildest dreams of any barbarian plunderer.

The fate of Constantine's 150lb (68kg) gold cross at the tomb of St Peter in St Peter's Basilica is still a mystery. Late in the nineteenth century, Lanciani noted that in the spring of 1594, while workers were flattening the pavement of the church on top of the Confession (the shrine of the tomb of St Peter), they also took away the base of Julius II's (1503–13) ciborium (vessel containing the consecrated bread or sacred wafers for the Eucharist). At that point, the floor caved in and the architect and sculptor Giacomo della Porta was able to see in the hole the tomb of the Galilean fisherman and the gold cross of Constantine and Helena. These had last been seen during the papacy of Sergius II (844–7), which meant – no less and no more – that the cross had survived the sack of Alaric in 410, that of Gaiseric in 455 and all subsequent raids.[62]

In a state of excitement, Giacomo della Porta brought Pope Clement VIII to the site. Cardinals Bellarmino, Antoniano and Sfrondato were also present. They were able to read on the golden cross the dedication with the names of the first Christian emperor and his mother. Very moved, Pope Clement VIII ordered the workers to seal the hole immediately. In support of this story, Lanciani mentioned a written statement by Torrigio, the seventeenth-century author of the first guide to the sacred Vatican grottoes, describing the unexpected discovery. He also noted that the materials used to close the hole were still visible.[63]

This was all very exciting, but the problem is that unfortunately excavations performed in the twentieth century found no trace of Constantine's copper cube or his gold cross.

Did the barbarians really return the vessels of St Peter, as Orosius exultantly proclaims? And if they did, was it a complete or a partial restitution? Moreover, it is not entirely convincing that the barbarians, Christian or not, put aside their urge to loot and rape only to escort St Peter's vessels on a lengthy trip through the city. What happened to St Paul's treasure?

Already in the sixth century, Cassiodorus, as evidenced in his *Variae*, found it hard to believe that Alaric, a barbarian who plundered the churches inside the Aurelian Wall, would abstain from looting the completely defenceless churches of the apostles located without its perimeter.[64] (The *Variae* is a collection of letters and proclamations prepared by Cassiodorus between 506 and 538, while he was in the service of the Gothic rulers of Italy.[65])

Davis concluded that during the papacy of Celestine (422–32) 'something was done also to compensate for losses at the basilicas of St. Peter and St. Paul'.[66] So it is not entirely certain that the Visigoths refrained from pillaging the basilicas of the Apostles, and Orosius' account needs to be taken with a pinch of salt.

What is definite is that the Visigothic hordes looted the shining metallic adornments of the pagan temples. The Christian churches lost their sacred gold and silver furnishings. The patrician houses lost their gold and silver fixtures, jewellery and other wealth.[67] As the story of St Marcella illustrates, the barbarians tortured the citizens of Rome in the hope of making them reveal the location of their money or treasures.[68] The runaway slaves probably led the plunderers to their former masters and helped find their hidden riches.

Discussing the fate of the *fastigium* of St John in the Lateran in the nineteenth century Gregorovius wrote, 'For the latter had been carried off by the Goths, in spite of their respect for churches, and since this treasure alone weighed 511lb (according to the Book of Pontiffs the weight of the *fastigium* was 2,025lb), we may imagine how rich were the spoils which the barbarians must have collected from the other churches of Rome.' The loot of the Visigoths has been described as, quite literally, 'incredible'.[69]

The opulence of the Visigothic booty from Rome and Italy is attested to by the gifts which Galla Placidia received from Athaulf, Alaric's successor, when he married her in January 414, in Narbonne, in what is now southern France.[70] Obviously, these gifts represented only a small fraction of the Visigothic loot from Rome and Italy. Basing his writing on Olympiodorus' account, Gibbon mentions that Galla Placidia received from Athaulf fifty basins filled with gold coins, and fifty basins loaded with precious stones of incalculable worth.[71]

The story goes that upon receiving these wedding gifts, the thought that they had formerly served to adorn the aristocratic ladies of Rome filled Galla Placidia with intense shame. Many treasures that were hidden only to be abandoned by the fleeing Romans remain lost forever. Stories of gold and jewels concealed in parks or houses persisted for a long time after the sack, but none were recovered.[72]

The fall of Rome, the mother-city of the empire and its symbol of law and civilisation, traumatised not only many in the city itself but also numerous citizens in the provinces of the empire. In remote Jerusalem, St Jerome lamented: 'My voice sticks in my throat, and, as I dictate, sobs choke my utterance. The city which had taken the whole world has itself been taken.'[73]

The sack of Rome, the downfall of a city that had for long been considered the centre of the civilised world, was a powerful symbol of the end of antiquity and the beginning of the Middle Ages.

After three long days, in the manner of their third-century ancestors, Alaric and his people left Rome and marched on to Campania.[74] The Visigoths did not leave occupying forces in Rome. They did not make changes to the local government, either. Although the damage caused by the barbarians was considerable, much of Rome remained intact. Certainly, the barbarians had been busier looting and raping than destroying, and Rome was simply too big to be completely ruined in three days.[75]

But gorged on Roman treasure, the Gothic king entertained grand dreams of future conquest. He could not know just how little time remained to him to enjoy the gilded fruits of his martial labours.

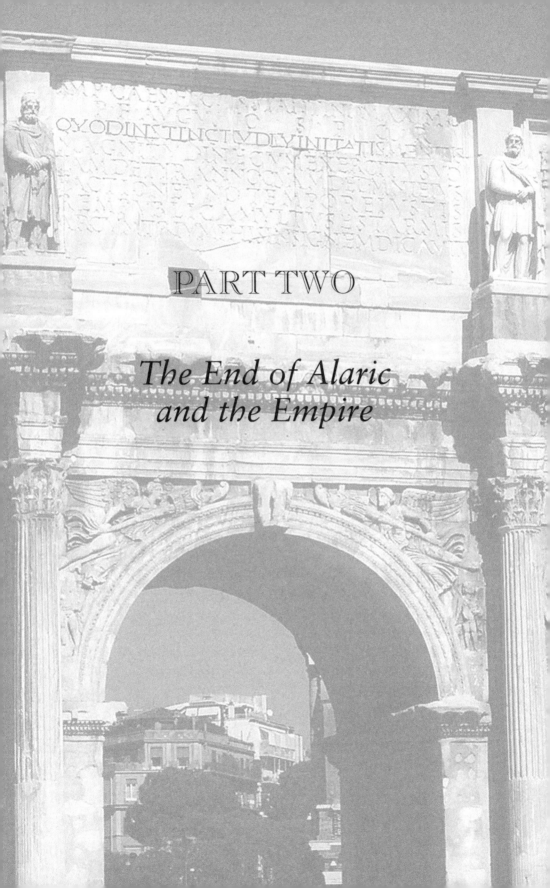

PART TWO

The End of Alaric
and the Empire

SIX

The Death and Burial of Alaric

Exasperated by the Roman reluctance to provide land for settlement, provisions for his people, or a high-ranking position in the Roman administration for himself, Alaric decided to travel from Rome to Africa via Sicily. He and his people had to find provisions and a place to spend the winter. On 27 August 410, the Visigoths moved south and pillaged Capua and Nola but failed to take Naples. Then they continued their ravaging march south. Eventually they arrived in Rhegium (today's Reggio di Calabria). But it was no longer summer. Their attempt to cross the 2½-mile (4km) wide Straits of Messina failed miserably due to an unexpected storm and a dearth of suitable vessels.[1]

The ancients wrote little, though, about what happened. Jordanes relates:

Now the land of the Bruttii is at the extreme southern bound of Italy, and a corner of it marks the beginning of the Apennine Mountains. It stretches out like a tongue into the Adriatic Sea and separates it from the Tyrrhenian waters. It chanced to receive its name in ancient times from a Queen Bruttia. To this place came Alaric, king of the Visigoths, with the wealth of all Italy which he had taken as spoil, and from there, as we have said, he intended to cross over by way of Sicily to the quiet land of Africa. But since man is not free to do anything he wishes without the will of God, that dread strait sunk several of his ships and threw all into confusion. Alaric was cast down by his reverse and, while deliberating what he should do, was suddenly overtaken by an untimely death and departed from human cares. His people mourned for him with the utmost affection. Then turning from its course the River Busentus near the city of Cosentia – for this stream flows with its wholesome waters from the foot of a mountain near the city – they led a band of captives into the midst of its bed to dig out a place for his grave. In the depth of this pit they buried Alaric, together with many treasures, and then turned the waters back into their channel. And that none might ever know the place, they put to death all the diggers. They bestowed the kingdom of the Visigoths on Atavulf his kinsman.[2]

Interestingly, Philostorgius, an Arian Christian who was born around 368 and lived in Constantinople after the age of 20, locates the death of Alaric in Campania, not in Lucania et Bruttii, the territory to which Cosentia (today's Cosenza) belonged in antiquity.[3] The ancient region (province) of Lucania et Bruttii extended all the way down to the tip of the Italian toe. The antique Campania was the area surrounding modern Naples.[4]

The flat treatment given by Jordanes to the demise of King Alaric, with no chronicle of at least some of his deeds and no commentary on his transgressions, comes as a surprise. Jordanes, himself of Germanic origin and a Christian, chose to say nothing of the man who was believed to have acted as the hand of God in punishing Rome for its terrible sins.[5] Perhaps Alaric ended up as a sort of theological embarrassment since his own death came so soon after his actions in Rome, an event difficult to explain away without contradicting to some degree the idea that Alaric was God's instrument. Or perhaps Jordanes' pro-Gothic sympathies prevented him from preparing an impartial memoir of Alaric, his co-national.

It has been proposed that, in fact, Jordanes' terse treatment of Alaric's death was a manifestation of an Augustinian view of history, according to which secular history has only one purpose: to punish people for their sins.[6] In Alaric's case, the storm at the Straits of Messina and his untimely death would have been punishment for his sack of Rome.

This seems a tempting explanation for Jordanes' unexciting rendition of Alaric's demise, as long as one ignores Jordanes' passages in which he seems pleased to relate rousing episodes, particularly when they bring to his readers' attention past triumphs of the Goths.[7] In such passages, Jordanes' expressed or implicit nationalistic pride would seem to contradict outright the Augustinian Christian concept of a lack of meaning in secular history.[8]

THE CAUSE OF ALARIC'S DEATH

Why did Alaric die so soon after raiding Rome? The contemporary chronicle of Philostorgius held that while in Campania, the Visigothic king 'died of a disorder which seized him there'.[9] As if to corroborate this view, Procopius, who flourished in the first half of the sixth century, wrote that Alaric died of 'disease'.[10]

According to the speculations of the Italian Angelo Raffaele Amato, both Alaric and Athaulf fell in love with the charming Galla Placidia, but Galla's choice fell on Athaulf. According to Amato, the two lovers decided to eliminate Alaric by poison because he was planning to use every means at his disposal to get the beautiful woman for himself.[11] Galla Placidia may have had an additional reason to poison Alaric. After all, she was a member of the imperial family and the daughter of Theodosius the Great, so, viewed in this light, she would avenge the Roman people were she to take the life of the Visigothic king. This poisoning hypothesis might seem compatible with the unexpected death reported by Jordanes. The fact that it has not been advanced in a serious academic study should not deter one from considering it. Indeed, in many cases of unexplained death, it is common practice to attempt to rule out poisoning of one type or another. (The toxic plants popular among ancient poisoners[12] included monkshood,[13] deadly nightshade[14] and hemlock.[15])

Galla Placidia was probably a woman of strong passions and capable of extreme actions, evidenced by her contribution to the execution of Serena, the woman who had recently been preparing to become her mother-in-law. The major problem, however, is that we have no description of the actual symptoms Alaric experienced before he died.

No one really knows for sure what caused Alaric's death. Sozomenus wrote that, when an Italian monk attempted to persuade Alaric, who was on his way to take Rome, not to become the person responsible for so many disasters, the Visigothic king replied that he did not feel disposed to start the blockade, but that 'some resistless influence compelled and commanded him to go against Rome; and this he eventually did'.[16] The same story can be found in Socrates' Scholasticus.[17] These authors seem to suggest that Alaric was possessed, but this is not a satisfactory explanation for his death.

Modern authors have considered the possibility that Alaric fell victim to a fever that infested the coasts of Calabria,[18] or to plague contracted during the sacking of Rome.[19] However, the incubation period of plague is between two and ten days. Since the death of Alaric probably occurred at least two months after he left Rome, even if we accept that there had been an epidemic of plague in Rome, the plague hypothesis does not seem attractive, particularly when there is no information to suggest that there were other cases of plague among his followers. The fact that the Visigoths did not hesitate to storm Rome also raises some doubts about plague being present at the time.

Cosenza's reputation as a malaria-infested place persisted until the middle of the nineteenth century, giving some support to the theory of Alaric's death from the mosquito-borne disease. Horace Rilliet, a Swiss military doctor in the service of King Ferdinand I, wrote that the memory of Alaric's death by malaria in 410 made the royal retinue cross the beautiful Cosenza without stopping.[20]

As we have no compelling information to suggest that Alaric died in battle, the Visigothic king's death might reasonably be attributed to disease (perhaps malaria), poisoning, or sudden death that was cardiac in origin. Of course, there is also the possibility of infected battle wounds, but there is no indication that Alaric had been wounded in combat. According to a lesser-known tradition, an invention of local historians, Alaric was killed by the javelin of a courageous Cosentine.[21]

ALARIC'S BURIAL WITH ROMAN TREASURES

However it happened, the king of the Visigoths was dead, leaving his devastated followers to plan his burial. Alaric's successor, Athaulf, probably played a key role in the organisation of Alaric's funeral.[22] Athaulf was Alaric's brother-in-law and had always been loyal to him.

Examining the patterns of behaviour later exhibited by Athaulf, in connection with precious items as symbols of his esteem and affection for another person, will help us picture what course of action he decided upon for the burial of Alaric. As we have seen, when Athaulf married Galla Placidia in Narbonne he presented her with a fabulous wedding gift. Besides indicating the monumental size of the booty which the Visigoths took from Italy and Rome, this suggests that in crucial moments, when Athaulf showed his respect for someone, he did it on a grand scale.

It is conceivable that, as a king who belonged to one of the most powerful Gothic clans, Alaric was buried with treasures commensurate with his status.[23] Also, Jordanes noted that the Visigoths felt great affection for King Alaric; after all, they had been together through so many adventures and dangers. This echoed the early lines of Tacitus, who noted the reverence of the Goths for their leaders long before the time of Alaric.[24]

In spite of fashionable legend, early German society was never a democratic organisation of equal 'warrior-farmers'.[25] The existence of a Gothic aristocracy is attested by written sources, such as the *Passion of St Saba*, which describes the persecution of the Christian Goths.[26] The early Germans thought that working the land was a manifestation of laziness and passivity.[27] Instead, they lusted after gold and treasure, and some sought to take their wealth with them when they passed from this life.[28]

In support of Alaric's burial with elaborate grave goods, the practice of wealthy interments by Gothic nobility is suggested by the rich graves found in today's Romania, such as those from Conceşti in the north-eastern county of Botoşani, Bîrlad-Valea Seacă in the Vaslui county in eastern Romania, and Târgşor, the latter located 3.7 miles (6km) west of Ploieşti in the south-east of the country.[29]

The treasure of Pietroasele (formerly known as Pietroasa) in the county of Buzău in south-eastern Romania provides strong evidence for rich burials by the Goths. A ring which forms part of this treasure displays the dedication *'gutane jer weih hailag'* – 'a blessing for a fruitful and prosperous year' inscribed with runes.[30] More rich interments have been excavated in other parts of Romania, such as those of Someşeni on the eastern end of Cluj Napoca and Şimleul Silvaniei in the north-west.[31]

According to Diaz, Alaric's burial, as reported by Jordanes, had more in common with a ceremony for a Germanic warlord than for a king, as understood by the Romans.[32] Indeed, the transition to kingship began with Alaric. Moreover, the fact that the Visigoths were a wandering people suggests that burials en route were not something new to them. Their intention to continue to migrate after the death of Alaric, as indicated by their historically recorded behaviour, must have had a significant effect on the way he was buried.[33] The Visigoths who buried Alaric probably knew that they were going to depart from southern Italy and, most likely, that they were never going to return. This fact must have added to the solemnity, grief and grandeur of the occasion. It also helps explain the secret character of the burial and the site of the grave.

ALARIC'S BURIAL PLACE: SECRECY AND WORSHIP

When Alaric died, the Visigoths needed to find a suitable location for his grave. Indeed, there was a real danger that after their departure Romans or grave robbers would desecrate it.[34] Grave robbers were a constant threat in ancient times, as Alaric's people were no doubt aware.[35]

Since Alaric was born in the vicinity of a great river and the Visigoths might have worshipped river gods in the not-too-distant past,[36] a secret burial under or near the bed of a local river must have seemed an appropriate tribute to the man who had led them so far. The ancient writer Jordanes held that the great king was laid to rest with his treasures in a tomb beneath a river's running waters, forever hiding from human eyes the last resting place of the barbarian who had sacked the mighty city of Rome. Marcel Brion, in his romanticised biography *La vie d'Alaric* narrates that the Visigoths buried their king with the 'treasure of Solomon' in the bed of the river 'Barentino'.[37]

Jordanes relates that the Visigoths killed all the gravediggers, presumably to keep secret the location of Alaric's tomb, but also perhaps in memory of early Gothic human sacrifices. Schwarcz did not rule out entirely the latter reason, and noted that the slaying of the captives could be seen both as a precaution and a ritual sacrifice.[38]

But did the Visigoths have the manpower to do the necessary work on a river tomb? Probably. They had a significant number of captives with them and they may have been able to take more prisoners from the region of Cosenza, where Alaric had died. Moreover, the rivers around Cosenza, including the Busento, are not very large. Alaric probably died during the last three weeks of the year, since it must have taken at least a few months from when they left Rome in late August to travel to the south, while stopping here and there to lay siege to cities and to plunder them. Moreover, the Visigoths made an about turn and marched north from Rhegium (Reggio di Calabria) to Cosenza, where Alaric died. The locals say that the water level of the rivers in the area may increase due to rainfall in the headwaters towards the end of the year.

But the Goths would have needed to understand riverbed erosion if they were to bury a man under a river and keep him buried there. Mountain rivers with abrupt gradients and plentiful precipitation in their headwaters can suffer substantial erosion of their beds.[39] The Busento and other rivers in the Cosenza area have a rather steep slope.

We do not know if the Visigoths were aware that there was a risk that the waters would damage Alaric's grave, particularly if it were not deep enough under the riverbed. It has been suggested that they did indeed consider this potential problem, ordering their captives to dig a tunnel advancing into the side of the riverbed, perpendicular to the direction of the stream, so that the burial chamber at its end would be at a safe distance from the flowing waters.[40]

As we have seen, Jordanes held that the Goths diverted the river to construct the tomb. Against this idea, the Hungarian archaeologist István Bóna thought that diverting a river in a short interval was unlikely in the time of Alaric, given the technology of that age.[41] When expressing such an opinion he perhaps had in mind the large River Tisza, which is huge in comparison to the rivers flowing in the vicinity of Cosenza. Given their smaller size, it does not seem implausible to achieve such a project, providing there are a sufficient workers. But what of the deeds of the Visigoths after the burial of Alaric?

THE VISIGOTHS IN GAUL AND SPAIN

After the death of Alaric, the wanderings of the Visigothic people continued under the leadership of Athaulf, their new king.[42] They did not have a homeland, food was scarce and there was the possibility of the Romans organising at the last moment a military intervention against them.

In 412, the Visigoths crossed the Alps into Gaul, after some more drifting and plundering through Italy, actions that are very poorly documented in the ancient sources.[43] In 414, as we saw, Athaulf married Galla Placidia in Narbonne according to the Roman tradition. Then Athaulf tried to develop a warmer relationship with Honorius, who had opposed the match but was now his brother-in-law; for her part, Galla Placidia seems to have entered into the marriage perfectly willingly. Honorius, who may have been in love with Galla Placidia himself, ignored Athaulf's overtures.[44] Frustrated, Athaulf imitated Alaric and proclaimed Attalus emperor once again, as the Visigoths had been carrying around the former Roman senator wherever they went.[45] This would be a completely pointless move.

Honorius reacted by sending to Gaul his new Master of Soldiers, Constantius, a Catholic who was, too, consumed by love for Galla

Placidia, with orders to defeat the Visigoths, get rid of the usurper Attalus and take Galla Placidia away from the barbarians.[46]

Constantius led a successful campaign against the Visigoths in southern Gaul. He organised a blockade of the coast of Narbonne, thus causing a shortage of supplies for the Visigoths. In 415, Athaulf and his people dumped the hapless Attalus and moved to Barcelona, Spain, hoping to improve their situation in that part of the empire after they had devastated south-western Gaul during their withdrawal. Possibly under the influence of his wife Galla Placidia, with whom he had a child that did not live long after birth, Athaulf now declared himself willing to submit to Honorius and the empire.[47] However, in an act of personal revenge, a Goth assassinated him in 415 in Barcelona.[48]

Eventually, the Visigoths remained in southern France for almost a century where they ruled a realm known as the Kingdom of Toulouse.[49]

Gibbon noted that the descendants of the Visigoths of Alaric and Athaulf possessed a massive gold *missorium* (a large ceremonial plate) weighing 500lb that had been given to the Visigothic king Thorismund by the Roman patrician Aetius. Aetius and Thorismund were allies in the great battle of the Catalaunian Fields/Troyes with Attila the Hun in 451. According to Gibbon, when the Arabs conquered Visigoth-ruled Spain in 711, they seized a table of substantial dimensions. This remarkable piece of furniture was made from a single great block of emerald and was decorated with superb pearls arranged in three circles. The incredible table stood on 365 legs, each made of precious stones and solid gold.[50]

Gregory of Tours reported the story of Amalaric, the son of the Visigothic king Alaric II. The latter had been defeated and killed by Clovis, the Frankish king, at Vouillé, France, in 507. Amalaric himself was killed in 531 in Barcelona by the soldiers of Childebert I, the Frankish king and son of Clovis, while trying to run away with his treasure. The Franks captured Amalaric's sixty chalices, fifteen patens, and twenty Gospel cases, all made from pure gold and decorated with precious stones.[51] Had he not returned to the city to retrieve the precious items, Amalaric might have survived.

This brief overview of the activities of the Visigoths in France and Spain indicates that they continued their longstanding interest in accumulating wealth. A similar preoccupation with amassing treasures during their migrations in the preceding centuries is well documented so their behaviour in France and Spain simply serves to reinforce what is a discernible pattern.

The Visigoths had huge piles of precious booty with them in Cosenza, and the Balthi clan of Alaric would not have lost the opportunity to bury him with stunning riches, perhaps with Roman war trophies as well, to emphasise their splendour as a clan by showing the rest of the Visigoths just how much they could afford to leave in a grave.

But the story of Alaric does not quite end with the Visigoths. Alaric's raid had a significant impact on the city of Rome and the western part of the empire. To gather more information in our search for Alaric's tomb, it is to this history that we now turn to see just how Alaric's breach of the Roman frontier played out in Rome and on the plains of Italy.

SEVEN

Restoring Rome

Alaric's raid did not bring about the collapse of the Roman Empire, but his incursion into the empire and sacking of its mother-city demonstrated the weakness of the imperial system and laid bare the empire's frailty. At the same time it encouraged the Catholic Church to take a more active role in the government of the city of Rome.

An overview of this period of restoration and decay can tell us much about the changing nature of power and the redistribution of wealth in early medieval Rome. It will help us begin to understand the changes Alaric's raid wrought and piece together the story of the treasures he left behind, enabling us to know more exactly what it was Alaric had taken from the imperial city.

ROME RECOVERS; HONORIUS DOES NOT

During the first few years after the departure of the Goths from Italy in 412, the people of Rome began to return in ever increasing numbers to the slowly recovering city, although many of the privileged among her citizens abandoned their vast palatial homes.[1] Between 412 and 416, the Romans repaired the offices of the Senate, the Suran Bath on the Aventine, and the Basilica Julia. The urban prefect restored the colonnade of his offices just as the rule of Honorius ended in 423.[2] The priest Peter of Illyria erected the Church of St Sabina (Piazza Pietro d'Illiria) on the Aventine in 425, putting to use twenty-five marble columns from the nearby Temple of Junona Regina.[3] This church, which still stands, is a fascinating example of an early Christian basilica. Its carved cypress wood portal dates to the fifth century and depicts scenes from the Old and New Testaments and is one of the treasures of this basilica. The face of the drowning pharaoh in the episode of the crossing of the Red Sea is in fact that of Napoleon Bonaparte. This was the doing of the restorer who worked on the portal in

1836. Napoleon, who had treated the papacy badly, was already dead at that time.

The myth of the empire's immortality seemed to regain its old place in the minds of the Romans. Orosius claimed that 'although the memory of this event is fresh, nevertheless, if anyone sees the multitudes of the Roman people themselves and hears their talk, he will think that nothing took place, as even they themselves confess, unless by chance he is informed by the ruins of the fire that still remain'.[4]

In 414, thousands of soldiers from the disbanded army of Count Heraclian, the African usurper defeated by the resurrected imperial troops in 413 on the Tyrrhenian Sea beaches not far from Rome, swelled the population of the city to the point that the grain allowance became insufficient.[5]

As Wolfram narrates, the Catholic general Constantius, who was himself profoundly enamoured of Galla Placidia,[6] defeated the Visigoths in Gaul in 416, and the beautiful widow of Athaulf was returned to the Romans later that year.[7] On 1 January 417 she tied the knot with Constantius who died in 421, after being Honorius' co-emperor for only a few months.

In 416, Honorius and Theodosius II, emperor in the East, prohibited the wearing of the traditional Germanic long hair and animal pelts. It was a rather desperate measure taken in reaction to the growing barbarisation seen in Rome among both free citizens and slaves six years after the sack by Alaric.[8] Valentinian I had made marriage between Romans and barbarians illegal, but half barbarian children continued to be born.

In 417, the cowardly Honorius 'triumphantly' entered Rome, the tragic figure of Attalus marching in chains ahead of his chariot. The debased Romans had to witness the embarrassing spectacle of a dull-witted emperor trying to hide his own disgrace by singling out for punishment another disgraced co-national. Honorius was greeted with insincere ovations and damning silence.[9]

Following the demise of Constantius in 421, Honorius engaged in very inappropriate behaviour with his half-sister Galla Placidia, who had two children from her marriage to Constantius. Honorius, who as we know had always liked Galla, kept kissing her in public in a manner that resulted in considerable public disgrace, intense court intrigue and urban battles between their respective supporters. Eventually, in 423 Galla was forced to move to Constantinople with her two children, where she joined the court of her nephew, Emperor Theodosius II.

Not long after Galla left, Honorius' disastrous rule was terminated when in 423 he succumbed to a disease associated with dropsy (oedema). According to Bury, he passed away on 15 August.[10] The Dewing translation of Procopius' *History of the Wars* indicates that he died on 27 August.[11] So it seems that Honorius' death occurred on the thirteenth anniversary of Alaric's sack of Rome or shortly before it, a strange coincidence. He was buried in a mausoleum near the old St Peter's Basilica.

RESTORING CHURCH AND STATE

In 417 the poet Rutilius Namatianus, a former prefect of the city, found it once again superb enough to describe it as 'the most beautiful Queen of the World, whose temples approach the skies'.[12] But the Queen of the World was changed. In 419, the number of people in Rome sufficiently poor to be entitled to assistance from the city, that is the right to receive meat, dropped to 120,000 from 317,333 in 386.[13] The reorganisation of the *annona*, accomplished that same year, suggests a decrease of some 300,000 people in the number of inhabitants.[14]

The Book of Pontiffs is surprisingly silent about the sieges and sack by Alaric when describing the incumbency of Pope Innocent I (401–17),[15] called the defender of the city (*defensor urbis*)[16] in recognition of his alleged urging of Alaric to show compassion to the citizens of Rome.[17]

During his pontificate Innocent dedicated the present church of St Vitale to Gervasius and Protasius, at that time believed to have been martyred in Milan during the first century. The description of its foundation given in the Book of Pontiffs provides the first detailed documentation of the process of founding a Christian church based on a will, in this case that of the 'illustrious' Vestina, a widow belonging to the highest echelons of Roman society. The new church was endowed with an assortment of Vestina's urban and rural possessions.[18]

The following facts give some idea of contemporary prices and relative incomes. We learn that the Roman bakery of Castoriani included in the endowment brought revenue of 61 *solidi*.[19] (1 *solidus* equalled about £155.59 or US $286.38 at 2005 rates.)[20]

From Harl, we know that in the period AD 325 to 625, a Roman cavalryman made 9 *solidi* per year, i.e. 56 per cent of the gold equivalent of the same yearly salary in the time of Emperor Augustus (27 BC–AD 14)

A Roman foot soldier made 5 *solidi* per year between 325 and 625, which was only 31 per cent of the gold equivalent of the comparable annual earnings under Augustus.[21] This was quite a drop.

An adult male Roman needed at least 48 *modii* (approximately 12 bushels or between 313 and 325kg) of wheat per year, which covered maybe two-thirds of his caloric needs. He got his remaining calories from oil, vegetables and protein. During the fourth century, 1 *solidus* would buy 30 *modii* (about 7½ bushels or 196–203kg) of wheat in government acquisitions and levies, while in the late fifth century and in the sixth 1 *solidus* would get 40 *modii* (about 10 bushels or 261 to 271kg) of wheat. Of course, these rates may not necessarily reflect the situation in the local markets.[22]

We may conclude tentatively that the money made by the Castoriani bakery translated into the grain requirement of about fifty-one Roman cavalrymen for one year. Based on the generosity of a Roman named Francesco Silla, the little church of San Vitale distributed free bread to the poor until the nineteenth century.

Through donations the Roman Church accumulated great riches. Moreover, most of the wealth of the pagan temples was transferred to her and stood as the basis of her worldly domains. Was this the fate of the Jerusalem Temple treasure?

Ever since the reign of Constantine the priests had been excused from paying taxes, even though the Roman state was chronically short of money for national defence and other governmental tasks. However, the church lands, like the imperial estates and private lands, were not exempt from the *annona*, which was paid in kind. Eventually, the clerics became responsible for running the affairs of the Church in the administrative units of the Late Empire, the dioceses and the provinces.[23]

The pope of Rome was the grandest property-owner of the empire, albeit he wielded no political power. With the emperors mostly absent from the city, the citizens of Rome looked to the popes more and more, their respect increasing particularly once they realised that they could count on them for the city's defence. The former imperial capital, ruled by the urban prefect and the Senate and receiving its spiritual guidance from the pope, evolved into a city that was rather disconnected from the affairs of the empire, inward-looking and concentrated mostly on the business of the Church.[24]

By the end of the first decade of the fifth century, the Christians had completely taken over control of the Senate.[25]

As Duffy notes, this dramatic change is reflected in an intriguing fifth-century apse mosaic in the Church of St Pudenziana (Piazza Sant'Uffizio), erected at the end of the fourth century. The Apostles, seated at the sides of the enthroned Saviour, wear the Roman senatorial toga. The message of the mosaic was plain: the eastern saints had been co-opted as Romans, and Christianity had taken over the ageing mother-city of the empire.[26]

No longer playing a significant role in the politics of the empire, the citizens of Rome immersed themselves in religious disputes.[27] Innocent I rejected the increasingly popular teachings of the British monk Pelagius, whose concept of free will in the matter of an individual's following or rejecting the way of Christ disregarded Augustine's doctrine that human behaviour is predetermined by God. Pelagius had initiated his campaign for asceticism in religious practice, in reaction to the corruption, worldliness and pleasure-seeking of the Catholic Christians of Rome. For St Jerome, who met the Briton when the latter visited Palestine, Pelagius was a 'corpulent dog' weighed down with 'porridge'.[28] Eventually, Pelagius was forced to leave Palestine and vanished from history. Traces of Pelagianism survived in the West until 540.

Innocent I continued the trend of his predecessor Siricius and proclaimed the supremacy of the bishop of Rome over all other bishops of the empire. In the West, the dominance of the pope was accepted without question outside Italy (in Gaul, Spain and Africa), but he intervened in provincial episcopal affairs mostly only on local demand. In nearly all peninsular Italy, the pope ruled effectively. However, in the Eastern Roman Empire, Rome was perceived as only one of the five higher-ranking patriarchates, and the belief of Constantinople that it was the 'New Rome' posed a permanent threat to the supremacy of the Roman popes.[29]

After the demise of Pope Zosimus in December 418, the Church of Rome was again divided by a double election of bishops, as in the time of Damasus and Ursinus.[30] The greater part of the citizenry elected the conformist Boniface, while a minority opted for the Pelagian Eulalius, who had the support of the pagan prefect Symmachus. To many Christians gone astray one way or another, Augustine's concept of predestination, according to which human behaviour is determined in advance by God, may have been a convenient justification for persistence in sin. If God determines one's acts in advance, why bother trying to improve one's morals? The Pelagian Eulalius posed a threat to the cosy Catholicism of the Romans and it is not surprising that he lost the election. After tense manoeuvres and negotiations requiring the intervention of Honorius, who was being advised by Galla Placidia, Boniface I (418–22) became pope.[31]

THE REGENCY OF GALLA PLACIDIA: MOUNTING FEARS AND DISASTERS

Following the death of Honorius, the ambitious Galla Placidia convinced Theodosius II in Constantinople to appoint her *Augusta* and protector of her son Valentinian in the West, and then sailed to Ravenna accompanied by her son and an eastern Roman armada. After the eastern soldiers apprehended and executed the usurper John, Galla and her son hurried to Rome, where the seven-year-old Valentinian accepted the imperial purple from an eastern Roman envoy and was proclaimed *Augustus* as Valentinian III in 425.[32]

Finally, Rome was involved again in the proclamation of an emperor, but this was a short-lived affair as Galla Placidia and Valentinian returned to Ravenna where she raised her son surrounded by the ladies and eunuchs of the imperial residence. Galla Placidia's deeds during her regency show that her governing abilities did not always match her legendary beauty. Gregorovius portrays her as fond of court intrigues and too feeble to steer the corrupt Roman state.[33]

In the fifty years before the fall of the last Western Roman emperor in 476, successive waves of panic hit the citizens of Rome and Italy, following the military and political disasters that beset other parts of the empire as they fell victim to barbarian assaults.

When Boniface, count of Africa, faced expeditionary forces sent by Galla Placidia in 428 to punish him for his rebellious behaviour, he perfidiously called the Vandals from Spain to come to his rescue, promising their king Gaiseric the three provinces of Mauretania in Western Africa in return. The crafty Gaiseric pretended to agree to the deal and landed in Africa with 80,000 Vandals and Alans, of whom 15,000 might have been warriors. In Bury's words 'the Visigoths were lambs compared to the Vandal wolves'. The latter subjected the defenceless Roman population to savagery and depredations never seen before. Ignoring the deal struck with Boniface, Gaiseric embarked upon a campaign to conquer the whole of Roman Africa.[34]

After halting Gaiseric at Carthage (located not far from today's Tunis in Tunisia) and Cirta (modern Constantine in Algeria), the remorseful Boniface travelled to Italy. Galla Placidia removed the consul Aetius (432) from his military appointment and replaced him with the contrite Boniface.[35] She could not forget that in 425, Aetius had showed up at Ravenna with 60,000 Huns to back the usurper John, but arrived a few days after the latter's capture by the eastern troops that had accompanied her to Italy. Galla could not forget either that, overwhelmed by the presence of the 60,000 Huns, she had had to put up with Aetius.[36]

Civil war broke out. After winning a battle against Aetius, Boniface died unexpectedly of disease. Aetius escaped to his friend King Rugila of the Huns and, with the latter's help, somehow regained his previous position and obtained the title of patrician in 434. Galla Placidia found herself again having to deal with Aetius; their mutual dislike was intense.[37]

Over the next few years, Aetius had to strike the aggressive Burgundians and Visigoths in Gaul. He summoned his friends the Huns of King Rugila to punish the first Burgundian Kingdom in Gaul and its king who ruled from Worms (on the Rhine in modern Germany), for invading the province of Upper Belgica (roughly, today's Belgium) in 435. The Huns killed 20,000 Burgundians, including King Gundahar, in 436. This historical event is at the root of the famous German legend, the *Nibelungenlied*, which was among the sources that inspired Wagner's cycle of operas known as *The Ring of the Nibelung*.[38]

Wanting to avoid a war on two fronts, the Romans had signed a treaty with Gaiseric at Hippo (Annaba in today's Algeria) in 435, but Gaiseric cared little about treaties and not long afterwards resumed his campaign to conquer Roman Africa.[39]

Against this threatening backdrop, in Rome Pope Sixtus III (432–40) carried out his programme of church building and endowments known today as the 'Sixtine Renaissance'.[40] He aimed at enhancing the citizenry's respect for the then mainly Christian Rome by a return to the sophisticated architecture and decorative style of classical antiquity, as Krautheimer noted. In the eyes of the popes, Rome was the successor to ancient Rome and the legitimate leader of the West. Perhaps the Romans also needed a distraction from the terrifying news coming from the borders of the remaining western imperial territories.

Sixtus III erected the Basilica di Santa Maria Maggiore in 432 in honour of Mary the 'Mother of God'. The concept of Mary as Mother of God had been imposed by the Council of Ephesus in 431, at which the participants had condemned the Byzantine patriarch Nestorius, who opposed it, based on his view that Christ was made up of two distinct persons, one divine and the other human. The splendid original mosaics located in the central nave and on top of the triumphal arch are the only ones in Rome depicting the growth of Christianity in a sequence of biblical narrations. These mosaics display no Byzantine stylistic features, thus having the distinction of being the last surviving examples of late ancient Roman art.[41]

Sixtus III managed to obtain donations from Valentinian III for his projects. The scarcity of endowments with gold furnishings after Constantine is striking. Indeed, the first pope who is mentioned by the Book of Pontiffs as providing gold furnishings is Sixtus III, whose reign was almost a century after the death of Constantine.[42] There was less and less gold in Rome after the sack of Alaric, but it was still enough to tempt the barbarians.

ROME UNDER VALENTINIAN III

In 437, Valentinian married the attractive Licinia Eudoxia, the daughter of Theodosius II, the emperor in the East. Around that time, Galla Placidia's regency ended and Aetius had to start dealing with the green, feeble and pampered Valentinian, who was also an incurable womaniser. Valentinian was unfit to govern, as Honorius and Arcadius had also been in their time. From 437 until his death in 454, Aetius was the real ruler of the West. His strategic abilities slowed down considerably the disintegration of the empire.[43]

Valentinian did not interfere with Aetius' decisions. Like Stilicho a generation earlier, Aetius developed a concrete and realistic political programme. Unlike the conservative Romans who lived in the past and profoundly despised the barbarians, Aetius, who in his youth had been a noble hostage of the Huns, realised that the only chance of survival the militarily inferior Romans had was to forge profitable political alliances with the barbarian nations.[44]

Again, because they were exposed on two fronts, in 442 the Romans could not avoid a new and detrimental treaty with the shrewd Gaiseric, who by then had a navy capable of challenging that of the Romans and endangering Rome itself. On advice from Aetius, Valentinian III offered the hand of his daughter Eudocia to Gaiseric's son Huneric. However, the latter was already the lawful husband of the daughter of Theodoric, king of the Visigoths in Gaul. Attracted by the idea of becoming related to the imperial family, Gaiseric made his son eligible again by accusing his wife of conspiring to kill him. The Vandals disfigured the Visigothic wife of Huneric by cutting her ears and nose and then shipped her back to Theodoric.[45]

These were the kind of people among whom Eudocia was expected to live. Africa, the granary of Rome, was almost completely in the hands of the cruellest of all barbarians. Rome waited anxiously. There was absolutely nothing else to be done. Then more frightening news came.

From the midpoint of Honorius' rule to the 440s, the Saxons, Picts and Scots continually made incursions into Roman Britain. The southern residents of that country escaped to the shores of Gaul or Armorica, thus founding Brittany. Aetius was faced with a serious fiscal situation: the finances of the Roman state, a state assaulted by barbarians at virtually every turn, were well below the requirements of national defence. This is why Aetius had been forced to agree to the unfavourable treaty with Gaiseric in 442, and why he had to abandon Britain at around the same time he lost much of Africa to Gaiseric.[46]

Then, of course, came Attila.

ATTILA HEADS FOR ROME

Valentinian's intelligent sister Honoria was very ambitious. She saw herself as capable of governing the empire as her mother Galla Placidia had done. Honoria had an affair with Eugenius, the steward of her house, in 449. In her plans, Eugenius was supposed to help her oust Valentinian. Unfortunately, their liaison was discovered. Valentinian put Eugenius to death and betrothed Honoria against her will to a senator of his own choosing.[47]

Outraged, Honoria concocted the stunning idea of summoning King Attila of the Huns, the strongest ruler in Europe at that time, to help her avert the unwanted marriage. Honoria must have remembered that, after all, her mother had been married to the Visigoth Athaulf and her niece

Eudocia had been betrothed by Valentinian to Huneric, son of Gaiseric, king of the Vandals. Involving barbarians directly in imperial business was far from a new strategy in the late Roman Empire.

The beautiful Honoria sent Attila a message, a ring to authenticate the message and an unknown amount of money. The astute Attila reacted as if Honoria's ring signified a marriage proposal. He wrote to the Eastern emperor Theodosius II, who was older than Valentinian III, that in the light of Honoria's request, she was his bride. Attila declared in no uncertain terms that he expected Valentinian to surrender to him half of his realm and began preparations to overrun Gaul.[48]

Jordanes left for posterity a description of Attila's appearance: 'He was haughty in his walk, rolling his eyes hither and thither, so that the power of his proud spirit appeared in the movement of his body. . . . He was short of stature, with a broad chest and a large head; his eyes were small, his beard thin and sprinkled with grey; and he had a flat nose and a swarthy complexion, showing the evidence of his origins.'[49]

Attila, a weak strategist according to Bury, invaded Gaul, but finding Aetius and his Visigothic and other Germanic allies prepared, decided to withdraw. In 451 Aetius engaged Attila in a colossal battle traditionally associated with Châlons (the Catalaunian Fields), but it is now believed that the battlefield was closer to Troyes.[50] Between 500,000 and 550,000 warriors participated in the confrontation. In the end, Honoria's letter resulted in 160,000 dead and wounded. The heaps of corpses were so high that the surviving horses could not advance. Aetius won, but allowed Attila and the remnants of his army to leave the battlefield.[51]

In Bury's opinion, the wise Aetius did not want the Visigoths to gain more status than they already enjoyed and he thought the Huns might be useful again to him, as they had been in the past.[52] To authors such as Bouvier-Ajam, it remains a mystery why the armies on the battlefield at Troyes left it one after the other, without being worried that the balance of power between the remaining forces was going to be dangerously altered.[53]

Attila was the nephew of King Rugila, Aetius' Hunnic friend, who had died some time after chastising the Burgundians on Aetius' behalf in 436. It may also help to know that between the ages of 13 and 17, Attila had been a noble hostage at the court of Honorius and spent a lot of time both in Ravenna and Rome, having thus plenty of opportunity to study the patterns of behaviour and motivations of the Romans. He learned some Latin and spoke it slowly but correctly. He studied Greek and became good at it.[54] As we know, Aetius had himself been a noble hostage of King Rugila between the ages of 15 and 19. During that period, he purportedly became friends with both Rugila and Attila.[55]

After his retreat from Gaul to Pannonia (roughly, today's Hungary), Attila continued to claim Honoria's hand and dowry. In 452, his pride severely wounded by his defeat at Troyes the previous year, the Hun and his restored army invaded Italy from the north-east. He devastated the towns of the old mainland region of Venetia, and completely destroyed Aquileia on the northern Adriatic Sea after a three-month-long siege. He made Mediolanum (Milan) pay him handsomely for its continued existence. The horrified survivors of Attila's onslaughts on the Venetian mainland poured into the neighbouring marshes, which were far more difficult to invade, and founded the future maritime city of Venetia (Venice).[56]

In accordance with Attila's plan, his general Onegesius had engaged in diversionary troop movements and an offensive south of the River Po, to create the impression that the main thrust of the Hunnic attack would be along the road running south by the western shore of the Italian peninsula. In this manner, Onegesius had succeeded in drawing west a large part of Aetius' forces, thus leaving the road to Rome via the Apennine Mountains open to the main body of Attila's troops. Mysteriously, Attila did not follow his own strategy and came to a complete stop south of Mantua, at the confluence of the Rivers Po and Mincio.[57]

Aetius, mostly for financial reasons, did not possess forces strong enough to stop the multiple attacks of the Huns. Realising that even Ravenna was no longer safe, Aetius brought the pusillanimous Valentinian to Rome, which was completely unprepared to face the invaders. Valentinian was thus less protected than Honorius had ever been during Alaric's invasion.[58]

The people of Rome were overwhelmed by terror, as Attila had a dreadful reputation. Unlike the heroic inhabitants of Aquileia, they never considered arming themselves and fighting the invaders. Desperate, Emperor Valentinian and the Senate decided to try their last card: they sued for peace through a distinguished delegation that included Pope Leo I, senator Avienus, the head of the Senate and senator Trygetius, former prefect of Italy.[59] Following the precedent set by Innocent I during the last siege of Rome by Alaric, Leo I became the second pope to participate in such an important political assignment.

Leo I was the first great pope in the long history of the Roman Church. Even the pagans respected him. A talented and sensible man, he had an almost magical belief that the papacy personified the apostle St Peter. He worked hard to bolster the power of the Holy See and dealt judiciously with several heresies, including that of the Manicheans, whose dualistic faith consisted of a hotchpotch of Zoroastrianism, Buddhism, Christianity and Gnosticism.[60]

Pope Leo was very disappointed that there were still pagan enclaves in Rome.[61] Like modern-day popes, he decried the low attendance at church services.[62]

His eloquence was spectacular. After the Council of Ephesus in 431, where Mary was proclaimed 'Mother of God', a new divisive controversy rocked Christianity. This time the debate centred around the exact nature of the union of the divine and human in Christ. It was opened by Eutyches of Constantinople who maintained that before the Incarnation (the event resulting in God taking human form in the body of Christ), Christ was both human and divine, but after the Incarnation, He was only divine.[63]

When Eutyches contacted Leo regarding his teachings, the Roman pope was dismayed. In the end he wrote the famous 'Tome', teaching that Christ's two natures were separate, eternally joined in a sole individual, with His human deeds fully explicable by virtue of His divinity, and the other way around. Leo's dissertation formed the basis of the settlement of the dispute at the General Council of Chalcedon in 451. The simplicity and fluency of Leo's formulations were so remarkable that the perpetually bickering Christian bishops of the empire felt compelled to agree with them.[64]

Let us turn our attention once more to the Roman delegation to Attila. Aetius met its members before they crossed the bridge leading to Attila's camp south of Mantua. Senator Avienus told the puzzled Aetius he should simply wait with his soldiers for the conclusion of the conference.[65] Perhaps the senators thought it better to exclude Aetius from the negotiations, given his past friendship with Attila.

The legendary meeting between the Romans and Attila took place at Peschiera on the River Mincio.[66] We owe our description of it to the secretary of the Roman delegation, Prosper of Aquitaine. The official dinner was an amazing spectacle. Attila, who was rather short, wore a white Roman toga that contrasted sharply with his dark complexion. Precious necklaces adorned his neck and ermine. For their part, the senators were dressed in white togas and displayed all the emblems of their high rank. During the dinner, Attila admired the elderly and dignified pope – and Leo was overwhelmed by the charm and confidence of the surprisingly civilised leader of the Huns.

The pope and Attila met in total privacy on 5 July 452. Nobody will ever know what was said in the tent where they conducted their negotiations. On 6 July Attila announced that he was going to leave Italy on 8 July the way he had arrived, and that Valentinian had agreed to pay an acceptable tribute for the next five years. Attila also declared that he renounced any intention of taking Gaul and Italy and that he expected Valentinian to convince Marcian, the emperor in the East, to pay the tribute promised by the latter's predecessor. In exchange, he, Attila, undertook to cause no problems to the Byzantines; but if Marcian failed to adhere to these terms, then Constantinople would no longer be safe.

Attila ended by saluting the pope, 'the wisest man of the world', and wished him a long life. Leo I was profoundly moved and could not say a word. To the astonishment of those present, the pope and Attila embraced each other in silence. Attila's last words were addressed to Trygetius. He told him to remind Valentinian that he was going to continue to wait for his fiancée, Honoria. Italy and Rome were safe, at least for the time being.[67]

The British historian Bury doubted that the pagan Attila really cared for what he, Bury, supposed were the Christian exhortations of Leo I; rather, he believed that the real reasons for Attila's change of heart were that his army was suffering from plague and lack of provisions. Moreover, Emperor Marcian's eastern Roman troops had reached the war zone.[68] Such circumstances could well explain why Attila came to a halt so unexpectedly near Mantua. Bouvier-Ajam, on the other hand, argued that Marcian's troops did not pose a danger to Attila and suspected that Attila may have been ill.[69] Attila's departure from Italy may well, of course, have been connected to Valentinian's promise to pay a tribute for five years. Naturally, a combination of reasons would not be surprising.

Jordanes narrates that it was Attila's own worried people who persuaded him to give up Rome, for fear that he would meet the same fate that befell Alaric, who had died a few months after sacking the city forty-two years earlier.[70] Attila stayed away from Rome, but he died all the same – in the arms of Ildiko, a mysterious beauty of unknown origin, and only a year later.[71]

His empire collapsed almost immediately. In 454, the Germanic tribes of the Gepids, Ostrogoths, Rugians, Heruls and others inflicted a severe defeat on the Huns, their former masters. As a result, the territories of the barbarians north of the Danube underwent major changes.[72]

The empire of the Huns delayed the disintegration of the Roman Empire: the Huns indirectly protected Rome by subduing the German tribes north of the Danube and by providing military help to the embattled imperials.[73] For instance, Stilicho's great victory against the hordes of Radagaisus in 406 was due mainly to the intervention of the Hunnic cavalry led by Uldin.[74] However, it was the Hunnic expansion that had pushed the Goths, Alaric's parents included, into the Roman Empire in the fourth century.

According to the legend illustrated in the bas-relief that can be seen today at his tomb in St Peter's Basilica, while Leo I was negotiating with Attila, St Peter and St Paul descended from heaven, swords drawn, to deter the Hun from marching on Rome.[75]

But once the Hunnic peril had receded, the citizens of Rome dedicated themselves once more to the passion of the chariot races and other public shows, neglecting to attend the services of thanksgiving for their deliverance which were held at the tomb of St Peter. Leo, as shown by his writings, felt humiliated and frightened by the ingratitude of the Roman populace. Other writers also expressed their shock at seeing the citizens of Rome totally absorbed by the rivalry between the chariot teams of the Greens and the Blues while the empire fell apart and their risk of being put to the sword or taken into captivity at the hands of the barbarians was no longer imminent.[76]

The emperor himself was a disaster waiting to happen.

COURT INTRIGUE AND VALENTINIAN

Mysteriously, the Book of Pontiffs is also silent about the church of St Peter in Chains (Piazza di San Pietro in Vincoli) founded by the empress Eudoxia and still extant today. Was it omitted because of Eudoxia's alleged role in the calamity that was to befall Rome in 455? This smaller church shelters the legendary chain which supposedly bound St Peter, and Michelangelo's famous *Moses*.[77]

After his victory against the Huns, Aetius had many admirers but, like Stilicho in his time, he also had many enemies and was suspected of plotting to seize the throne with the help of his barbarian friends. There were courtiers who still blamed him for siding with the usurper John in the years after the death of Honorius and for his double-dealing with the late Boniface, Placidia's favourite.[78]

Valentinian III was in the habit of coming to Rome quite often. During a visit to the imperial palace there in 455, Aetius challenged the emperor to marry one of his daughters, Eudocia or Placidia, to one of his sons, Gaudentius or Carpilion, as he had solemnly undertaken to do some time earlier. Aetius probably wanted to consolidate his position by cementing relations with the imperial family.

The spineless Valentinian, surrounded by a large number of eunuchs and courtiers, surprisingly drew his sword and pierced the general's flesh. Taking their cue from their dishonourable master, the eunuchs and courtiers immediately began to run through the last great Roman general. Aetius' supporters were also assassinated methodically, which suggests that this was a carefully planned move.[79]

In 454, the previous year, the Huns had been defeated by their German subjects, and disappeared from history; perhaps this event encouraged the enemies of Aetius to strike. Thus, like Honorius, the incompetent and debased Valentinian III murdered his best general and, as happened after Stilicho's death, the consequences would be terrible.

But the immorality and foolishness of the Roman emperor went far deeper than the assassination of his most talented general. The worthless Valentinian, although married to the beautiful Eudoxia, had continued his womanising little suspecting that one day he would pay a very heavy price for seducing the wives of Roman patricians. He had been irresistibly attracted to the wife of the senator Maximus, the head of the famous house of Anicii, but she steadfastly rejected his advances. With the help of his retainers, Valentinian found a way of bringing the virtuous woman to a secluded area of the palace where he raped her.

Learning of what had happened to his wife, Maximus carefully orchestrated Valentinian's assassination, which took place on 16 March 455. Next day, Maximus was proclaimed emperor with the help of his money, thus winning the competition with Majorianus. Then, Maximus interred Valentinian III near the tomb of St Peter. In the meantime, Maximus' wife died heartbroken.

Only a few days after the death of Valentinian, which meant the end of the Theodosian male line, Maximus coerced the widowed Empress Eudoxia to marry him, hoping to gain the allegiance of those who had followed the house of Theodosius the Great for so many years. Soon after that, he supposedly revealed to Eudoxia that it was he who had been behind the plot to end Valentinian's life.[80]

Maximus also married his son to Eudocia, the daughter of Eudoxia and the late Valentinian III. The Vandal King Gaiseric declined to acknowledge Maximus as emperor and made outrageous territorial demands. Gaiseric was probably furious that Maximus had wedded Eudocia to his son, after the late Valentinian had betrothed her to his own son Huneric.[81]

Several Byzantine historians narrate that Eudoxia wanted revenge on Maximus by all means and summoned King Gaiseric of the Vandals to come immediately to Rome. Gregorovius and other authorities cited by him believed this was legend,[82] and indeed there are modern texts that do not mention this story. Nevertheless, during the second month of Maximus' rule at Rome, news reached the city that the mighty fleet of Gaiseric, whether by invitation of Eudoxia or not, had appeared at the mouth of the Tiber.

THE VANDALS SACK ROME

The reaction of Maximus was similar to that of the other Romans. He ran for his life without doing anything at all to organise the defence of the city. His outraged servants caught up with him in the streets, stoned him to death and dumped his corpse in the Tiber. His assassination took place in June 455.[83]

Only the elderly Pope Leo I and his retinue of priests marched south on the Via Portuensis and courageously stopped the loot-hungry hordes of Gaiseric. Unfortunately, Leo's legendary powers of persuasion were not of much help on this occasion. All he could extract from the greedy Gaiseric was a promise not to harm the citizens, not to set Rome on fire, and to spare the basilicas of St Peter, St Paul and St John in Lateran.[84]

The hordes of Gaiseric stole methodically anything of value they could find. Every region of Rome was plundered simultaneously. The Vandals seized furnishings of gold and silver, precious stones and necklaces.[85] Of Gaiseric's ships that sailed to Carthage laden with booty, only one, which was carrying statues, sank in the Mediterranean.[86]

The barbarians stripped the imperial palaces of the riches that remained. While ransacking those palaces they apprehended the unfortunate Empress Eudoxia. The Vandals plundered the sacred furnishings of the Temple of Jupiter on the Capitoline Hill, sheltered there since the time of Theodosius' edict banning public and private pagan worship in 391 – items that ended up in Gaiseric's palace in Africa. They also removed the gilded bronze tiles from half the roof of this famous temple.[87] The buildings in the Roman Forum and everywhere else were systematically pillaged. The furnishings of the Christian churches fell into the hands of the rapacious invaders, who also plundered the synagogue in Trastevere.[88]

Gregorovius found it difficult to believe that the Vandals, Arian Christians, and their African allies did not touch the basilicas of St Peter, St Paul and St John in Lateran.[89] Yet, he uncovered information indicating that, somehow, precious objects had indeed survived, especially in St Peter's, such as a gold relief placed above the memorial of the apostle by Valentinian III.[90]

The Vandals left Rome after fourteen interminable days, taking with them the Empress Eudoxia, her daughter Eudocia, and Gaudentius, one of the sons of Aetius. Moreover, they took into captivity thousands of Romans: it has been suggested that Rome lost nearly 200,000 of her citizens during the two weeks of the sack.[91] Exactly as the Visigoths had behaved forty-five years earlier, they forced no changes in the government and did not initiate a military occupation.[92] But they left behind a profoundly humiliated and impoverished city with ugly scars caused by their rapacity and dead bodies decomposing in the streets.

Eudocia ended up as the wife of Gaiseric's son Huneric. Somehow, after sixteen long years she managed to escape her horrible situation and reached Jerusalem, where death put an end to her nightmarish existence.[93] Placidia, the younger daughter of Valentinian III and Eudoxia, recovered her freedom after the demise of the eastern Emperor Marcian in 457. She travelled to Constantinople with her mother Eudoxia where she found her husband Olybrius, who had arrived earlier.[94]

The horrific behaviour of the Vandals during their ransacking of Rome left permanent traces in our vocabulary. To us, a vandal is someone who intentionally or ignorantly devastates or damages something beautiful or precious. Yet, while the Vandals departed with Rome's treasures and works of art, they left the city mostly intact. Indeed, the buildings and the infrastructure did not sustain catastrophic damage.[95] The fires set by the invaders were few and limited. Amazingly, the Ulpian Library in the Forum of Trajan and its statues survived the sack of Gaiseric.[96]

However, the other losses were enormous. In Africa, Rome's granary, the Vandals had taken over the lands of the Roman nobility and the Roman Church. Most of the senatorial families were now destitute, and famous ancient families vanished. Many fled the severely damaged city or were taken into slavery, which resulted in serious depopulation. Many immense palaces and streets were deserted. In this forlorn atmosphere, bewildered survivors wandered like ghosts through the ravaged city.[97]

Unbelievably, Rome recovered once again after the horrendous sack of Gaiseric. In 500, the bishop Fulgentius, a refugee from Vandal-controlled Africa, was in Rome and came out to greet King Theodoric the Great. On seeing the spectacle of the royal reception, he exclaimed: 'How beautiful must Paradise be, if Rome, which is only a city, and therefore corruptible, is so great and wonderful!'[98]

EIGHT

Rome and the End of the Empire in the West

The antagonistic presence of the Vandals in Africa, their control over the grain supply to Rome and Italy, and the vigorous raids of their navy seriously enfeebled the Roman strength in the Western provinces. Moreover, during the four decades that followed the rapid disintegration of the Hunnic Empire in 454, the Germanic barbarians gradually expanded their territories in Gaul and Spain.[1] And with the assassination of Aetius by Valentinian III in 455 the Roman power in the West had received a last, violent body-blow.

The continuing crisis in the Western Empire, fuelled by unremitting barbarian incursions, the haemorrhaging of her once great wealth through raids and to the Church, and the growing power of Christian leaders, finally drove the empire over the edge. Its demise paved the way for the complete triumph of the barbarians and the onset of the Middle Ages.

RICIMER SACKS ROME, 11 JULY 472

After Valentinian's long rule, Ricimer, a Germanic general of Suevian extraction, was, until his death in 472, the real master of what was left of the Western Roman Empire. The much-diminished Roman state could not do without the rude Germanic mercenaries.[2]

No longer was there an imperial family commanding respect and obedience. After toppling Avitus, the first post-Valentinian emperor after Maximus, Ricimer brought Majorianus (457–61) to the throne. Ricimer decapitated him on 7 August 461.[3]

The powerful Germanic general then found himself another puppet-emperor in the person of Severus (461–5), but after four years he overthrew him as well. At that point, all non-Italian western provinces were mostly in the hands of the Burgundians, Franks, Visigoths and Vandals. Eventually, under pressure from the eastern emperor Leo and the Senate, Ricimer agreed to the election of an emperor of Greek origin by the name of Anthemius.[4]

While the Empire was disintegrating, the Church was gaining strength. By the time of Sixtus III the popes had assumed leadership in the building of churches. After Sixtus III, through the building projects of Leo I (440–61), Hilary (461–8), and Simplicius (468–83) the papacy continued to act as custodian of the classical tradition.[5] St Stephen of the Ethiopians (Santo Stefano degli Abissini, Vatican City), St Bibiana, and Round St Stephen (Santo Stefano Rotondo), the Roman home to Hungarian Catholics, date back to this period.[6]

Some time in the fifth century, the Romans also erected St Anthony Abbot (Sant'Antonio Abate), dedicated to the hermit Anthony (251–356) who lived in the Egyptian desert and is revered as the founding father of Christian monasticism. St Anthony of Egypt is also considered the protector of animals. Romans still enthusiastically celebrate the blessing of their pets and other animals by St Anthony on 17 January. St Anthony Abbot is the Roman home to Russian Catholics.

After the sack of Gaiseric, Pope Leo I and his successor Pope Hilary worked tirelessly to make good the losses caused by Gaiseric's hordes to the churches of Rome. The gold furnishings were finally reinstated in even larger quantities than previously because the estates of the Roman Church continued to be a source of gold, silver and precious stones.[7] Jewellers, brass founders and mosaic designers adorned the churches, but the Roman sculpture was no more. The city of Rome showed the ugly blemishes of decline, though the baths of Diocletian, Nero and Alexander continued to function.[8]

The shrinking western Roman Empire could not raise the money to send an army against the African Vandals. Then, in 468, a joint East–West expedition for the reconquest of Africa failed and the reputation of Anthemius plummeted. Ricimer increasingly sought to tighten his hold over the hapless Greek, which led to a military confrontation. Ricimer began to lay siege to Rome in 472. Famine and pestilence haunted the city. Eventually, the mercenaries of Ricimer broke through the city's defences. They robbed her citizens and put them to the sword. Detailed information about the sack of Ricimer is lacking, but it seems that Trastevere and the Vatican areas were not affected. Olybrius became Ricimer's new puppet-emperor.[9]

Ricimer, an Arian Christian, died unexpectedly on 18 August 472, supposedly of plague. He had decorated the mysterious Church of St Agatha of the Goths with a splendid mosaic that was lost during the restoration of 1589. St Agatha eventually became the national church of the Arian Goths.[10]

According to a tradition narrated by Rendina, when the church was blessed by Pope Gregory the Great in 593 and thus restored to Catholicism, a sow possessed by the devil ran amok emitting terrible groans. For three days, clouds of sulphur surrounded the area of the church and blood-curling screams were heard at night. On the third day, the great altar was covered by a cloud that descended from the heavens. This second cloud brought with it a perfume of lilies, roses, violets and incense.[11]

THE FALL OF THE LAST EMPEROR

Olybrius also died of pestilence, on 23 October 472. Glycerius followed him on the throne in Ravenna in 473. In 474, Julius Nepos ousted Glycerius with support from Constantinople.[12]

Orestes, general of the army in what was left of Roman Gaul and former secretary to Attila at the time of the latter's meeting with Pope Leo the Great, headed a rebellion against Nepos, who ended up in exile in Salona, where Glycerius had also found refuge and was a bishop. Orestes set his son Romulus Augustulus on the imperial throne. Thus, Romulus Augustulus was a usurper, because Nepos was still alive and had a justifiable claim to the throne. What a destiny: the name of one of Rome's legendary twin founders, Romulus, joined with that of her first emperor, Augustus, as the last puppet-emperor.[13]

The downfall of the last Roman emperor in the West, Romulus Augustulus, was caused by his refusal to grant the Regional Army of Italy, made up almost entirely of barbarians, one-third of each Italian landowner's property.[14] The Germanic chieftain Odoacer, who was also an officer in the Roman army, promised to get the Germanic mercenaries what they wanted, and under his command they toppled Romulus Augustulus on 22 August 476 in Ravenna, on the anniversary of the day on which Stilicho had been beheaded sixty-eight years earlier.[15] Odoacer kept his word. The landowners who wished to maintain their property intact had to pay a new tax.[16]

Odoacer assumed the title king of Italy with a not very clearly defined legal framework. He was not interested in ruling a practically non-existent empire and returned the imperial symbols to Emperor Zeno of the East.[17]

Furious at the Roman Senate for recognising the barbarian as king of Italy, Emperor Zeno eventually acknowledged Odoacer only as 'Patrician of the Romans'.[18] This meant that, at least in theory, Italy was still part of the Roman Empire. However, any remaining hopes of reinstating imperial rule in Italy disappeared with the assassination of Nepos in 480.[19]

The Book of Pontiffs has not a word to say about the end of the Roman Empire in the West. It also makes no mention of how the Germanic barbarians Odoacer, then Theodoric, took over the rule of Italy.[20] This may indicate that these events, which many of us tend to view as traumatic for those living in Rome at the time, had in fact only limited immediate impact on the lives of the church and lay people of the former imperial capital.[21]

ROME AND THE END OF THE EMPIRE IN THE WEST

Liebeschuetz explains that the situation of the city of Rome and other western urban systems deteriorated gradually over time, as a consequence of the establishment of Constantinople as the imperial seat in the East, the conquest of Africa by the Vandals and the foundation of several barbarian kingdoms within the confines of the old empire; it was a downturn that culminated in the breakdown of commerce in the western half of the Mediterranean Sea. However, the Christianity of the new barbarian rulers of Italy had a protective effect on Rome and other urban centres, as Christianity was then a mainly urban religion.[22]

The debasement of classical Roman citizenship was a major factor in the decay of Rome and other Roman cities.[23] During the early empire, Roman citizenship had constituted a formidable unifying force. According to Liebeschuetz, 'Citizens felt a sense of obligation to the Roman state very much like that inspired by [the] patriotism of the European nations of modern times.' But Emperor Caracalla had been keen to find new sources of revenue.[24] With this short-term gain in mind, in 212 he made Roman citizens all the inhabitants of the empire except the *dediticii*, slaves who had been freed after being punished for committing a felony.[25] After that, the now heavily diluted attribute of Roman citizenship became less and less relevant.

Liebeschuetz observes that the legislation of the Late Empire documents increasingly numerous categories of people with diverse advantages, limitations and duties, a situation which did little to promote a commitment to one society and state. Among the many different status groups of the Late Empire, when it came to choosing between collaborating with foreign aggressors or putting their lives and wealth on the line for the good of the country, short-term gain rather than patriotism ruled their decisions.[26] And while the egalitarian Christian teachings furthered social cohesion, it was not in a direction that overlapped with that required for the survival of the empire. Indeed, the practice of Christianity resulted not in underpinning the state, but rather in increasing the power and wealth of the Church.[27] Allegiance to the empire gradually died out and new bonds, more local and ethnically based, replaced it. A new Western Europe would come into being after more battles with the barbarians.[28]

The city of Rome, nevertheless, survived the demise of the Roman Empire in the West. Bankrupt, its life was now completely provincial, its once splendid buildings lying in ruins or decrepit. Rome's ancient political institutions were but a faint shadow of their former glory. But the Roman Church was well organised, prosperous and capable of leading Rome and the western European peoples, the new Germanic inhabitants included, into the future, while preserving as much as possible of the Roman heritage.[29]

Yet it was Alaric, and not Gaiseric or Odoacer, who came to symbolise the end of the Empire in the West. Alaric was the first to ravage the mother-city of the empire and the subsequent disasters to befall the city did not surpass in psychological impact the trauma of his sacrilege.

Looking at what happened in Rome and Italy during the early Middle Ages may help our search for Alaric's tomb. A number of people and locations involved in the events of this nebulous period in the history of Rome and Italy are relevant to our investigation.

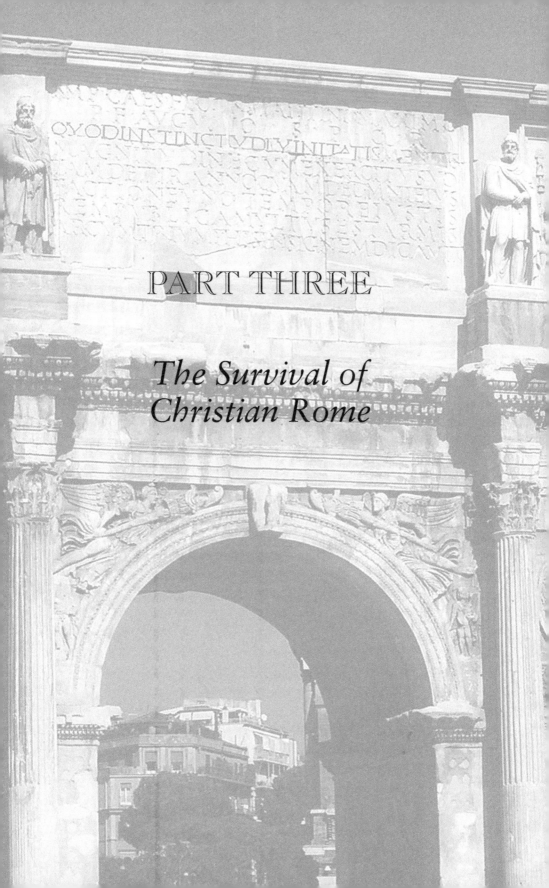

PART THREE

The Survival of Christian Rome

NINE

Rome under the Ostrogoths

After the German defeat of the Huns in 454, the Ostrogoths took over Pannonia, migrating into the Balkans in 473.[1] To rid himself of the troublesome Balkan Ostrogoths of Theodoric, who in 487 had marched to the walls of Constantinople, the eastern Emperor Zeno supported the idea of their departure for Italy in 488. The Ostrogoths were to snatch it from Odoacer and rule it under eastern imperial control. Zeno was clearly not in a position to reconquer Italy himself. As for the Ostrogoths, they lacked provisions and had been longing for many years to settle.[2]

According to Burns, in 488 approximately forty thousand Ostrogoths began advancing towards Italy along the old Roman roads, accompanied by their wagons. Food was scarce. After marching past cities with locked gates and defeating the fierce Gepids, another Germanic tribe, Theodoric finally led his famished people into Italy.[3] Strangely, Alaric himself had been followed by some forty thousand people into Italy and the whole story of the Ostrogoths seemed a re-enactment of the saga of the Visigoths.[4] But Theodoric was marching towards lands no longer ruled by the Roman Empire.

It took Theodoric three and a half years and several vicious battles in Italy to win the war with Odoacer. On 25 February 493, Theodoric concluded a treaty with Odoacer whereby they were to rule Italy as co-regents. Only ten days afterwards, Theodoric ended the life of Odoacer with his own hands during a shared meal in Ravenna on 5 March 493. Theodoric refused to allow Odoacer a Christian burial. He then orchestrated a campaign of killings aimed at eliminating the former supporters of Odoacer and ordered barbaric measures against his family: Odoacer's widow Sunigilda died of starvation and Theodoric's soldiers assassinated Hunulf, Odoacer's brother. The barbarian warriors of Odoacer were forced to flee or were eliminated.[5]

THE REIGN OF THEODORIC

Theodoric was one of the few barbarians who saw both Constantinople, where he had been held as a noble hostage in his youth (459–*c*. 469),[6] and Rome.[7] Incredibly, the city of Rome and Italy as a whole prospered during the rule of this ruthless and illiterate Germanic warrior. His reign (493–526) was remembered as a golden age in the following centuries, when contrasted with the calamities that had preceded it. Zacharias of Mytilene left for posterity a depiction of Rome during the reign of Theodoric:

> It contains 24 churches of the blessed apostles, Catholic churches. It contains 2 great *basilicae*, where the king sits and the senators are assembled before him every day. It contains 324 great spacious streets. It contains 2 great capitols. It contains 80 golden gods. It contains 64 ivory gods. . . . It contains 3,785 bronze statues of kings and magistrates. It contains, moreover, 25 bronze statues of Abraham, Sarah and Hagar, and of the kings of the House of David, which Vespasian the king brought up when he sacked Jerusalem, and the gates of Jerusalem and other bronze objects.[8]

While Theodoric did not meet the senators every day in Rome, this description does show that Rome and the treasure of the Jerusalem Temple remained an inexhaustible source of fascination at the beginning of the sixth century, including in the East.[9] Contrasting the number of statues given by Zacharias with information found in Cassiodorus, Gregorovius did not find it unbelievable. He also concluded that even in the depressed times of Pope Gregory the Great, Rome was wealthier than all the modern European capitals put together.[10]

Theodoric, an uneducated barbarian who spoke bad Latin,[11] set out to develop a government that protected the power and customs of the Ostrogoths within Roman society.[12] Theodoric made existence somewhat easier for the culturally and numerically superior Romans by not interfering with the barely surviving Roman establishment and by frequently complimenting them. He shrewdly hid the military supremacy of the Goths under the rather empty forms of the old Roman institutions. In this context, the Church of Rome became even more powerful.[13]

During his reign, the Christian community of Rome experienced bitter internal divisions. The pagan fertility festival of Lupercalia was still celebrated a century after Theodosius had banned pagan rituals, and the Christian nobility of Rome were not willing to give it up, in spite of pressure exerted by Pope Gelasius (492–6). The participants ran around almost naked and smacked any women in their way with shreds of goat hide to guarantee their fertility and prosperity.[14]

Theodoric played a major role in the protracted and often violent confrontation between Symmachus (498–514) and Laurence (498 and 501–5), who were both elected pope on the same day in 498. He recognised the anti-Monophysite Symmachus as pope after it was determined that he had not only been the first to be consecrated, but also had a more sizeable group of supporters.[15] In 499, Symmachus organised the first Roman synod (conference or council of bishops). Rendina notes it was at this meeting that it was decided that in future the populace would be excluded from papal elections.[16] The modern papal election process thus gained its first endorsement during the synod held under Theodoric.

Harmony seemed to have returned to Rome by 500. That year, Theodoric visited the city with the goal of buttressing the peace and boosting his own popularity. The first thing the politically astute Theodoric did once in Rome was to pray on his knees at the tomb of St Peter. After him and throughout the Middle Ages, all the emperors who arrived in Rome began their visit with a procession to St Peter. In the Forum, the distinguished writer Boethius greeted him with the traditional panegyric.[17] The king dwelt in the aged and empty imperial palaces. He offered public shows in the amphitheatre of Titus, known today as the Colosseum, and at the Circus Maximus, much to the delight of the pleasure-deprived Romans.[18]

Soon after Theodoric's departure from Rome, supporters of Laurence accused Pope Symmachus of destroying church property and of illegal relationships with women. Theodoric convened a council in Rome to examine the accusations against Pope Symmachus. There was violence in the streets and the intimidated bishops of the Council declared themselves unable to pass judgement on the pope, who barricaded himself in St Peter's. After four long years of bloody street battles between the two factions, in 505 Theodoric ordered Laurence to leave Rome.[19]

Theodoric resided in Ravenna but seemed to show genuine interest in the situation of the Senate, Church and citizens of Rome.[20] He recognised the importance of provisions for the hungry of the city, but the amount of grain he distributed, while significant, was enough for only about two thousand people.[21] To explain this limited quantity of grain, according to Gregorovius, Gibbon hypothesised a major drop in the number of inhabitants.[22] The maritime transportation of supplies continued up the Tiber up to the century of Theodoric.[23]

Theodoric did not restrict his concern for Rome's citizens to their physical needs. He supported too the maintenance of Rome's ageing monuments through various measures,[24] allocating funds for the restoration of the imperial palaces and repairing the Theatre of Pompey. Theodoric also appointed a Superintendent of Aqueducts for the city – Cassiodorus described with admiration the still functioning Aqua Virgo and Aqua Claudia. These and the other aqueducts continued to bring water to the many baths and fountains of Rome. The surprising 'barbarian from the Danube', as some would call Theodoric, also repaired the Aurelian Wall and the city sewers. In defiance of the centuries and in spite of the barbarian sacks, the Forum of Trajan was still standing.[25] Moreover, Theodoric maintained the institution of the public doctors.[26]

But the lamentations in the letters of Cassiodorus contribute to a more complete image of Rome in his time, an ageing city that was falling to pieces while its inhabitants looted statues and valuable construction materials such as lead, marble and brass, thus ignoring the prohibition of such practices by the government. The empty clamp holes in the surviving structures of the Colosseum are the result of centuries of such defacement. From the time of Constantine to well beyond the Middle Ages, the Church was the main perpetrator in the demolition of ancient Rome. For example, the beautiful church of St Augustine was built in the early Renaissance (1483) using travertine from the Colosseum. The ruin of the ancient city ensured the growth of Christian Rome, as Krautheimer so aptly put it.

The traditional forms of Roman entertainment survived the fall of the last emperor in the West. During the age of Theodoric and Cassiodorus, the Roman theatres produced comedies or mimes full of language and gestures that were outright pornographic.[27] Three centuries of Christian preaching failed to eliminate obscenity from the Roman theatre. Procopius describes in detail the controversial performances given by the Empress Theodora, such as her famous 'geese and bailey' act.[28] She had been a Roman actress and that was what Roman actors and actresses were called upon to perform in those days. Salvian could not find words to describe the obscenity displayed in the Roman theatres. Even the 494 proclamation by the eastern Emperor Anastasius I failed to curb lewdness in theatrical performances.[29]

The tradition of staging public shows continued during the reign of Theodoric. There had been fires in the Colosseum in 217 and 250. This famous venue had also been hit by lightning in 320 and shaken by earthquakes in 429, 443 and 486. Repairs are documented in 438, after the earthquake of 443 and in 470. Venantius carried out the last recorded restoration in 484, which is mentioned in an inscription that can still be seen in the Colosseum.[30]

Inside the Colosseum, the modern-day visitor encounters the fascinating remnants of the *corona podii*, the marble protective wall separating the seats of the senators and their families from the arena. During the shows, a net of 13ft (4m) was erected between the tier on which the senators were seated and the arena, to prevent the animals attacking the privileged of Rome. When a senator died or was promoted, his name, which was inscribed on his place, was erased to make room for those of other senators. It is because of this practice that researchers have been able to discover the names of 195 senators active after the fall of the last emperor in 476.[31] A piece of marble exhibited in the Colosseum displays an inscription indicating Senator Marcellus' seat in the early sixth century. The shows there continued, seemingly unaffected by the disappearance of the Roman Empire in the West.

Cassiodorus describes in somewhat disturbing detail the horrors of the hunting shows in a letter he wrote on behalf of his master Theodoric around 523. While the king apparently disapproved of these spectacles, he permitted the consul Maximus to provide one in the Colosseum for the Roman populace. After 523, there appears to be no more documentation relating to public shows in the Colosseum.[32]

Within the Colosseum, the visitor can see the name of the gladiator Vindicomus, carved on a marble slab. The Greek letter *theta* Θ, known as *theta nigrum*, next to the name, indicates that Vindicomus perished in battle inside the great amphitheatre. But gladiatorial combat was no longer permitted after the visit of Honorius in 404 to Rome. In Constantinople, it was prohibited only in 494.[33]

The aged and dilapidated Circus Maximus was still in use, but spectators filled only about a quarter of the available seats. The Egyptian obelisk of the pharaoh Sethi I, brought to the city by Emperor Augustus, was still standing. Only in 1588 did Pope Sixtus V move it to Piazza del Popolo, where it can be seen today.[34] Rome's oldest obelisk, made of red granite and erected at Aswan by pharaoh Tuthmosis III in the fifteenth century BC, then moved to Egyptian Thebes (today's Luxor), adorned this circus as well. Constantius II transported it to Rome in 357. Since 1587 it has been in Piazza San Giovanni in Laterano.

Theodoric is remembered as tolerant and impartial in his treatment of Christians and Jews.[35] As Leon tells us, a Jewish population had existed in Rome since the first century BC. Julius Caesar rewarded the Jews with many favours for the support they had given him during his confrontation with Pompey. These privileges survived under the pagan emperors, with brief interruptions caused by sectarian violence within the Jewish community, such as that mentioned in Acts 18:2, and too much proselytising. During the Early Empire, while Rome was the imperial capital, the city's Jewish community numbered about fifty thousand and was concentrated in Trastevere and prospered.[36]

Under the Christian emperors, the Jews of Rome must have been affected by such laws as those limiting their recruiting of new converts, banning intermarriage with Christians and prohibiting them from owning Christian slaves, as described in the Theodosian code. However, there are no data referring explicitly to the Jews of Rome during the reign of the late Roman emperors in the West and they are last mentioned under Theodoric. Until the twelfth century, their history is shrouded in darkness, although we know that they continued to live in Trastevere.[37]

The last stage of Theodoric's rule was, however, noted for its cruelty. But this cruelty could not stem the tide of the terrible events that followed.

THE END OF THEODORIC

In 519, the Eastern emperor Justin (518–27) spearheaded a council that produced an authoritative denunciation of Eutyches' Monophysitism. The aim was the reconciliation of the Eastern imperials and Church of Constantinople with the Church of Rome and the Roman senators.[38] At the same time, Justin muddied the political waters in Italy and Rome by issuing a proclamation against the Arians, and the Ostrogoths were Arians, who did not accept the full divinity of Christ.[39]

The Byzantines, as the Eastern Romans came to be known, saw themselves until their end as inheritors of the Roman Empire, but this was a cultural Christian concept and not based on the old idea of Roman citizenship, in which was implicit the commitment to protect the empire from foreign aggressors.[40]

Thus, in the time of Theodoric, the Byzantine emperor Justin sent Pope Hormisdas (514–23) and Pope John I (523–6) very rich gifts. After the death of Theodoric, Emperor Justinian (527–65) sent Pope John II (533–5) more gifts for St Peter.[41] It was as though the Byzantines were attempting to stake out and claim territory. But even the Frankish King Clovis, who had chosen to convert to Catholic Christianity from the start, sent St Peter's a tiara encrusted with gems, a harbinger of the great role that the Franks were to play in the life of Rome.[42]

Theodoric felt himself targeted by the anti-Arian edict of Justin. He accused of sedition and executed the innocent writer Boethius, Consul Albinus and Symmachus, head of the Senate and father-in-law of Boethius. Before being put to death, Boethius spent time in prison, where he wrote his famous *De consolatio philosophiae*. In an attempt to reverse the anti-Arian edict, Theodoric ordered Pope John I (523–6) to travel to Constantinople and persuade Justin to annul it. The Roman Pope John I was given a triumphal reception in Constantinople but chose to remain silent about Theodoric's desire to see the edict rescinded. He returned to Rome where Theodoric, furious that his strategy had been thwarted, imprisoned him. Pope John died as a result of the treatment meted out to him in prison. The Ostrogothic king then imposed Felix IV as pope.[43]

On 30 August 526, Theodoric died of dysentery, like Arius, the founder of his brand of Christianity. His passing inspired legends of demonic death and countless rumours about the manner of his demise. In the 800s, his porphyry casket could be seen next to the entrance of the monastery of St Mary, which had been built next to his mausoleum. The fate of his remains is, however, a mystery.[44]

Until he died in 526, Theodoric was king of Italy. From 511 to the time of his death, he was also regent of the Visigoths.[45] After the death of Theodoric, the sorely tried inhabitants of Rome and Italy waited anxiously to see what would happen to their Gothic masters and to themselves.

AMALASUNTHA AND THE BYZANTINE–GOTHIC WAR

After Theodoric was gone there ensued a period of relative calm ushered in by the regency of Amalasuntha, his widowed daughter, who reigned in the name of her 10-year-old son Athalaric. Amalasuntha reconciled the Gothic crown with the papacy.[46] In 527, she allowed Pope Felix to erect the Church of St Cosmas and St Damian incorporating what was left from the library of the Temple of Peace built by Vespasian.[47]

Amalasuntha made peace with the Senate, too. She returned the property of the late Boethius and Symmachus to their sons. She wrote to the eastern emperor that she did not favour the harsh policies her father had adopted in his last years.[48]

But the clergy and the Senate were not on good terms. To a certain degree, the Roman populace continued to resent the Goths. The papal elections, affected by simony and corruption, were a battleground between the pro-Gothic and pro-Byzantine factions. After a tumultuous contest, Athalaric confirmed Pope John II (533–5) as bishop of Rome.[49]

In 532–3, Amalasuntha had to deal with a dangerous group of Gothic nobles who opposed her policy of friendship with the Byzantines and had previously incited Theodoric to carry out cruel anti-Roman measures before his death. They wanted to manipulate Athalaric, who by then was 16 years old. To justify their interference, they claimed his education contravened Gothic tradition.

Amalasuntha panicked. She asked Emperor Justinian of the East to receive her as a political refugee and then sent a ship with the royal treasure to Durazzo (Dures in modern Albania), where Justinian had reserved a palatial home for her use. The ship was laden with 40,000lb (18,000kg) of gold. The annual budget of the Empire in the West in its last stages amounted to approximately half that amount. Amalasuntha also offered to vacate the throne of Italy in favour of Emperor Justinian. The vessel arrived safely in Durazzo. Justinian duly invited her to travel to Constantinople.

But Amalasuntha, displaying a streak of her father's resolute character, did not leave Ravenna and weathered the crisis. As the Franks had attacked the Burgundians in 532 and temporarily taken over Arles in Gaul (France), which had been under Gothic control, she sent to war the three troublesome noble Goths from Ravenna. They were killed at a later date.

Surprised by her bold move, Amalasuntha's opponents stayed their hand. She appointed men she trusted to high-ranking positions, among them Cassiodorus who became praetorian prefect of Italy.

Then something totally unexpected happened. Athalaric died in 534. To consolidate her position, Amalasuntha, a widow since 522–3, entered into an alliance with her cousin Theodahad and made him co-regent in the year of her son's death. This would prove a serious mistake.[50]

Theodahad was among those hostile to the Romans. The revitalised Byzantines were at war with the Vandals of Africa. Their emperor, Justinian, worked towards the reconquest of the former Roman lands in the West.

Theodahad made a move, the result of which was to give Justinian the pretext he needed to attack the Goths in Italy. Theodahad banished Amalasuntha to the island of Martana on Lake Bolsena. Some sources relate that the Byzantines tried to rescue her, but that the Empress Theodora, Justinian's wife, was so envious of the attractive and learned Gothic queen that she took steps to ensure she was never freed. Eventually, Amalasuntha was murdered in mysterious circumstances on Martana.[51]

In response to the assassination of Amalasuntha, Emperor Justinian opened hostilities against the Ostrogoths in Italy with the goal of returning the former imperial lands to his rule. To ward off so powerful a threat to himself and to his people, Theodahad engaged in frantic negotiations with the Byzantines, undertaking to send to Constantinople a 300lb gold crown every year, 3,000 Gothic warriors to serve in the Byzantine army and even to renounce the throne of Italy so Justinian could take it over, in exchange for being appointed senator in Constantinople. In response, Justinian promised only to leave the royal domains in Italy under Theodahad's control, but under imperial authority, and declined to appoint him senator in the East. When Theodahad became openly hostile to Justinian, a Byzantine fleet swiftly conquered Dalmatia and General Belisarius invaded southern Italy. The Ostrogothic commander of Rhegium (Reggio di Calabria) Ebrimund, Theodahad's son-in-law, surrendered without a fight.[52] This was not Belisarius' first campaign. The contributions of this talented and loyal general to the survival of the Byzantine Empire were crucial. Previously, he had defeated the Persians, put an end to the Nika rebellion that almost cost Emperor Justinian his throne and with only a small army vanquished the north African Vandals.

The cornered Theodahad sent Pope Agapitus I (535–6) to Constantinople on a mission to persuade Justinian to give up the offensive. Agapitus was well received, but his intervention failed to stop the war. Moreover, he became ill and died in Constantinople. The by-now despairing Theodahad imposed Silverius (536–7) on the throne of St Peter, perhaps in the hope that the new pope could miraculously help him.

Belisarius advanced unimpeded to Naples, which he took after a ferocious battle. Theodahad left Ravenna and brought most of his army to the outskirts of Rome. At the end of November 536, the Gothic warriors rebelled and elected Witigis (536–42) as the new king of the Ostrogoths, on whose orders Theodahad was assassinated.[53]

Witigis urged the Senate to oppose the Byzantines, and then withdrew to Ravenna. He left in Rome only 4,000 warriors. Pope Silverius exhorted the Senate not to fight a battle that was already lost. In fact, he invited Belisarius to advance to Rome. The famous general marched with his forces into the city during the night of 5/6 December 536 through the Porta Asinaria, which still stands on Via Sannio, not far from St John in Lateran. Simultaneously, the last Gothic warriors left Rome via Porta Flaminia (today's Porta del Popolo). The Ostrogothic rule in Italy and Rome had come to an end.[54]

What followed was something that neither Goths nor Romans could have predicted.

TEN

Rome, the Byzantines and the Lombards

After Constantine, the emperors of the East continued to see themselves as the lawful heirs of Rome. Even in the eleventh century, Michael Psellos taught his imperial pupil Michael VII that the foremost person in his ancestry was Augustus, because his rule coincided with the incarnation of God, the most important episode in the history of the world. The people under Byzantine rule called themselves *Romaioi* (Romans) long after the use of Latin became a thing of the past.[1]

But the sixth-century Italians did not view the Byzantine army as their allies, coming to rescue them from a despotic regime. They were more concerned about the safety of their towns and loved ones. It did not matter to them whether their town was taken by the barbarians or by the Byzantines. The Italians frequently took part in the resistance of their cities to the eastern Romans. While the indigenous inhabitants were prepared to defend their city against any attacker, they were not prepared to become legionaries and leave their homes and families to reinstate the rule of the lawful imperials in Italy.

There was a shocking disparity between the seemingly endless recruiting capability of the Senate in times of war with Carthage and the almost total absence of native Italians from the imperial troops fighting the Goths in Italy. In the minds of the Italians, the Roman Empire no longer existed.[2]

THE BYZANTINE–GOTHIC WAR

Once in Rome, Belisarius prepared the city as best he could against attack by the Goths. For example, he repaired the Aurelian Wall and replenished the grain stores of the city. In March 537, Witigis encircled Rome with 150,000 men. The siege would last about a year.[3]

Like Alaric before them, the Ostrogoths took over Portus and began starving the city by blocking the transportation of grain to its quays.[4] The famine reached horrific proportions. The senators were purchasing sausages prepared from carcasses of dead mules. The price was equal to the weight of the sausage in gold. The stench of the rotting cadavers strewn all over the city and the oppressive heat of the Roman summer were hellish.[5]

In one of the most famous episodes of this siege, the Byzantine soldiers defending the Mausoleum of Hadrian, included in the Aurelian Wall by Stilicho in 402–3, broke the marvellous statues that embellished the tomb of the emperor into pieces, and hurled the marble chunks at the Goths who were trying to scale the wall.[6]

In an attempt to break the resolve of the besieged, Witigis cut the aqueducts so exuberantly praised by Cassiodorus during Gothic rule and made the area surrounding Rome marshier than it already was. The Roman baths ceased to function and gradually fell into ruins. The mills in Trastevere, on the slope of the Janiculum, came to halt.[7] Ironically, the Janiculum aqueduct, which provided water to the grain mills, had been restored in 537, the year the siege began.[8] The aqueducts were gradually dismantled during the Middle Ages and in modern times; the Ostrogoths only cut them. Inside Rome, Belisarius closed the openings of the aqueducts. He knew only too well that they could be used to break into the city, as he and his men had used a similar ploy when they took Naples.[9]

In February 538, another Byzantine army led by General John conquered Ravenna. Outmanoeuvred, Witigis broke off the siege of Rome and advanced towards the second imperial army. He lost the ensuing battle and was taken prisoner. While Rome was under siege, Belisarius unseated Pope Silverius on 29 March 537 after the latter was unjustly accused of conspiring to aid the Goths' entry into the city.[10]

Vigilius, the scheming papal ambassador to Constantinople, had earlier tried to seize the throne of St Peter with the help of Empress Theodora, after Agapitus had died in Constantinople. By the time he arrived in Rome loaded with money from Theodora, an enthusiastic Monophysite, the late Theodahad had already made Silverius pope. Vigilius had promised the empress that once he was elected pope he would condemn the authors of some old anti-Monophysite writings as a form of opposition to the rulings of the Council of Chalcedon, which had used the Tome of Leo the Great as the basis of its decision to outlaw Monophysitism in 451.[11]

While Witigis' siege of Rome continued, Antonina, Belisarius' wife and a close friend of Empress Theodora, together with the incorrigible schemer

Above: St Paul's Gate (Porta Ostiense), with the nearby pyramid-tomb of Cestius incorporated into the Aurelian Wall. The vanished Salarian Gate (Porta Salaria) was similar to it. The Visigoths kept a close watch on the gates during their siege of Rome.

Below, left: Constantine the Great. *(Courtesy of Musei Capitolini, Rome. Photographic archives)*

Below, right: The Arch of Constantine and the Colosseum. The mysterious words QVOD INSTINCTV DIVINITATIS have been enhanced to make them more visible.

St John in Lateran, the cathedral of Rome, endowed by Constantine with fabulous riches and plundered by Alaric, in an etching by Domenico Amici, 1832–40.

The western end of the Roman Forum:
1 Temple of Dei Consentes
2 Palazzo Senatorio
3 Tabularium
4 Temple of Vespasian and Titus
5 Temple of Concordia
6 Temple of Saturn
7 Rostra
8 Arch of Septimius Severus

The Roman Senate.

Remains of the imperial palaces on the Palatine. In the foreground, the Basilica Aemilia which the Visigoths set on fire.

Arch of Titus, displaying furnishings from the Temple of Jerusalem looted by the Romans in AD 70. Alaric is thought to have seized at least part of the Temple treasure.

Bridge of Fabricius (Ponte Quattro Capi), built in 62 BC; the oldest surviving bridge in Rome.

Fifth-century mosaic of Christ and the Apostles in the apse of St Pudenziana. The senatorial togas of the Apostles symbolise their naturalisation as Romans. The missing Apostles were lost during restoration. *(Courtesy of Ministerio del'Interno, Direzione Centrale per l'Amministrazione del Fondo Edifici di Culto, Rome)*

Below, left: An ivory diptych of General Stilicho, arch-enemy of Alaric, with his wife Serena and son Eucherius. *(Courtesy of Museo del Duomo di Monza e Biblioteca Capitolare)*

Below, right: Aqueduct built by Nero and working at the time of the sacks of Alaric and Gaiseric.

Above, left: The hordes of Alaric sack Rome. Etching and printing by Adriaan Schoonebeck, Tsar Peter the Great's chief printer. (From '*Alaric ou Rome Vaincu*', an epic poem by Georges de Scudery, The Hague, 1685)

Above, right: Alaric confronts a bear. Etching and printing by Adriaan Schoonebeck. (From '*Alaric ou Rome Vaincu*', The Hague, 1685)

Marks on the pavement of the Basilica Aemilia left by coins melted in the fire during Alaric's sack of Rome. *(Courtesy of Soprintendenza Archeologica di Roma)*

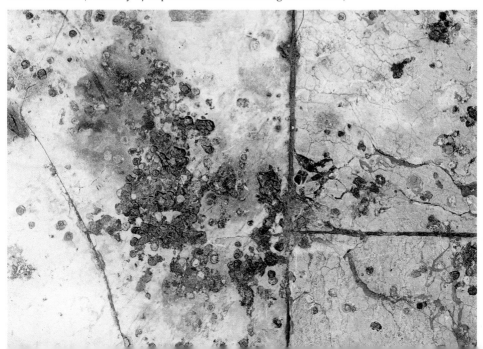

Above: The burial of Alaric under the Busento riverbed near Cosenza. Lithograph by Anton Ziegler, 1850.

Left: St Gregory on the Celian Hill. From here Christianity was exported to England in 597. At that time, the site was occupied by St Andrew's, Pope Gregory's own monastery.

St Mary in Cosmedin with its Romanesque belfry. A mosaic from old St Peter's and a faun with a mouth of stone known as the *Bocca della Verità* can be seen inside the church. The famous stony mouth no longer works as a lie detector after a clever adulteress tricked it.

Old St Peter's as it would have appeared to the devout Charlemagne when he approached the basilica built by Constantine the Great. *(Istituto Nazionale per la Grafica, Rome; Courtesy of Ministerio per i Beni e le Attività Culturali)*

The Coronation of Charlemagne by Pope Leo III at Old St Peter's on Christmas Day 800 (drawing by Philippoteaux and etching by Rebel, 1852). The tomb of St Peter was desecrated on 25 August 846, 436 years after the sack of Alaric.

The mosaic of Theodora Episcopa (the female pope), the mother of Pope Paschal I (817–24), in the Chapel of St Zeno in the church of St Prassede. Theodora was the only woman to be called pope. *(Courtesy of Ministero dell'Interno, Direzione Centrale per l'Amministrazione del Fondo Edifici di Culto, Rome)*

Above, left: St Paul's Without the Walls (xilography by Ottavio Panciroli, *c.* 1670). The tomb of St Paul and the basilica were desecrated on 25 August 846.

Above, right: Busento in Cosenza.

Below: The historic centre of Cosenza.

Vigilius, persuaded Belisarius to detain Silverius. Belisarius knew that the imposing wall of Rome had been made irrelevant by betrayal in the time of Alaric and took extraordinary precautions.[12] Silverius ended up as a simple monk exiled to Anatolia (modern Turkey). The frightened clergy elected Vigilius pope (537–55), who thus saw his dream finally come true.[13]

Duffy says that in the East, Silverius managed to see Justinian in person and convinced him that he was an innocent victim. The emperor shipped him back to Rome for a fair hearing. But Vigilius detained and banished him to the island of Palmaria, the largest of the three islands in the small gulf of La Spezia in the Ligurian Sea. After a few months, Silverius succumbed to starvation.[14] Others state that he was murdered by Eugenius, a man in the service of Antonina, Belisarius' wife.[15] For the next six years, Vigilius did not have to do anything for his Byzantine masters.

We will return to Vigilius in a little while, as he too is connected with the story of Alaric's treasure.

In 539, the imperials were once again in control of Italy. Belisarius placed a garrison in Rome and left for Constantinople to celebrate his victory. His departure would be a major miscalculation.[16]

TOTILA'S SACK OF ROME

Under their new king Totila (541–52), the revitalised Goths marched south and inflicted a crushing defeat on the Byzantines at Faenza. The imperial forces retreated inside Ravenna, Rome and Naples. In 543 Totila took Naples. The following year, Justinian ordered Belisarius to return to Italy. The general was forced to remain in Ravenna, not having the means to recruit an army strong enough to oppose the Goths and protect Rome. The sorely tested city once more endured a long siege at the hands of the barbarians.[17]

The moment of truth finally came for Pope Vigilius. In 543, in the wake of the resurrection of the Gothic army, Justinian was eager to placate the Monophysite faction in an attempt to boost the cohesion of the empire. Grudgingly, his bishops helped him by signing a denunciation of the anti-Monophysite texts identified as 'The Three Chapters', the ones that Vigilius had promised Theodora to attack in 536, after the death of Pope Agapitus. This way, Justinian hoped to dissociate his rule from the directives of the 451 Council of Chalcedon, without having openly to reject its conclusions.

Unfortunately for Vigilius, the West was unanimously opposed to Justinian's initiative and the intimidated pope refused to sign the condemnation.[18]

In November 545, the soldiers of Justinian apprehended Vigilius and shipped him off to Constantinople.[19]

Those who had been caught inside the walls of Rome suffered horrendous deprivation. Affluent or destitute, citizens were forced to eat grass and nettles. Many died of starvation and there were cases of suicide. Thousands of Romans, especially senators, aristocrats and great land-owners, bought their freedom and left Rome, marching south on the Via Appia and Via Latina. But there were still people remaining inside the city. Eventually, Belisarius tried but failed to bring food to the unfortunate besieged. To make matters worse, he himself fell ill.[20]

In the end, the Isaurians, mercenaries in the pay of the Byzantines and on duty at Porta Asinaria, opened negotiations with Totila and reached an agreement with him. The traitors opened the gate on 17 December 546. Those Romans still inside fled in panic, if they had the strength to do so, apparently warned by the Gothic trumpets. The scenes on the streets of Rome were horrifying. The city was severely depopulated, and probably many Romans already weakened by starvation died. Gatto believes that thousands were murdered during the storming of the city and that Procopius' figures are questionable.[21] (Procopius may have accompanied Belisarius during the war with Totila and may have been under pressure to play down the Byzantine failure to protect Rome.[22])

The Ostrogoths engaged in plunder and destruction on an unprecedented scale – well beyond the ravages inflicted during the sacks of Alaric, Gaiseric and Ricimer. While Rome contained fewer riches than at the time of the previous sacks, the houses, public palaces and churches were subjected to systematic pillaging. The Ostrogoths obliterated many buildings. They hacked down and set on fire many areas never previously touched by barbarians, including the avenues in the historic centre of the city.

On the steps of old St Peter's, the deacon Pelagius, clutching a Bible in his hands, implored Totila to have mercy on the Romans. The king agreed, but the wretched survivors had to sell their properties to purchase grain and meat and the pass allowing them to quit their city.[23]

At the time of Totila's sack, Rome's population plummeted, some say to a mere thirty thousand.[24] Pope Pelagius wrote to the bishop of Arles in Gaul, requesting clothes and money for the many impoverished Romans.[25] The activities of the Senate ground to a halt. The water lost by the severed aqueducts caused the already wet area around Rome to become a malaria-infested marsh that was not drained until the time of Mussolini.[26]

Believe it or not, there were still ancient riches to be plundered in Rome.

THE END OF THE BYZANTINE–GOTHIC WARS

The overconfident Totila, infuriated by the Byzantines' lack of enthusiasm for negotiations, threatened the total destruction of Rome should Pelagius and Belisarius try to deceive him. To demonstrate his resolve, he demolished a portion of the Aurelian Wall and set Trastevere on fire.

Belisarius wrote Totila a modern-sounding letter in which he explained to the barbarian that if he were to demolish Rome completely, he would go down in history as the man responsible for the destruction of a city that belonged to the universal patrimony of all times, irrespective of whether he emerged as the winner or loser. Totila's reply has not survived. Belisarius' memorable epistle saved the city.[27]

Totila left Rome, taking with him senators and rich Romans as hostages. An additional number of inhabitants left the city at this point.

Belisarius entered the deserted and filthy former imperial capital, repaired the wall as best he could, and followed Totila, who had moved south to subdue the rest of Italy. But Belisarius did not have the forces required to challenge the Goths. Around this time, his presence at the head of the Byzantine army in Italy came to an end.

According to the inscription on a twelfth-century memorial stone at the Church of St Mary in Trivio, Belisarius was its founder; he supposedly erected the church to expiate his guilt for unjustly unseating Pope Silverius.[28] But a legend mentioned by Rendina tells us that a destitute and blind Belisarius ended up begging near the still existing Porta Pinciana, called Porta Belisaria in the past.[29]

Totila then returned to Rome and subjected it to a third Gothic siege, in the autumn of 549. This time the city was better prepared. The Romans had grown grain, vegetables and fruit inside the walls. However, the chronically perfidious Isaurian mercenaries, unhappy again at their Byzantine masters for failure to pay them, opened St Paul's Gate on the Via Ostiense and the Aurelian Gate (replaced eventually by St Pancratius' Gate

– Porta S. Pancrazio)[30] on Via Aurelia, allowing the barbarians to storm the city on 16 January 550.[31]

Totila tried to normalise the life of the city. In 550 and 551, he reconquered Sicily, Sardinia and Corsica. In 552, the Goths confronted a new Byzantine army led by Narses at Gualdo Tadino in Umbria, 32 miles (52km) north-east of Perugia. They were defeated and Totila lost his life. The Goths elected Teias as their new king, but they were vanquished again, in 553, in the area of Vesuvius near Naples. Teias, too, died in battle.[32]

The surviving Ostrogoths did not elect a king. After the Visigoths and the barbarians of Odoacer, the Ostrogoths were the third Germanic group that failed to settle in Italy. As Wolfram observed, their 500-year-long history had come to an end.[33]

Rome and Italy were utterly devastated. But the destruction was not only physical.

JUSTINIAN HUMILIATES THE PAPACY

In Constantinople before the end of the war the fickle Vigilius gave in and in April 548 denounced in writing 'The Three Chapters'. He tried desperately to hide his blatant volte-face by claiming that his statement did not affect the conclusions of the Council of Chalcedon.

In the West, absolutely everybody was outraged and denounced Vigilius as a turncoat. Shaken by this violent response, Justinian permitted Vigilius to rescind his statement, on condition that he republish it when the time was ripe. The emperor also agreed that a general council of bishops was needed to tackle the problem. However, in 551 the impatient Justinian published his own proclamation criticising 'The Three Chapters'.

At that point, Vigilius no longer felt he had the resources to carry on playing games with Justinian and decided to rescue whatever authority he still had back home. To this end, he called on the clergy to resist the imperial decree. He gathered in council all the bishops present in Constantinople and renewed the excommunication of Patriarch Menas. Vigilius had to seek asylum in the palace church of Sts Peter and Paul in an attempt to avoid arrest by the imperial soldiers.[34]

Evidence that we will examine in the section dedicated to the lost writings of Cassiodorus suggests that the Jordanes who wrote about the burial of Alaric was a bishop from Crotone, a town that still exists in southern Italy, not far from Cassiodorus' monastery and Cosenza, where Alaric is alleged to have been buried. This Jordanes may have been among the bishops who accompanied the controversial Vigilius in his church sanctuary.

At one point, the people of Constantinople witnessed an incredible spectacle: the old pope desperately clinging to the columns of the altar, while the soldiers tried to drag him away, pulling at his hair, beard and garments. The columns of the altar moved and crumbled. Disgusted, the bystanders mobbed the soldiers and rescued the elderly pope. During the night, Vigilius crossed the Bosphorus and sought safety in Chalcedon (modern Kadiköy near Istanbul). The supreme irony was that he found sanctuary in the very church where the 451 council, the one he had been indirectly attacking, held its meetings.

Incredibly, Vigilius once more capitulated to Justinian, thus rendering worthless his recent brave resistance. In May 553 the expected General Council, the fifth, met in Constantinople, but there were few Westerners among the participants and all its business was conducted under heavy imperial pressure. Vigilius refused to join the council and published his own statement, in which he dissented partially.

But Justinian was now in full command of the situation. His army had at last inflicted a final defeat on the Goths in Italy and he wanted an obedient pope in Rome. To rid himself of Vigilius once and for all, Justinian sent the council the confidential letters in which Vigilius had repeatedly promised to attack 'The Three Chapters'. Justinian cut off all communication with Vigilius, but not with the papal see. The totally dishonoured Vigilius was arrested, and the clergy accompanying him sent to hard labour or imprisoned. In 555, Justinian allowed the wretched Vigilius to leave. The former pope died in Syracuse, Sicily, on his way to a Rome that did not want him.[35]

The new pope Pelagius (556–1), who had previously firmly opposed the pressures exerted by Justinian, stunned everyone by accepting the fifth council's denunciation of 'The Three Chapters'. The Westerners declared him a traitor as well. Milan, Aquilea and Istria severed all ties with the Holy See. Milan would take half a century and Istria 150 years to reinstate relations with Rome. The bishops in Gaul no longer trusted Pelagius.

At the bottom of this unprecedented debasement of papal prestige was a major difference of perspective between the pope and the Eastern emperor.

The deeds of Constantine the Great gave a solid foundation to the Eastern concept of the emperor as the higher-ranking colleague in the coalition with the pope. Justinian was simply abiding by that tradition. Indeed, the Byzantine emperor was responsible for the appointment and demotion of bishops, and for overseeing the churches and matters of doctrine. The Byzantine emperor was God's representative on earth, not the pope of Rome. Byzantine court ritual reflected the nearly divine nature of the emperor's position.[36] This Byzantine concept of the role of the emperor in the world would form the basis for the relationship between the papacy and Constantinople for decades.

JUSTINIAN NORMALISES ITALY

After almost twenty years of war, Rome and Italy were in chaos. Rome's population had shrunk to fifty thousand.[37]

In August 554, Justinian intervened and published a lengthy decree known as the Pragmatic Sanction. Italy became part of the Eastern Empire. The edict regulated the legal situation generated by the war. It also made the pope and the Senate responsible for the selection of weights and measures for all provinces of Italy. This meant that the Senate was resurrected. The pope became more influential. He was now able to intervene in the administration of the city and to exercise legal powers. In terms of practical measures to benefit the city, the Pragmatic Sanction revived the institution of the fourteen public doctors paid in kind.[38] Some of the aqueducts were repaired later, but use of the public baths declined considerably following the drop in the number of inhabitants.[39]

However terrible what had gone before, what happened next made many Romans believe that the end of the world was at hand.

THE LOMBARDS MARCH ON ROME

In the second half of the sixth century, after the devastating Byzantine–Gothic Wars, the population of Rome swelled to between eighty thousand and a hundred thousand, mostly as a result of the influx of a new wave of refugees.[40]

By eliminating the Gothic power in Italy, the Byzantines made it vulnerable to invasion by the part-pagan, part-Arian Lombards from the area which is today's Austria. These wild tribesmen took Milan in 569. By 574 they controlled half of Italy. The Byzantines were left only with Rome, the exarchate of Ravenna and the Pentapolis (Rimini, Ancona, Fano, Pesaro, Senigallia, today's Marche region). The Lombard king Alboin made Pavia his capital and styled himself 'Lord of Italy'. From their bases, the Lombards raided the lands under Byzantine control. In 573, Faruald, Lombard duke of Spoleto, besieged Rome and laid waste to the surrounding area.[41] The Lombards would dominate Italy for the next 200 years.

GREGORY SAVES ROME FROM THE LOMBARDS

Gregory the Great (590–604) came to the throne of St Peter in what was thus an extraordinarily difficult period for the city of Rome. The sixth century was a turning point in the history of the world. It was the age when the people of the former Roman Empire witnessed the downfall of classical civilisation, a disaster that convinced many of them that the end of the world was at hand. Epidemics and other calamities threatened the survival of the barbarians and the remnants of the peoples of the old empire alike.[42]

But the descendants of the barbarians who had devastated the Empire in the West would gradually become agents of rebirth, united and guided by Catholic Rome after the disappearance of Arianism. Together, Rome and these barbarians would raise a new Empire in the West, after the forces of the recently born Islam compelled the Byzantines to fight for survival and invaded many of their Christian lands, including Palestine and North Africa.[43] Thanks to Gregory, Rome became the missionary headquarters of Western Europe and the executive centre of its Church. It was his achievement that Rome became the capital of Western Christianity and an important player in the politics of medieval Europe.

Many aristocrats embraced the monastic life in those terrible years, among them Gregory, a monk of senatorial origin. He was very pious and engaged in arduous fasting, which ruined his health. He preferred the contemplative life of a monk, but the Church had need of his talents. Pope Benedict I (575–9) appointed him against his will as deacon of Rome's 7th district. So highly was he regarded that Pope Pelagius II (579–90) sent him as ambassador to Constantinople, at a time when Rome badly needed military backing. Gregory spent seven years there but refused to study

Greek and distrusted the theological restlessness of the Easterners. To him, the Eternal City had the sacred primacy, not Constantinople. By all accounts, the only thing Greek he liked was retsina.

In the winter of 589, the Tiber flooded Rome and destroyed the city's provisions. There were three or four major floods every century until the Italian state erected massive protective walls on the riverbanks in the late 1800s. Famine was followed by plague, which killed Pope Pelagius among many other Romans. The clerics and citizens of Rome elected Gregory as the new pope. He engaged in a gigantic effort to restructure the rich papal patrimony, which consisted of lands dispersed all over the former empire, and made the papacy the greatest property-owner in the West.[44]

We learn from Duffy that, as part of his religious programme, Pope Gregory I personally initiated the conversion of the barbarian kingdoms of England to Christianity. To this end, in 597, Augustine, the prefect of Gregory's own monastery of St Andrew, today's church of St Gregory on the Celian Hill, arrived with forty companions at Thanet in Kent.[45]

In Rome, Gregory organised in minute detail the feeding of the poor in the city. Every day, twelve indigent Romans were invited to share a meal with him.[46] The seven ecclesiastical departments introduced by Pope Fabian (236–50) had already replaced the ancient Roman division into fourteen regions. These ecclesiastical districts were not, however, identical with the *diaconiae*, food distribution centres, which were first recorded under Pope Benedict II (684–5).[47]

According to Lepri, a *diaconia* distributed food to the poor, preserved the foodstuffs and bathed those in need, usually once a week on a Thursday. It also saw to the needs of pilgrims. The Church funded the *diaconia*, but it was managed by a layperson. As a rule, it had a chapel, but it was not a church. The activities of the *diaconiae* are well documented from the end of the seventh century. They tended to be located near the Tiber, which still served as transportation route for foodstuffs. They also tended to cluster in groups near the road that brought the pilgrims to old St Peter's, called Via Francigena because many pilgrims were Franks.[48]

The last documented urban prefect, Iohannes, held his post in 599, during the Byzantine era in Italy and in the reign of Pope Gregory the Great[49] at a time when the popes had gained complete control of Rome.

In Gregory's time, the rundown buildings of Imperial Rome were still standing and structurally safe. The Aurelian Wall, repaired by the

Byzantines, was intact. The main roads were usable, although other streets were covered with dirt and debris. The aqueducts continued to provide some water to the city. The Byzantines restored them and they worked for two more centuries. Some of the baths may have continued to function before being eventually abandoned. The Roman Forum was still a place where one could purchase goods and slaves and get the news. Until the seventh century, the Forum of Trajan served as backdrop for literary gatherings. The imperial palaces on the Palatine were also maintained and housed Byzantine officials. A keeper of the palace was responsible for the venerable buildings until 687. But vast swathes of Rome were already deserted and the inhabited areas were mostly concentrated around the S-shaped loop of the Tiber.

Pope Gregory defended Rome to the best of his ability. In 592, using money from the wealthy papal treasury, he paid off Ariulf, the new Lombard duke of Spoleto and, in 593, Agilulf, king of the Lombards, to discontinue a new siege of Rome.[50] The Byzantines, albeit they left some troops to defend the city (paid for by Gregory out of church funds),[51] were more concerned with the defence of other cities, which was a source of great disappointment to Gregory.[52] But their attitude may be understood in the light of the difficulty for the Byzantines in stomaching his claims that Rome had the supremacy.

Gregory realised that it would to be to Rome's advantage to evangelise the 'unspeakable' Lombards, whom he abhorred.

The population saw in Gregory a worker of miracles. Tradition has it that in 590, while awaiting his consecration as pope, he put an end to the epidemic of plague that followed the famine caused by the flood. He led an enormous procession comprising absolutely everyone in the city, even pagans, with many participants dropping dead as the convoy wound its way towards its destination. When Gregory arrived at the bridge leading to St Peter's, the crowds saw the archangel Michael descending from heaven. Hovering above the mausoleum of Hadrian, Michael was seen to sheathe a blazing sword as an indication that the plague was over. The name Castel Sant'Angelo given to the old mausoleum owes its origin to this tradition, as does the statue of the archangel Michael placed above the building.[53]

Gregory's was a time when reason was overwhelmed by the adversities that followed hard, one upon another, in the real world: a constant source of horror and hopelessness. Those who survived created an imaginary world in which miracles and ancient beliefs in magic provided some hope and alleviated the fear of renewed calamities and their consequences. Moreover, the classical language and pagan-influenced, sophisticated cultural traditions of educated Christians, which had been prevalent in the fifth century during the Sistine Renaissance, did not mean very much to the masses of the sixth century, who were culturally deprived after so many years of devastating war and invasions. Thus in the time of Gregory, while still using Latin, the focus of the Church was more on faith, practical goals, sound reasoning and Roman administrative know-how, as opposed to classical studies. The clerics maintained an interest in history, with its emphasis on Rome as the centre of the world. Most importantly, they were also bearers of classical academic learning and fundamental concepts.

THE BYZANTINES WANT ROME'S TREASURES

Duffy tells us that during the seventh century, the Byzantines provided many Greek-speaking popes. Indeed, the senatorial families of Rome, from whose ranks had come many talented and capable popes in the past, were extinguished or had moved east.[54] Gregory the Great and Honorius (625–38) were the last popes to originate from the ancient Roman aristocracy.[55]

By the end of the seventh century the Greeks dominated the Roman clergy. The Byzantines erected many churches dedicated to eastern saints. The Greeks exerted a strong influence on music, the visual arts and the liturgy. Before their arrival, Roman rituals were sober and rather plain affairs. The Byzantines brought with them music and ceremonial originating in the East. The ceremonies involving the pope highlighted his sacred role and imitated Byzantine court observance.

Rome was very cosmopolitan in those years. A group of Irish monks encountered in their hostel pilgrims from Egypt, Palestine, the Greek East and southern Russia. The Anglo-Saxon Benedict Biscop, abbot of the twin monasteries of Wearmouth and Jarrow, travelled five times to Rome between 653 and 680. The Anglo-Saxon Ceolfrid, who was abbot of the same twin monasteries after Benedict Biscop, came to Rome to be interred there. In 689, King Ceadwalla of Wessex journeyed to Rome to be baptised.[56]

In 727, King Ina of Wessex arrived in Rome as a pilgrim. Pope Gregory II allowed him to erect a *schola Saxonum*, near old St Peter's, for the benefit of those Saxons interested in receiving a Christian education. Moreover, Ina built a church to provide funerals for the Saxon pilgrims who died in Rome. These projects were the starting point of the British Saxon Borgo near old St Peter's, an area immediately to the west of the Tiber (number 4 on the map in figure 2). On his return to Wessex, the devout Ina introduced the rome-scot, a tax aimed at providing funds for the poor and the lights of the newly erected Saxon church in Rome. The pope was much impressed by the devotion the Saxons showed to St Peter and for that reason chose them to be the first to have a national *schola* in Rome.

Lepri narrates that King Offa of Mercia (757–95) added a *xenodochium* (guesthouse) to the *schola Saxonum*. Because the Saxons called their Roman settlement a *burg*, the Romans also used this name for the other national *scholae* located near old St Peter's. Eventually, the entire urban development in the vicinity of St Peter's was called *burg*, which became Borgo in Italian, a term still in use. The *schola Saxonum* was strategically located. Indeed, it controlled access from Trastevere, the Tiber and Rome itself to the Vatican.[57]

Today's Church of Santo Spirito in Sassia stands on the site of the old St Mary in Saxia, which formed part of the *schola Saxonum* in the seventh and eighth centuries.[58] This neighbourhood witnessed what may well be one of the most hushed-up misdeeds in the history of humanity.

The distinct identity of Rome survived even as Byzantine power gradually decayed. The Byzantine emperors neglected Italy and the former imperial capital, as they had to use most of their resources in the effort to oppose Muslim offensives in the East. In that context, the political tendencies of Rome became more and more independent.

Only Emperor Phocas (602–10) was actively involved in the life of Rome. Phocas acknowledged the primacy of the bishop of Rome over the other bishops. In the years of Boniface IV (608–15), Phocas permitted the transformation of the Pantheon (Piazza della Rotonda) into a Christian basilica. Initially built in 27–25 BC by Marcus Vipsanius Agrippa, son-in-law and prefect of Augustus, the Pantheon took its present circular shape during the reconstruction carried out by Emperor Hadrian in 118–25. Tradition has it that Pope Boniface brought twenty-eight wagons full of martyrs' bones and buried them under the superb building, which was to become a church. During the consecration ceremony, while the pope was sprinkling holy water on the walls that had been stripped of every pagan vestige and the priests were chanting, the Romans saw hordes of terrified demons escaping through the opening in the dome. The appreciative Romans erected a modest column in the Forum in honour of Phocas and placed his statue on top of it. The statue has not survived, but the column still stands. It is the last monument built by Rome in the derelict Roman Forum to celebrate an emperor.[59]

Some time after the Senate had ceased to convene, in the time of Pope Honorius (625–38) the Senate building (Curia) was converted into the Church of St Adrian.[60] To bring back to light the ancient Roman Senate, Honorius' additions were removed in 1931 during the rule of Mussolini. Still under Honorius, the basilica of St Agnes outside the walls, originally erected by Constantine's daughter Constantina, was reconstructed in Byzantine style and its apse decorated with an impressive mosaic representing Agnes, the 12-year-old girl martyred during the persecution of Diocletian.

Often relations between Rome and the imperials became confrontational. Emperor Constans II (630–68), who had Monothelitist sympathies, sent Olympius, exarch of Italy, to Rome to assassinate Pope Martin I (649–55), whose opposition to Monothelitism challenged the religious authority of the emperor. Monothelitism, which held that Jesus has two natures but one will, was an attempt to reconcile Monophysitism, the belief that Christ has one, divine nature, with the teachings of the Council of Chalcedon that Christ has both a divine and a human nature and, accordingly, two wills.

The exarch's personal attendant had orders to assassinate the pope as the latter was about to give communion to the exarch. When the opportunity to strike presented itself, the attendant went suddenly blind and was unable to carry out the murder. Much shaken, the exarch revealed to the pope what his secret mission had been.[61]

Determined to rid himself of Martin, Constans II dispatched another exarch who succeeded in secretly arresting the pope. The exarch eventually shipped Martin to Constantinople. All the while the people of Rome were unaware of what was going on. His gaolers cruelly mistreated him. For example, while he was ill with dysentery, they did not permit him to wash for forty-seven days. Once in Constantinople, the imperials subjected him to a show trial on trumped-up charges of treason. The unfortunate Martin I died as a result of ill treatment at the hands of the Byzantines, which included a public flogging.[62]

The brutality of Constans II shocked Rome. Pope Eugenius I (654–7) agreed to compromise in his desire to save the papal see, but then reverted to an anti-monothelite position. In 663, Constans II came to Rome in person, allegedly to pay his respects to Pope Vitalian (657–72). In fact, he came to plunder what pagan treasures were still left in the city. The eastern emperor looted the gilded roof tiles of the Pantheon and some bronze statues. On his way home he was assassinated and Muslim pirates seized his booty. Constans II was the last Roman emperor to visit Rome. The previous imperial visit to Rome had taken place almost two centuries earlier.[63]

The struggle for supremacy between Rome and Constantinople culminated in a new battle in 692, which would mark the beginning of the end of Byzantine control over Rome. Pope Sergius I (687–701) opposed some of the decisions of a council that had been held in Constantinople, among other things its proclamation that the clergy were free to marry – something that went entirely against the views of the Western Church.[64] (The conference of bishops of the Roman Catholic Church that ended on 22 October 2005 reaffirmed the celibacy of Roman Catholic priests 1,313 years later.)

Emperor Justinian II (685–711) sent to Rome the Chief of the General Staff of the Byzantine army, Zachariah, with orders to arrest Pope Sergius and frighten him into submission. The people of Rome and the Pentapolis rushed in large numbers to rescue their pope. Zachariah panicked and sought sanctuary in the papal bedchamber. Sergius had to order his saviours to allow the terrified Byzantine general to return home.[65]

In 695, Byzantine nobles discontented with matters in Rome ousted Justinian II, severed his nose and ears and exiled him to the Crimea.[66] In the end he returned to the throne and invited Pope Constantine (708–15) to Constantinople in an effort to normalise relations between the imperials and Rome. In 710, Constantine, the last pope to visit Constantinople, was received with pomp and pageantry, but nothing substantial resulted from his meeting with the imperials. The first pope to visit Constantinople (modern Istanbul) after Constantine in 710 was Paul VI in 1967.[67]

THE MUSLIMS AND A DISPUTE OVER ICONS

In 717, the Muslims began to lay siege to Constantinople with a gigantic expeditionary force comprising an army of 120,000 soldiers and a fleet of 1,800 ships. The city of Constantine and its remaining empire were in mortal danger. After a siege lasting thirteen months, during which they employed the mysterious Greek fire, the Byzantine Christians under Emperor Leo III (717–41) won a magnificent victory. That was the last major Arab attempt to conquer Constantinople.[68]

Unfortunately for the Byzantines, Muslim incursions into Anatolia continued in spite of the formers' brilliant victory.

Examining at length the difficult military situation of the empire, Leo III and his advisers somehow reached the conclusion that God was angry with the Greeks because they were venerating icons. In fact, the Old Testament prohibits the veneration of images. In 730, Leo III ordered the destruction of all icons.[69]

The Christians of the West were furious. When the exarch of Ravenna tried to destroy icons, the crowds murdered him.

Pope Gregory II (715–31) proclaimed iconoclasm (the destruction of the icons) a heresy. This dramatic divergence of views created a new schism between the Churches of East and West. In 732 or 733, the steadfast Emperor Leo III seized the papal properties in southern Italy and Sicily, the chief income generator for the Holy See, and removed the Greek-speaking lands of Sicily, meridional Italy and Illyricum from papal jurisdiction. The Byzantines seemed to concentrate on keeping control of Sicily and southern Italy, while leaving the exarchate of Ravenna to its fate.[70]

Leo III also sent agents to assassinate the pope, but the Lombard dukes of Spoleto and Tuscia thwarted all these efforts to eliminate Gregory II. The inhabitants of the Duchy of Rome, as the writers of the time already called it, developed a sense of common national Christian values embodied by the papacy and manifested in their resistance to the pressures for change coming from Constantinople.[71]

What followed would shape the future of Europe.

ELEVEN

The Franks Restore the Roman Empire

Aware of the weakening of Byzantine power in Italy, Liutprand, king of the Lombards (712–44), attacked Rome repeatedly.[1] In reaction to these aggressive acts, Pope Gregory III (731–41) made a fateful decision. He dispatched a letter to Charles Martel (717–41), the Mayor of the Palace of the Merovingian kingdom in Gaul and the real power behind the Frankish king. The papal delegates also carried with them the keys to the shrine of St Peter. The letter requested Martel to act as defender of the Roman Church, appealing to his reverence for St Peter.[2]

In 711, Muslim armies had invaded Spain and brought to an end Catholic Visigothic domination of the Iberian Peninsula. In 732, at Poitiers Charles Martel had vanquished a Muslim force headed for Tours. This was a crucial battle in the continent's history as it checked the Arab advance into Europe. The Catholic Charles Martel was not only a mighty warrior, but also a pragmatic politician. He declined the title of Consul of the Romans proffered by the pope, as well as his invitation to act as defender of the Roman Church, keen to avoid antagonising both Lombards and Byzantines, even if that meant disappointing St Peter.

At the beginning of his reign, the remarkable Pope Zacharias (741–52) was able to deal more successfully with the then aged King Liutprand. Somehow, the pope regained castles lost previously and received some Lombard territories. In his dealings with secular powers, Zacharias was the first pope to display the real-world attributes of a duke.[3]

Pope Zacharias reorganised the administration of the territory around Rome into *domus cultae*, ecclesiastical domains that fed Rome and also functioned as bases from which to enlist the local militia in times of peril.[4]

Almost miraculously, Rome was resurrected as a city–state three hundred years after the fall of the last Roman emperor in the West and two hundred years after the devastating Byzantine–Gothic War. But as we shall see, the creativity of papal politics during those years went well beyond seeking favourable alliances. In fact, it did not scruple to embrace the shady world of forgery.

THE FRANKS AND THE DONATION OF CONSTANTINE

The Lombards now had a new and vigorous king, Astulf. He conquered the Byzantine exarchate of Ravenna in 751, thus capturing the last Byzantine possessions in northern peninsular Italy.[5]

Another turning point in the history of both the papacy and Europe came in 750 when Pepin, son of Charles Martel and the new Mayor of the Merovingian Palace, dispatched a chaplain to Pope Zacharias seeking a definitive answer to the following question: Pepin was the true authority in the Merovingian realm; should he not be king as well? Zacharias, who had been diligently trying to recruit the military help of the Franks to combat the increasing Lombard menace and the receding power of the Byzantines, replied that he certainly should. Feeling his aspirations legitimised by the papal response, Pepin had himself formally elected and anointed king in 751. The English bishop Boniface, who had been consecrated by Pope Gregory II in Rome, carried out the official ceremonial.[6]

The restive Astulf marched south and within a year had encircled Rome and exacted tribute from the powerless city. In the process, his men caused additional devastation to the city's catacombs, which had already been raided by the Goths centuries before. Zacharias, who passed away before Astulf surrounded Rome, was the last Greek pope and, as the last pontiff still faithful to Constantinople, had worked tirelessly to keep East–West communications open.[7]

The Patrimony of St Peter, as the duchy of Rome was already called in those years, was an empty designation as there was no legal basis for the secular rule of the popes. Some historians believe that the famous document the *Constitutum Constantini*, also known as the Donation of Constantine, opportunely surfaced in the time of Pope Stephen II (752–7), Zacharias' successor, to give legal foundation to the territorial claims of the popes and protect them from the aggressive Lombard king, Astulf. Other historians think it was formulated after the time of King Pepin to legitimise the domination of Pepin and Charlemagne over Italy in the face of Byzantine protest.[8]

The unknown forger was very inventive. According to this document, allegedly issued by Constantine after he was healed of leprosy through baptism in the Holy Font of Lateran, the duchy of Rome was the property of St Peter and the popes. The Church of Rome was seen as a religious state ruled by Christ represented by the popes, who had the same duties as the secular emperor. The document stated that Pope Sylvester (314–45) was the rightful owner of the imperial crown, but he did not wish to take it and kindly permitted Constantine to assume it. The twice-grateful Constantine donated the territories that would belong to the Papal State. The Lateran Palace was sovereign over Rome, Italy and the entire West. The military protection of the Papal State was the task of a *Patricius Romanorum* (Patrician of the Romans), to be appointed by the pope.

King Pepin had the opportunity to see the document and decided to meet Pope Stephen II in France. Did Pepin ask himself where this document had been for the previous four centuries? In April 754 Pepin and the pope concluded a pact in Querzy.

After its conquest by Pepin, the pope was to receive the island of Corsica, the cities south of a line linking Parma, Reggio and Mantova, including Tuscia (today's Viterbo and Civitavecchia) and the former Byzantine exarchate of Ravenna, Venice, Istria and the duchies of Spoleto and Benevento. While this was very impressive, the Holy See never ruled all those territories. Pope Stephen II anointed Pepin, his wife Bertha and his sons Charles (742–814) and Carloman (751–71). As expected, he designated Pepin as Patrician of the Romans.[9]

The tireless Stephen II would also dedicate the ancient mausoleum of Alaric's feeble adversary, the emperor Honorius, to a mysterious saint.

THE BIRTH OF THE PAPAL STATE

King Pepin vanquished Astulf in 756 after two campaigns. The victorious Pepin made a solemn vow at the grave of St Peter and a new treaty was made. Pope Stephen II was to receive the former Byzantine exarchate, the Pentapolis, part of Umbria and Marche and, of course, the Duchy of Rome. Obviously, this was a substantially less generous donation when compared with the terms of the previous agreement.

From remote Constantinople, Emperor Constantine V (741–75) protested and claimed those territories were legally his. According to

Rendina, Pepin shrewdly replied that he had gone to war twice because of his reverence for St Peter, who, represented in the person of the pope, was the rightful owner of those lands. The Christian West and East were once again at odds.[10]

In 756, shortly after his resounding defeat, the Lombard king Astulf died in a hunting accident. Pope Stephen II reacted with simultaneous anger and delight, which he expressed in a letter to the king of the Franks: the late Lombard king had failed to cede some of the territories he was supposed to; and Stephen interpreted the death of Astulf as divine endorsement of the papacy's worldly powers.[11]

Desiderius, duke of Tuscany, became king of the Lombards with the support of Pope Stephen II. In exchange, Desiderius made territorial concessions that marked a high point in the expansion of the papacy.[12]

Pope Stephen died in 757 at the peak of his success. Stephen II founded three *diaconiae* that also served as hostels for pilgrims, and a hospital for the latter.[13] In his time, the Vatican had already acquired the dimensions of a town. A variety of religious buildings, mausoleums and a community of diverse groups of people who made their living in the area encircled old St Peter's. Stephen II also erected a monastery, the fourth in the environs of the Vatican.

Pope Stephen II built a belfry near old St Peter's and covered it with silver and gold. While it would appear that Stephen's belfry was the first to be erected in Rome, many such belfries still stand in the venerable city, including that of St Mary in Cosmedin. They are square and of equal dimensions at the base and the summit and their pillars are characteristically short. From this point on, church architects discarded the design of the ancient Roman basilica and developed the Romanesque style of the Middle Ages.[14]

Still adjacent to old St Peter's, Stephen II founded a chapel dedicated to St Petronilla, who, according to tradition, had been St Peter's daughter or godchild.[15] Indeed, both Tertullian and St Jerome mention St Peter's wife. To De Rossi, Petronilla was rather the spiritual child of the Apostle Peter and derived her name from a man named Flavius Petronius. An old legend tells how a pagan aristocrat by the name of Flavius Petronius fell in love with the beautiful woman and proposed to her. Petronilla told him she needed three days to make up her mind. After three days of prayer, she died.

Petronilla's bones were brought to old St Peter's from the catacombs of Domitilla on the Via Ardeatina, after the Lombards had ransacked Rome's catacombs. Her chapel was erected in the then ruined, round structure built by Emperor Honorius for himself and his wives Maria and Thermantia, Stilicho's daughters. Since Stephen II erected the chapel of St Petronilla in honour of Pepin, the monarchs of France became its patrons until the demolition of old St Peter's in the sixteenth century. It is a mystery why the French were so keen to venerate Petronilla, St Peter's supposed daughter.

The workmen of Stephen II covered up with bricks and masonry the sarcophagi of Honorius, Valentinian III and other members of the house of Theodosius the Great. Some sarcophagi were discovered in this area in 1458 and 1519 and the graves of Maria and Thermantia, the wives of Honorius, were found in 1544. Robbers stole and then melted down the gold grave goods and no scientific investigations have been performed at the site.[16]

Writing about the tomb of Maria, discovered in the foundations of old St Peter's, Lanciani noted that 'a greater treasure of gems, gold, and precious objects has never been found in a single tomb'. The late imperial gold of Rome ended up being looted again more than 1,100 years after Alaric.

Paul the Deacon (720–99) wrote that Honorius had been buried next to his wife Maria. The fate of Honorius' casket is unknown; Lanciani was of the opinion that it is probably buried under the floor of present-day St Peter's.[17]

In the time of Pope Paul I (757–67), the Lombard king Desiderius had second thoughts about the territorial gifts he had pledged to the duchy of Rome and, to recover them, engaged in military campaigns against lands belonging to the Papal State.[18]

Paul I had all the bones of the dead still remaining in the catacombs carried into the city and distributed among the churches and convents. This great transfer of holy relics happened after the Lombards of Astulf had plundered what was left in the catacombs following the previous barbarian sacks. At that point, every church in Christian Europe desired to obtain these priceless relics and sent emissaries to implore the Roman authorities to grant them such holy gifts. This was how even remote areas of Western Europe managed to acquire sacred remains of Romans from every conceivable background.[19]

As Rendina narrates, a confusing and violent period lasting some thirteen months followed the death of Paul I. This civil strife involved the usurpation of the papal throne by two individuals, the layman Constantine and the priest Philip, and illustrates just how important the role of pope was and how the power groups of the time vied to control it. The first usurper, Constantine, was imposed by force as pope. In the end, his opponents gouged out his eyeballs and eventually he disappeared without trace after being dragged and then tortured before the members of the 769 Lateran Council. Philip, the second usurper, finished his days as a monk. The two are now classified as anti-popes.

Pope Stephen III (768–72) was elected with the support of the Francophiles Christophorus, a minor church administrator, and his son, the sexton Sergius. In the meantime Pepin died and his sons Charles and Carloman sent a dozen bishops to Rome to investigate the usurpations. The Lateran Council of April 769 proclaimed that henceforth only members of the clergy could be elected pope.

At this point, Stephen III wished to escape the domination of Christophorus and Sergius. As Charles and Carloman were busy settling the disputes that ensued from the death of their father Pepin, Stephen summoned the Lombard king Desiderius to his aid. A popular revolt contributed to the pope's success. The victors removed the eyeballs of Christophorus who died three days later. Sergius' eyes were also put out, but he survived until after the death of Stephen III.[20]

The grisly punishment meted out by the Romans to Christophorus and Sergius, who had done the same thing to Valdipert, the Lombard sent by Desiderius to impose Philip as pope, was not something likely to please the Franks. In a letter to Charles and his mother Bertha, Pope Stephen III, whom Gregorovius called 'the unscrupulous Sicilian', claimed to have been unaware of what had befallen the hapless pair.[21]

CHARLEMAGNE AND POPE HADRIAN I

Carloman passed away and Charles, or Charlemagne (Charles the Great), a devout Christian who dreamed of resurrecting the majesty of the Roman Empire in his own lands, became the sole ruler of the Franks. At that point, Charlemagne finally decided to confront the Lombards in Italy, displeased with the interference of King Desiderius in the affairs of the papacy.[22]

But Charlemagne had first to overcome a major obstacle: he was married to Ermengarda, daughter of Desiderius. However, the incredibly flexible Pope Stephen III took care of his worries. He wrote to him that it was sacrilege for a Roman patrician to be on friendly terms with an enemy of the pope and St Peter, a sacrilege that would damn him to eternal hell fire. The suddenly and conveniently enlightened Charlemagne promptly divorced his wife in December 771. Stephen III died the following year.[23]

The favourable moment Charlemagne was waiting for came in 773, when Desiderius began his march on Rome. Charlemagne clashed with Desiderius at Susa, west of Turin, which lies at the eastern end of the valley from where Hannibal and the Carthaginians had crossed the Alps in winter during the Second Punic War (218–202 BC). The victorious Charlemagne then travelled to Rome with his wife and children, where he remained over the Easter, 774.[24]

Pope Hadrian I (772–95) organised a splendid reception to welcome his august guest. Charlemagne showed sincere respect for St Peter, kissing every step leading up into his basilica. Hadrian confirmed Charlemagne's title of Patrician of the Romans and in return, Charlemagne reconfirmed the territorial donations of his father Pepin and personally placed the deed on the tomb of the Apostle.[25]

Charlemagne returned to his war with the Lombards and eventually conquered Pavia and assumed the iron crown of the Lombard kings.[26] That was the end of the Lombard kingdom in Italy, but the Lombards remained on Italian soil and were assimilated into the ethnic fabric of the modern Italian people. Today's Lombardy is named after them. The Lombards were the only Germanic tribesmen who managed to settle in peninsular Italy. They contributed words to both Latin and vernacular Italian, for example, *scherzare* (to joke) is derived from the Lombard *skerzan*,[27] while *scherzoso* (playfully) is a direction frequently seen on musical scores.

Pope Hadrian I still needed Charlemagne to make official the territorial donations to the papal state and inundated him with letters requesting him to do so. Charlemagne, who was unable to write[28] and relied on the counsel and secretarial services of learned men such as the monk Alcuin of York, was an excellent negotiator and diplomat, besides being a talented general.

Charlemagne eventually came back to Rome in 781 and formally endowed the papal state with the Roman duchy, the former Byzantine exarchate of Ravenna, the Pentapolis and Sabina. He kept Tuscia and Spoleto for himself. After putting down the rebellion of a southern Lombard duke in 787, Charlemagne ceded to the pope Tuscia, Amelia, Todi and Perugia, but took over Capua, Salerno and Benevento.[29]

The Seventh General Council, convened by the Byzantine Empress Irene at Nicaea in 787, adopted the position of Pope Hadrian and approved the use of images and icons, thus ending the East–West Christian conflict over this issue. However, Charlemagne was worried by this reconciliation between Rome and the Byzantines. Moreover, he disliked the fact that he had not been involved in the discussions, feeling he had been excluded because he was a barbarian.

Charlemagne summoned his ecclesiastical scholars to study the decree issued at Nicaea. To their surprise, they discovered that the Latin translation indicated that the Council had endorsed the adoration of images, a practice which Charlemagne and his theologians rejected. Eventually, this disagreement between emperor and pope was settled at Charlemagne's synod in Frankfurt in 794. In the event, it was not unduly contentious since the Greek text spoke only of veneration and not adoration of images, albeit the difference is a subtle one.[30]

POPE HADRIAN I RESTORES ROME

Pope Hadrian I enlarged the church of St Mary in Cosmedin, which in the sixth century had been a *diaconia* built on top of the Ara Maxima, an altar dedicated to Hercules.

The round Temple of Hercules Victor (Victorious Hercules), erroneously called the Temple of Vesta on some maps, still stands in front of St Mary in Cosmedin (Piazza Bocca della Verità) in the area of the ancient Forum Boarium (cattle market).[31] Only a select few know that it is the oldest marble building surviving in Rome, having been erected in 179–142 BC.

The church of St Mary in Cosmedin, a name alluding to the beautiful decorations of the church (Greek *kosmetikos*, the source of the English word 'cosmetic', means 'relating to adornment') and perhaps to the Church of St Mary in Kosmidion in Constantinople, was assigned to the Greeks who fled the persecution resulting from the controversy surrounding the veneration of icons in the East. The area around this church was known as *schola Graeca* (the Greek Community).

The *Bocca della Verità* (the Mouth of Truth), a large sculpted image of an acquatic god's head with gaping mouth, made famous by Gregory Peck and Audrey Hepburn in *Roman Holiday*, which is located in the portico of the church, has spawned an ancient tradition. Legend has it that those who lie while their hand is inside the stone mouth are not able to extract it unless the hand is cut off.[32] Pope Stephen III should have had the veracity of his claims of innocence in relation to the horrific treatment meted out to Christophorus and Sergius tested here, but after a shrewd adulteress tricked the acquatic god, the spell was broken and it lost its lie-detecting abilities.

The indefatigable Hadrian I repaired the severely damaged Aurelian Wall by mobilising a huge army of workmen, reminiscent of the construction crews of the emperors of antiquity. While the quality of the restoration may not have been equal to imperial standards, the reinstated wall with its 387 towers offered better protection. However, Gregorovius lamented that during this gigantic reconstruction effort, many ancient monuments and relics were lost for ever.

Hadrian I also renovated the aqueducts Aqua Trajana, Claudia, Jovia, and Virgo. Aqua Trajana ran from the vicinity of Lake Bracciano to the Janiculum Hill. From there, large pipes carried water to the atrium of old St Peter's, thus feeding its fountains and the baths of the *diaconiae* serving the pilgrims.[33]

Hadrian also reorganised the *diaconiae* already existing in the vicinity of old St Peter's. He created six new church estates, the latter being much needed since the Byzantines had appropriated the former papal estates in Sicily, southern Italy and the Balkans. Historians have thus called Hadrian I 'restorer of the city'.[34]

Literary and scientific accomplishments were less favoured than the religious arts. The barbarians were now beating the Romans at their own old game. For example, the Lombards, initially considered culturally inferior by the popes, refined the liberal art of oratory such that the monks and priests of Rome could not then equal them. Thus, the Romans had no one to delegate to debate with the Lombard Paul the Deacon, noteworthy for his account of Alaric in his history.

The best-known authors of the day, among them the Venerable Bede, Alcuin of York, Aldhelm, Theodulf of Orleans and Isidore, had no connection with Rome. The popes no longer supported the composition of scholarly theological treatises as had their predecessors, Leo the Great and

Gregory the Great. Adalberga, daughter of Desiderius, the last king of the Lombards, was famous for her superior intellect and dedication to learning. Together with the cultured Amalasuntha, the daughter of Theodoric the Great, she stands out as one of the few women noted for intellectual refinement in the centuries that followed antiquity.

There were, nonetheless, still grammarians and mathematicians in Rome, which continued to be considered the protector of classical studies, although native Romans did not excel at them. Sacred music continued to flourish, taught in the school opened by Gregory the Great in the Lateran, which provided singing and organ instructors and training to the Franks. Charlemagne took with him two much admired Roman singers, Benedict and Theodore, and appointed them as professors of singing at Soissons and Metz respectively. They tried very hard, but in the end they complained that when the poor Franks tried to sing like larks as the Romans did, they sounded more like ravens. Roman poetry was extinct. Use of Latin declined dramatically in the eighth century, but what was then debased Latin would gradually evolve into the wonderfully musical Italian language.[35]

The popes finally had an officially recognised state, the Patrimony of St Peter, the fisherman from the Lake of Galilee.[36] The sacristy of St Mary in Cosmedin shelters the Epiphany, a mosaic transferred there from old St Peter's basilica. This mysterious mosaic, with its glittering golden background, must have witnessed many of the great events that took place in old St Peter's. It leads us on towards modern St Peter's.

POPE LEO III ON TRIAL

Pope Hadrian I died in 795. On the wall of the majestic colonnade surrounding the piazza of the basilica of St Peter is displayed his epitaph inscribed in Latin in golden letters on a marble plaque sent to Rome by the grief-stricken great emperor. The moving text was composed by Alcuin of York.[37]

Immediately after his election, Leo III (795–816) took steps to define the position of the papacy in its relations with Charlemagne. He sent the Frankish king a letter accompanied by the keys of St Peter and the banner of Rome. In this letter, the pope proclaimed Charlemagne armed defender of Christianity and that the Mother Church (*Mater Ecclesia*) symbolised the worldly and spiritual authority. To a minority of Roman clerics and nobles, the pope was too humble in these, his first dealings with Charlemagne. Discontented, they formed a conspiracy and concocted false accusations of lust and perjury against the pope and made them known to the court of Charlemagne, which dismissed them as slander.

But the pope continued to be in grave danger. On 25 April 799, Leo was riding in a procession that was moving from the Lateran to St Laurence in Lucina (Piazza San Lorenzo in Lucina). Suddenly, the conspirators toppled him from the saddle and tried to remove his eyeballs and cut out his tongue. They failed, but were able to confine the pope in the monastery of San Silvestro in Capite (Piazza San Silvestro), today dedicated to English-speaking Catholics, but then run by Greek monks, which would suggest Byzantine involvement in the plot. Then, during the hours of darkness, the conspirators moved the pope to another monastery, Sant' Erasmo al Celio, which no longer exists. Frightened, Leo III miraculously escaped through the window, using a rope to lower himself to the ground, whence he ran to the safety of St Peter's. Next day, he left for Paderborn (now in Germany).[38]

In Paderborn, Leo III met Charlemagne, at that time at war with the old Saxons (not to be confused with the subsequent Electorate of Saxony or the more recent Saxonies), whom he eventually defeated, Christianised and made into defenders of the Holy Roman Empire. Through the Ottonian dynasty, these Saxons ensured the longevity of the new Roman Empire.[39]

At about the time that Leo III and Charlemagne met, the court of Paderborn received a letter from the plotters in Rome containing specific accusations against Leo III and requesting that he be brought to trial. Alcuin of York counselled Charlemagne that such a trial would be greatly to his disadvantage and would also discredit the papacy, to which he was so closely tied.

In Paderborn, Charlemagne and Leo III held confidential talks, and then the pope travelled to Rome accompanied by Frankish bishops and nobles. The majority of Romans greeted Leo III and his entourage with enthusiasm. The accusers were sent to Paderborn, where they were expected to formulate the charges against the pope. In November 800 Charlemagne himself left for Rome accompanied by soldiers, Frankish bishops and the conspirators.[40]

The party arrived in Rome on 23 November. On the 24th, Charlemagne convened a parliament of the entire clergy and people, which met on 1 December in front of the great basilica of St Peter. The trial lasted twenty-one days. The Frankish bishops unanimously insisted that the Holy See could not be put on trial.

On 23 December, Leo III suddenly stood up in front of the multitudes, swore on the Gospels that he was innocent and declared that God was his witness. It is hard to judge just how convincing Leo III was in his so-called 'Oath of Purification', but nobody dared to cross-examine his invisible witness. Charlemagne condemned the conspirators to death, but the pope intervened in what was intended to show papal compassion and they were all banished to the Frankish lands.[41]

CHRISTMAS DAY, 800

Soon after the visitor enters the modern basilica of St Peter, built during the Renaissance in place of the basilica Charlemagne would have seen, he or she is overcome by awe at the grandeur of the architecture. Some visitors happen to stand on a porphyry disc about 8ft 10in (2.7m) in diameter, located in the middle of the central nave, not far from the entrance. Most are completely unaware of it.

The majority in the crowd of sightseers will concentrate on getting as close as possible to the pope when he is in the basilica. Others will wish to be as near as possible to St Peter's tomb or to touch the toe of his bronze statue. We will make a different choice. We will stand on the porphyry disc and close our eyes, in an effort to travel back in time to Christmas Day, 800.

Perhaps we can see Charlemagne kneeling humbly in prayer before old St Peter's basilica. The porphyry disc, known as the *Rota Porphyretica*, is believed to mark the spot where he knelt. While Charlemagne's head is still lowered in prayer, Pope Leo III places upon it a golden crown. As Heer narrates, at that moment, the Romans gathered in the basilica give vent to a thunderous shout of acclamation: 'To Charles Augustus, crowned by God, the great and peace-giving emperor of the Romans, life and victory!'[42] Twice the crowds repeat their powerful shout. Next, Pope Leo III presents Charlemagne with the imperial mantle and kneels before him in an attitude of adoration.

Following mass, Charlemagne and his son Pepin offer a silver table with gold vessels to St Peter's basilica; similar gifts for St Paul's; a gold cross, encrusted with gems for the Lateran basilica; and other precious items for Greater St Mary.[43]

The coronation ceremony was probably planned in advance by Charlemagne and Leo III during their secret talks at Paderborn, contrary to the claims of the Book of Pontiffs that those assembled in St Peter's were inspired by God and St Peter, and those of Charlemagne's biographer that the emperor was taken by surprise by the ceremony.

The make-believe of improvisation may have been meant to pre-empt Byzantine objections, as the Byzantines considered themselves the rightful successors to the Roman emperors, even in the West. Eventually, in 812, Charlemagne recognised the dominion of the Byzantine emperor Michael I Rangabe over Venice, Istria, the maritime cities of southern Italy, Sicily, the Balkan peninsula and Asia Minor.[44]

During the Middle Ages, the Holy Roman emperors and the popes were frequently at odds due to the uncertainties surrounding the coronation of Charlemagne, but when the ceremony took place, it was seen as a credible promise of future understanding and collaboration.[45] However, even Leo III and Emperor Charlemagne did not always see eye to eye.

Leo III erected the Church of St Michael and St Magnus at the beginning of the ninth century and dedicated it to St Michael in Sassia (Saxia) as a church reserved for those of Germanic origin. Santa Maria dell'Anima is today considered the national church of Germany.

The Franks and the papacy resurrected the Roman Empire in the West 324 years after the fall of Romulus Augustulus, in a form that put great emphasis on Christian values, as indicated in the new name by which it became known to history: the Holy Roman Empire. In this framework, the emperor, the protector of the Roman Church, was holy. God had anointed him through the hand of Leo III in Rome, the home of the Church established by Christ and guided by St Peter and the bishops who came after him. Therefore, the emperor was sacred. The Mother Church was the source of everything, spiritual and worldly. The pope designated a ruler of his choice to be the backer and defender of the Church.[46]

In this way did the idea of a unifying Roman Empire survive in Europe. The Franks may have seen in the coronation of Charlemagne the fruits of their faith which proved that Christ, king of the Franks and warlord of the God-chosen Frankish tribe, had elected Charlemagne to guide them. In the person of Charlemagne, who was dressed as a Roman emperor, the Romans perceived a protector from the Lombards and Byzantines and the domination of the popes.[47]

Charlemagne's conquest of other Germanic tribes such as the old Saxons and the tribes of Bavaria resulted in the creation of a German-dominated Europe. Although the Carolingian Empire disintegrated soon after the demise of Charlemagne, its heritage influenced fundamentally the society, politics, religion and culture of Europe, up to the dissolution of the Holy Roman Empire in 1806. In the end, the words 'Roman', 'Frankish' and 'Christian' came to be used interchangeably.[48]

Like the French and Spanish monarchies, the popes of Rome would be perpetual rivals of the Holy Roman emperors. The latter firmly believed they were the highest-ranking guardians of the Church and this belief was the source of interminable disagreement.[49]

In the European mind, Charlemagne is forever associated with the idea of a resurrected European unity. Thus, in 1945 he was chosen as the patron of the European Economic Community. Winston Churchill was presented with the Charlemagne Prize at Aachen, Charlemagne's capital.[50]

Rome was only the religious centre of the Carolingian Empire, and it remained a papal city with a population of about forty thousand. The new nobility had no connection with the ancient patricians and included the city magistrates, army commanders and great landowners. The popes and the members of the papal Curia, the epicentre of Roman authority, were recruited from among these noble families that wanted greater independence from the Franks.[51]

In a show of power, one of these popes did something extremely unusual for his mother.

ROME AFTER CHARLEMAGNE

Leo III, who had crowned Charlemagne with such adoration in old St Peter's, showed his true colours soon after the emperor died in 814 by subjecting the followers of the plotters of 799 to a summary trial and then executing them. In 815, Emperor Louis the Pious (814–40), the son of Charlemagne, sent his nephew Bernard (810–18), king of Italy, to investigate, but the king only succeeded in putting an end to the urban warfare between various Roman factions.[52]

On the death of Leo III, the Romans hurriedly elected Pope Stephen IV (816–17) to pre-empt the imposition of a Frankish-backed candidate. Pope Paschal I (817–24) received from Louis the Pious a promise (*Pactum*) to cede to the papacy those lands repeatedly offered by Pepin and his son Charlemagne, but also the Byzantine territories of Calabria, where Alaric is buried, Naples, Corsica, Sardinia and Sicily. In addition, Louis guaranteed that there would be no Frankish intervention in the papal elections. It is suspected that this *Pactum* originally referred only to the lands already donated by Pepin and Charlemagne and that the other territories were additions made later by the papal Curia.

The reign of Paschal I is shrouded in relative mystery due to a lack of sources. In one of the legends, during the 817 fire that engulfed the district inhabited by the Saxons of Britain, the pope walked barefoot over the burning rubble while holding high his pastoral staff. Miraculously, the fire, generally considered a demonic manifestation in that period, immediately went out.[53]

The disillusioned emperor Louis the Pious, betrayed by almost all those who owed him allegiance and deeply hurt because of the discord in his own family, passed away in 840. After his death, his son Lothar became sole emperor, according to Louis's wish, but the civil war resumed with renewed vigour. Finally, in 843 Lothar and his brothers met at Verdun and divided the empire between them. The 843 Treaty of Verdun led to the formation of modern France and Germany. Strangely, during the First World War, 1½ million French and German soldiers perished at Verdun, the birthplace of their countries.[54]

In 822, Lothar had been in Rome in his capacity as king of Italy and made himself unpopular by intervening in the business of the papal Curia. After his departure, encouraged by Lothar's show of force, pro-Frankish Romans rebelled, but the Curia captured their two leaders Theodore and Leo, put out their eyes and beheaded them. Lothar sent envoys to Rome to put Paschal I on trial. Imitating Leo III, Pope Paschal I spontaneously took the oath of purification and Lothar's judges closed the trial.

This pope, whom Lothar had suspected of abusing the prerogatives of his position, would go down in history for something that no pope before or since has done. He commissioned a mosaic still extant in the Chapel of St Zeno in the Church of St Prassede, which portrays his mother Theodora, and names her an '*Episcopa*', a female pope. The square around Theodora's head indicates that she was alive when the mosaic was created.

In the time of Pope Eugenius II (824–7), the Franks strengthened their influence in Rome. Lothar came in person to the papal city and imposed a constitution that once more permitted laymen to be elected pope and required imperial confirmation of the individual so nominated.[55]

Frankish churchmen immediately exploited papal weakness to obtain a number of Rome's most precious possessions, the remains of the Christian martyrs. This way, Abbot Hilduin of St Médard from Soissons took home the remains of St Sebastian.[56]

Pope Gregory IV (827–44) rebuilt the basilica of St Mark, possibly in response to the daring translation of St Mark's remains from Muslim-ruled Alexandria to Christian Venice in 828.[57] Gregory IV also repaired the Aqua Trajana,[58] a long tract of which was discovered in 1912 beneath today's American Academy on Via Angelo Masina.[59]

During the reign of Pope Sergius II (844–7), Rome was forced to accept that a new pope could be consecrated only with imperial mandate and that the consecration ritual could be performed only with the participation of the imperial representative. Alas, this brought back the limitations and humiliations of the Byzantine era.[60]

But in St Peter's, the porphyry disc which had seen so many consecrations and coronations lies at the centre of a very old mystery of Christian Rome.

TWELVE

Looting the Last Ancient Riches of Rome

L et us return to the porphyry disc in today's St Peter's. We will stand on it once more and close our eyes in an effort to travel back in time to 25 August 846, exactly 436 years after the sack of Alaric.[1] It is the scene of the last important sack of Rome in the first millennium and the last looting of the city's ancient riches.

We are now in front of the old St Peter's basilica. The building we see is five centuries old. Constantine the Great, Leo the Great, Theodoric the Great, Pope Gregory the Great and Charlemagne walked on its hallowed grounds. In the time of Pope Hadrian I, Charlemagne kissed every step leading up to it. On Christmas Day 800, Pope Leo III crowned Charlemagne inside the sacred shrine.

Hot and humid, the August air coming from the Tyrrhenian Sea lingers above the basilica built by Constantine and above the Borgo, the quarter that gradually developed around it. The façade displays Christ and the Apostles arranged in three rows, with Christ, St Peter and St Paul at the top.[2]

In the middle of the reception area we see the fountain of Pope Symmachus, a contemporary of Theodoric the Great. In this oppressive heat, the fountain is a beautiful sight. It is a square structure with eight red porphyry columns, which are topped by a dome in the shape of a half-cylinder. The dome is covered with gilded bronze that shines mystically in the twilight. The horizontal marble lintels carrying the dome are decorated with gilt bronze peacocks, flowers and dolphins. The lintels give forth jets of water that fall into the basin at the bottom. The edge of this basin is covered in bas-reliefs displaying complete coats of arms and griffins – fabled creatures with the head and wings of an eagle and the body of a lion. Peering inside the basin, we see a huge bronze pine cone standing at its base. The monogram of Christ crowns the dome on both its vertical sides.

We are now approaching the five doors of the basilica. The main door is covered in 975lb (442kg) of glistening silver. As we enter, our eyes fall on the statues of St Peter and St Paul, their halos heavily encrusted with gems that glitter mysteriously in the candlelight. The air inside the old building is a bit musty but is much more pleasant than outside. The lights of the basilica illuminate softly the columns and other ancient Roman structures that bear the names of pagan emperors and that of Constantine.

A triumphal arch separates the five naves of the basilica from the apse (the vaulted semi-circular or polygonal termination of a church). This arch gleams with golden mosaics that represent Constantine in the act of offering a model of the basilica to Christ, while St Peter presents Constantine to the Saviour. At the northern end of the transept (the transverse arm of a cross-shaped church) we note the baptistery built by Damasus, the 'ladies' ear tickler'.[3]

The gold cross of Constantine and Helena is on the coffin of St Peter. The basilica also shelters the Pharus (lighthouse) of Hadrian and the silver table with the relief of Constantinople given as an offering by Charlemagne on the day of his coronation.[4]

Suddenly, we hear shouts of alarm inside the basilica and we see the clergy frantically running towards the doors. As we ourselves approach the doors, we hear in the distance sounds of battle. The clergy are running east towards the River Tiber, hoping to cross the bridge and thus reach safety behind the walls of Rome.

On 23 August 846 a foreign expeditionary force brought by seventy-three ships landed at Ostia, the old port of Rome, with 11,000 fighting men and 500 horses. The invaders sacked the deserted Ostia. The new fortified city, erected by Gregory IV near old Ostia and renamed Gregoriopolis, had been abandoned by its cowardly garrison. The aggressors then stopped in Portus, the new port of Rome, which had also been abandoned by its inhabitants. On 24 August the foreign brigands returned to Ostia.

Next, the militia of the Frankish, Frisian and British Saxon Communities, sent by the Romans to check the aggressors south of Rome, took over Portus.[5] On 24 August they engaged in a battle with some of the brigands. All the while, the Romans manned the gates of the Aurelian Wall. Eventually, on the same day, when the expected help failed to materialise, a detachment of Romans marched to Portus and engaged in skirmishes with the foreign plunderers.

Realising their numerical inferiority, the Romans left the militia of the Saxons, Frisians and Franks to defend Portus and went back to Rome. On 25 August the raiders surprised the Christian militiamen in Portus while they were eating and killed most of them. Finally, the invaders began moving by ship towards Rome. At twilight, they stopped at prearranged points. The horsemen landed and mounted a surprise attack on old St Peter's basilica.[6]

On their way to old St Peter's, the new wave of barbarians desecrated and pillaged St Paul's basilica and the tomb of the Apostle Paul.[7]

Before reaching old St Peter's, the invaders came across the quarters of the Franks, Frisians and British Saxons. These neighbourhoods had expanded from west to east in the direction of the Tiber, starting with the Frankish community situated immediately south of the basilica, followed by the Frisian community in the middle, and the British Saxon one bordering on the river, with the church of St Mary in Saxia (replaced later by today's Santo Spirito in Sassia), close to the river bank. The Lombard quarter was located north of the basilica.[8] The Frisians were inhabitants of an ancient territory located in what is today the Flemish part of Belgium and that extended into what is now Holland and Germany, all the way to Denmark.

The foreign warriors surrounded the buildings of the *scholae* and slaughtered the numerous Christian pilgrims caught inside.[9] They damaged the *schola* of the Saxons.[10] Eventually, the pirates marched on St Peter's basilica and finally reached its reception area. There they halted.

Perhaps now we can catch sight of an unarmed old man who has a long white cloth wound around his head. He walks towards the intruders and stops in front of them. He speaks briefly. Passionately he shouts several throaty phrases and we are able to distinguish the words '*Al-Kafiroon*' (Those who reject the faith).[11] Next, the impassioned multitude of brigands, many of them also with similar head wear, utter a mighty battle cry: '*Allahu akbar!*' (Allah is the Greatest).

Then they begin removing the silver plates from the main entrance door. They carry away the statues of St Peter and St Paul; the gold from the floor of the shrine of St Peter; the high altar; the massive gold cross of Constantine and Helena; the great Pharus of Hadrian; the silver table of Charlemagne. Once more, the riches of Rome end up in the hands of foreign invaders.

In our mind's eye we can see the brigands making for the huge coffin of the Apostle Peter and furiously trying to remove it. Unable to dislodge it, they break it open. This was the episode during which the tomb of Peter sustained the serious damage observed by archaeologists.

Nobody has been able to determine exactly what was removed from the tomb when it was plundered. As Davis indicates in his review, the sources do not discuss it and the contemporary church leaders would not have been very eager to publicise it, even had they been fully informed about it.[12]

According to Letizia Pani Ermini, professor of medieval archaeology at the University of La Sapienza in Rome, the Muslims looted the sanctuary of St Peter and desecrated the altar placed above his tomb. In commemoration of this dreadful Muslim offence, the grief-stricken Roman Christians left a lengthy inscription.[13]

The bones of Peter have never been found.[14] Did the Muslims scatter or destroy them? In Gregorovius's opinion that is exactly what they did:

> They violated the grave of the Apostle, and, unable to remove the huge bronze coffin, they broke it open and destroyed or scattered its contents. We must remember that this mysterious vault, according to the universal belief, contained the remains of the Prince of the Apostles, whose successors the bishops of Rome claimed to be, and before whose ashes all peoples and princes came to prostrate [themselves] in the dust. We must bring this belief home to our minds in order to fully understand the atrocity of the outrage and the grief of Christendom.[15]

Yet, in *The Arabs: A Short History* Philip K. Hitti writes that 'In 846 even Rome was threatened by Arab squadrons which landed at Ostia and, unable to penetrate the walls of the Eternal City, sacked the cathedrals of St. Peter beside the Vatican and St. Paul outside the walls, and desecrated the graves of the pontiffs.'[16] If the reader believes this account without additional research, he or she will be left thinking that the Muslims violated the tombs of some popes and not those of the founders of Christianity.

On 10 August 846, Adalbert, governor of Corsica, had written to the Romans that the Muslims were approaching their city on galleys laden with men equipped for war. Indeed, a fleet of seventy-three ships fitted out by the Ahglabid Emir of Kairouan (Tunisia) arrived at Ostia.[17] Adalbert had also recommended the transfer of the relics of St Peter and St Paul, together with the treasures of the respective basilicas, to a safer location.

Initially, the Roman authorities did not react with much concern; they contacted the neighbouring cities with plans to organise an alliance. But it was too late. The Book of Pontiffs blames the disaster on Pope Sergius II's incompetence and rampant simony: bishoprics were being put publicly up for sale.[18]

Following the desecration of old St Peter's, the Muslims seized and pillaged other towns, setting buildings on fire and butchering the inhabitants.

Not long after the sack of old St Peter's, a numerically inferior Christian force under Louis II, son of Emperor Lothar, fought the Muslims on the Meadows of Nero near the Vatican Hill. The Christians lost the battle, and Louis only saved his life by fleeing. Later, in November, a second Christian army led by Louis II lost another battle with the Muslims, at Gaeta, a Byzantine protectorate. Caesarius, the son of Duke Sergius, came to Gaeta with ships from the Byzantine protectorate of Naples and Amalfi and prevented the Muslims from taking it and putting to flight the Frankish survivors. Eventually, the Muslims sailed away, after requesting an armistice from Caesarius.[19]

The same year, three other Muslim fleets attacked the coast of Italy. One plundered Brindisi and conquered Taranto. Two others took the island of Ponza halfway between Rome and Naples and Miseno near Naples, but the navy of a maritime league uniting Naples, Gaeta and Amalfi soon liberated them.[20]

In 847, a severe earthquake devastated half of Rome and the Borgo was again engulfed by fire. There is a legend that Pope Leo IV (847–55) brought the fire to an end simply by making the sign of the cross.

In 849, the sorely tried Romans learned that another Muslim fleet was sailing from Sardinia in the direction of Portus. Pope Leo IV summoned to Rome's aid the maritime cities of Naples, Amalfi and Gaeta. Helped by a storm, the allies defeated the Muslims at Ostia. The miracle of the Borgo fire and the victory of Ostia were immortalised by Raphael in the 'Sala dell'incendio' (Room of the fire) in the Vatican Museum. In 852, Pope Leo IV finished the construction of a defensive wall intended to protect the Vatican and the basilica of St Peter.[21]

Since the time of Alaric, those who had invaded Rome had been Christians who probably never touched the tombs of St Peter and St Paul because they held them sacred. But the Muslims of the Aghlabid Emir Abu al-Abbas Muhammad I (841–56) of al-Ifriqqiya (Tunisia) did not scruple to violate the tombs of both Apostles.[22] They had done so in the spirit of the Abbasid Caliphs of Baghdad, who ruled over an immense territory that extended from Central Asia to Tunisia, and who considered the takeover and conversion of the Christian world to Islam as one of their fundamental goals. The Abbasids advocated *jihad*, the struggle against people of other faiths, as a way to achieve religious salvation.[23]

Understandably, the Church has not been keen to publicise these desecrations because of the immense shame involved and the loss of prestige that goes with it. Indeed, the physical presence in Rome of the remains of St Peter and St Paul has been a fundamental concept in the functioning of the Church as the New Jerusalem for many centuries.[24]

How did foreign invaders come to violate the tombs of the Apostles? They had taken advantage of the disintegration of the Roman Empire in the West and the increasing weakness of the Byzantine Empire in the East. Like a tsunami wave, Muslim forces occupied Byzantine Palestine and Syria. They also took Mesopotamia (an ancient region between the rivers Tigris and Euphrates in today's Iraq). Armenia, which was the first nation to embrace Christianity in 301, also fell into Muslim hands. As we have seen, in 717 the Byzantines won a great victory at Constantinople, where they had been besieged by colossal Muslim forces, but even that was not enough to put a stop to the Muslim raids into Asia Minor.

Within a relatively short time, Muslim forces overwhelmed Byzantine Egypt and all of Byzantine North Africa. In 711, the Muslims defeated the Catholic Visigoths of Spain. In 732, they advanced into what is today France. The Catholic Franks of Charles Martel, who had one of the strongest armies in western Europe at the time, stopped them at Poitiers. Obviously, the expansionist Muslim powers wanted to conquer the whole of Europe. Between 827 and 902 the Muslims occupied Byzantine Sicily. The Muslim threat to Rome and Italy continued until 912. Indeed, a Muslim settlement persisted until that year just 93 miles (150km) south of Rome at the mouth of Garigliano, when Pope John X, allied with southern Italian rulers, expelled the Muslims from the Italian peninsula.[25]

In 1009, the men of the Fatimid Caliph al-Hakim entered the Holy Sepulchre in Jerusalem and shattered into smithereens the rock tomb of Christ.[26] The Shi'ite Fatimid Caliphs of Cairo were the most powerful

Islamic rulers of that time. Al-Hakim engaged in the systematic destruction of synagogues and churches.[27]

The first crusade began in 1096, after the Muslims violated the three holiest Christian shrines and subjugated vast territories inhabited by Christians in Asia, Africa and Europe.

After the Muslim invasion, Rome would occasionally suffer again the indignity of sieges and the intermittent sacking of its newly accumulated riches. The sack by the Normans in 1084 and that of the troops of the Holy Roman Emperor Charles V in 1527 stand out as the most devastating.

During the Renaissance, some of the denizens of Italy began to look back to Rome's ancient glories, and they started to wonder what had happened to the wealth her first barbarian conqueror, Alaric the Visigoth, had stolen from the former imperial capital. Unlike subsequent invaders, whose spoils were gone for ever, lost or melted down, at least a part of Alaric's treasure might still exist and, if it existed, then perhaps it could be found. But to do so, Alaric would need to be rediscovered and tracked down in his hidden tomb.

For all the devastation after Alaric's sack of Rome, he had lived to see none of it. By rights, Alaric should have been the man to become Italy's king and the harbinger of a new order. Unfortunately, Alaric was a half-forgotten shadow who barely outlived his moment of infamy. Dead, just months after his triumph, his lost grave alone stood as mute testament to his war. His grave, though, was more than just a talisman to the Goths; for centuries it would inspire those who went in search of Alaric and his treasure.

PART FOUR

On the Trail of Treasure

THIRTEEN

The Thousand Faces of Alaric's Cosenza

For anyone interested in the story of Alaric's treasure, a trip to Cosenza is a must. All travellers should take the opportunity to go for a long walk around the historic centre both during the day, preferably before it gets too hot, and after dark.

As Gabriela de Falco tells us, old Cosenza has been dubbed 'The City with One Thousand Faces'. It perches on the *Colle Pancrazio* (Pancrazio Hill), and is joined to the new city by the *Ponte Mario Martire* (The Bridge of Mario the Martyr). In particular, the tourist who wanders off the beaten track will be rewarded with countless mesmerising and memorable vistas. Many of the old buildings in the historic centre of Cosenza are empty. While some of them are certainly dilapidated, they are not in a state of advanced ruin. They are largely built of tuff, called *tufo* in Italian, a fragmental rock made up of small pieces of volcanic material. The tuff used to construct the buildings of Cosenza came from the local quarries of Mendicino and San Lucido. Its colour ranges from rosy red to almost white.[1]

The most characteristic feature of the panoramas in old Cosenza is the golden or reddish colour of its walls, *la foglia morta* (dead leaf) colour, best seen from the Triglio Hill or the bridge of Alaric, especially at sunset. The architecture of Cosenza is austere and simple, and its styles range from the medieval to that of the seventeenth, the nineteenth and the first decades of the twentieth centuries.[2]

There are no buildings that stand out in terms of structural grandeur or decorative lavishness. After all, Cosenza has always been much smaller than the former Italian city-states of the North. However, the continuously varying proportions and the vertical solidity of the structures combine with beautiful loggias located at different heights and graceful, single or twin railings made from wrought iron, to fill the viewer with a deep sense of peace and harmony.

The walls and the columns show traces of beautiful frescoes consisting of *trompe l'oeil* landscapes, now almost completely faded. On the external walls, the tourist can see coats of arms and icons, at times illegible and with their colours muted. There are also arches and portals built of tuff and mysterious inner courtyards. It is quite a thrill to venture inside them, particularly at night when the buildings are flooded with light. Finally, the tourist will discover niches sheltering symbols of Christian veneration, frescoes, or small statuary groups.[3]

As in many other old European and Italian cities, the division of the quarters reflected the local social structure. The aristocratic districts occupy the highest levels. The merchant and the bourgeois areas are in the middle. And the neighbourhoods of the craftsmen are located on the shores of the River Crati.[4]

Some of the vacant palaces and houses, a few storeys high, have no glass in their window-frames and look haunted.

At night, old Cosenza comes across as a ghost city suddenly invaded by light and crowds of curious visitors. The experiences to be had in the *Centro Storico*, particularly after dark, are unique in the world of tourism. Only some sections of Venice, abandoned by their inhabitants, give a similar impression of a living ghost city, but that sensation is not as persistent as in Cosenza, where one feels, for the entire duration of one's visit and throughout the old city, like a flying spirit nostalgically seeking its long-lost body among the puzzling buildings. In our perpetual and painful search for immortality, old Cosenza is a place where mortality does not seem so frightening.

The area of the old, twelfth- to thirteenth-century Gothic cathedral and the surrounding network of medieval alleys and lanes captivate both visitors to the old city and the locals, who like to go out for an evening *passeggiata*. The façade of the cathedral is partly sombre and imposing, partly pleasant and inviting in character, as attested by the crowds thronging the plaza in front of it and the restaurants located in its immediate vicinity. It has three portals and three Gothic rose windows. Many businesses, including coffee shops and quaint little restaurants, have established themselves in the old quarter of Cosenza, and they bring life and colour to the old, mysterious buildings.

The cathedral shelters valuable works of art, including a beautiful Madonna by Luca Giordano, and a funerary monument to Isabel of

Aragon, a French contribution dating back to the late thirteenth century. The rich treasury of the cathedral is located in the nearby Bishop's Palace and at the Office of the Superintendent for Historic and Artistic Goods. Other churches of interest to the visitor include those of St Dominic (fifteenth century), St Francis of Assisi (with Gothic, Renaissance and Baroque features), and that of St Francis of Paola (eighteenth century). Piazza XV Marzo is home to the local theatre, the gardens of the Villa Communale and the Archaeological Museum. The Palazzo dell'Accademia Cosentina is at the heart of the great humanist cultural tradition of Cosenza. Paulo Giano Parrasio founded the local Academy in the sixteenth century.[5]

The mystery that envelops the ancient buildings of Cosenza and the grave of Alaric also surrounds the origins of the city. We know nothing definite about the circumstances and time of its foundation, or of the etymology of its name. As in many other Italian cities, the ancient urban area has been continuously inhabited, a factor that has prevented archaeological research aimed at answering these questions. However, de Falco writes that Cosenza was the only province strictly native in character of the three Calabrian provinces of antiquity, that it has never been subject to feudal bondage and that it has the most pronounced cultural traditions.[6]

The ruins of the Roman city of Cosentia are well below the ground level of today's Cosenza.

It is this city that many suppose houses the centuries-old grave of Alaric and his timeless treasure; this city that the ancient writers believed was the last resting place of the Visigothic king. As we shall see, exciting recent discoveries have lent some credence to this belief. But before we explore Cosenza further, we must take a look at those who came to Cosenza in search of Alaric, and trace their adventures as we embark on our own quest.

FOURTEEN

Himmler's Quest for the Lost Tomb

On 7 October 1900, a boy was born in Munich, Germany, to a classics teacher at a local school and the daughter of a shopkeeper. This boy became a bespectacled adult with the mild appearance of a lowly office worker.[1] As a young man he had difficulty establishing relationships with girls and, to many women, probably did not come across as very attractive. He was clumsy and of delicate health.[2] He was also prim and finicky.[3]

Many years later this man had found himself in a position of power. In his uniform emblazoned with swastikas, SS Reichsführer Heinrich Himmler had come to the region of Cosenza in the south of Italy on Hitler's orders, travelling in search of history and glory, in search of the lost tomb of Alaric.

Perhaps Himmler saw in the fifth-century Gothic king a reflection of himself and his Führer, all of them bold heroes engaging in an epic struggle against the diseased powers of decadent civilisation. Alaric had made the ancient city of Rome his plaything. The Nazis wished to bring the entire world to its knees.

Himmler had experience defying the civilised world. He conceived new rites to replace Christianity.[4] He was interested in the occult[5] and ordered his men to pursue all sorts of increasingly strange ideas, such as finding a legendary red horse with a white mane.[6] And this unstable man had an obsession with gold, an obsession that led him to seek it in the Nazi concentration camps when, inevitably, his other schemes failed.[7]

As the Nazi Reich began to crumble, Himmler delegated a geophysicist by the name of Karl Wienert to find gold in Munich's Isar river. When Himmler learned that someone named Tausend had allegedly mastered the secrets of alchemy, he imprisoned him and attempted to coerce him into obtaining gold from base metals. Karl Wienert, fully aware of the futility of searching for gold in the Isar, proceeded with the project to please Wolfram Sievers, Himmler's chief of staff. Eventually Wienert had to admit that he had failed. At that point, Himmler recruited Dr Josef Rimmer, a geologist reputed to have divining abilities. Emboldened by Rimmer's optimism, Himmler recommended that all geologists should be trained in divining and then continue the search for gold. This quixotic scheme also failed.[8]

But Himmler was also very keen to find the tomb of Alaric and the treasures reportedly buried with him. He was familiar with the background to the futile search for Alaric's gold, and he must have reviewed several times the long history of the quest to uncover the treasures of the barbarian king.

EARLY TREASURE HUNTERS

As Himmler would have been well aware, the legend of Alaric's tomb and treasure has a long history dating back to antiquity. But the first attempts to find them began in the Middle Ages, after the barbarian invasions had finally ground to a halt and romantics, historians and treasure seekers could begin to pull themselves out of the Dark Ages and look back to what must have seemed a more glorious era.

In 1858 Tommaso de Felici published a short story entitled *Il romito del Basento* (The Hermit of Basento), reportedly based on a fourteenth-century manuscript. In the story, a young Cosentine aristocrat discovers the treasure of Alaric thanks to a hermit's guidance. De Felici preserved in the story some of the phrases he had found in the fourteenth-century manuscript: 'The marvellous way in which the treasures of Sir Alarico, whose treasures were hidden with his body under the river Vasiento, near the noble and magnificent city of Cosenza'.[9]

Cornacchioli writes that in the sixteenth century, a humble family in the Cosenza region managed to escape their modest circumstances thanks to the discovery of a large quantity of silver and gold. The family's house was located near the River Crati, which merges with the Busento in Cosenza, legendary resting place of Alaric and his treasure. This intriguing story was found in a manuscript dated to 1764 and preserved in the Biblioteca Civica di Cosenza (Municipal Library of Cosenza). But the spectacular find left no trace in local folk memory.[10]

However, some Italians continued to write of Alaric and his treasure. As Cornacchioli narrates, among the first Italian authors to discuss the burial of Alaric was the meticulous Dominican monk Alberti in his *Description of*

All Italy, published in 1546. He dutifully mentions his sources, namely Paul the Deacon, the historian of the Lombards (*c.* 720–*c.* 799); Sabellicus, an Italian historian (1436–1506); and Flavio Biondo, an Italian archaeologist and historian (1388–1463).

Alberti's scholarly rigour is evident in the careful way he corrects an ancient error that confused the River Busento of Cosenza with the similar-sounding Basente/Basento, a river ending in the Gulf of Taranto over 62 miles (100km) north of Cosenza. Alberti, not a native of the Cosenza region, comments that Alaric was obviously buried in the Busento, as he died in Cosenza, far away from the Basente/Basento.[11]

Fioriglio brings to our attention the fact that one of the oldest maps of Cosenza (1584) features the confluence of the Busento and Crati marked by a text describing it as the suspected location of Alaric's mythical treasure.[12]

Later, in 1588, the Cosentine G.P. d'Aquino made a speech at the funeral of the renowned Cosentine philosopher Bernardino Telesio. Telesio had been the teacher of the philosopher Giordano Bruno (1548–1600) – burnt at the stake in Rome for his belief that Christ was only a clever magician,[13] his views about the Holy Virgin[14] and other doctrinal 'errors'.

D'Aquino briefly mentioned the burial of Alaric in Busento near Cosenza, which shows how persistent was the memory of the Visigoth among educated locals. For some reason D'Aquino used the name of Basento for the river, although he specifically referred to Cosenza. His pronunciation was explained as the manifestation of a classicist trend. Spelling, it seems, was not quite settled yet.

In a book published in Messina, Sicily, in 1693, Valente also wrote that Alaric was buried with a treasure under the confluence of the Busento and Crati.

The ultimate source for all these – and other – stories of Alaric was not some surviving folk memory, or even necessarily truth, but the historian Cassiodorus (490–583) filtered through the work of Jordanes.[15]

Unfortunately, Renaissance reliance on the authority of classical authors left the testing of their claims to a later era, after the upheavals of the eighteenth century. As in Himmler's time, the turmoil of the eighteenth century saw the spread of conflict on a global scale. The War of the Spanish Succession (1701–14) was the first world war of modern times, with armed conflict in Spain, Italy, southern Germany, the Netherlands, on the oceans and in the North Sea.

Following this period of great trouble and turbulence, in the southern Italian region where Cosenza stood, the Italians engaged in the first large-scale programme of excavations to find the tomb of Alaric.[16] If the Italians retained a folk memory of the troubled years of decline when Alaric had come out of the north and smashed the pitiful Roman Empire in the West, perhaps this new world war spurred thoughts of Alaric's treasure as the people strove for comparisons to the calamity that had befallen Italy yet again.

Complex dynastic intrigue and warfare had caused southern Italy to change hands several times following the war. By 1735, the people living in the area of Cosenza saw the Austrians leave and the Spanish arrive in the shape of the Bourbons.

In 1747, when the Italians of Cosenza undertook the first excavations to find Alaric's tomb, Europe was approaching the end of the War of the Austrian Succession (1740–8), a bloody conflagration that pitted France, Spain, Naples (under the Spanish Bourbons), Bavaria and Sweden against Austria, Russia, Britain, the Netherlands, Hanover and Savoy. The War of the Austrian Succession did not, however, affect the government in the area of Cosenza.[17]

To the modern eye, it is somewhat surprising that anybody would remember Alaric's centuries-old burial during those turbulent times. But in 1747, more than a hundred Italians led by Ettore Capecelatro, the *Preside* (Master) of the administrative region of *Calabria Citeriore* (Hithermost Calabria), took part in a costly campaign of excavations aimed at finding the grave and treasure of the Visigothic king Alaric at the confluence of the Rivers Busento and Crati in Cosenza, where legend placed his grave. Capecelatro and his army of diggers failed.[18] The excavations lasted only four days because of increasing suspicion that the confluence of the rivers had in fact been located elsewhere in Alaric's time. Capecelatro had one of the most serious cases of what Fioriglio aptly calls 'Alaric fever'.[19]

One wonders what prompted Capecelatro to initiate the expensive project. Did he have access to secret information that compelled him to mobilise more than a hundred workmen? Perhaps he had seen the map of 1584; maybe there was something else. Capecelatro's attempt to find the grave occurred thirteen years after the end of the two-decade long Austrian administration. Did he learn anything important in those twenty years, something that he felt comfortable putting to the test only after the departure of the Austrians? If he did, he never said, and that gave Himmler little more to go on than the Italian excavators' failure.

Not long after, Duret de Tavel, a French officer serving in southern Italy with the armies of Napoleon, wrote in his letters penned between 1807 and 1810 that Alaric's remains had been found one thousand years after his death, buried between two shields in the bed of the river. De Tavel's sources remain unidentified and the story is mere legend.

NINETEENTH-CENTURY SEARCHES

Still dreaming of the fabulous treasure concealed in Alaric's lost resting place, Himmler would probably have reviewed the other literary clues he had at his disposal, including an important poem by a German author.

August Graf von Platen's poem '*Das grab im Busento*' (The tomb in Busento), printed in final form in 1834, coupled with its subsequent translation into Italian by Giossuè Carducci in 1855,[20] had a significant impact on the search for the Visigothic king's tomb. After reading this poem, many treasure hunters travelled to Cosenza to find Alaric's grave. With the help of Axel and Ursula Stuck, here is the poem in my own translation:

> The Tomb in Busento

> A soft, nocturnal song on the Busento
> By Cosenza's heard and its refrain,
> Reflected by the waters bounces back,
> Then in the eddies it is heard again.

> The shadows of the bravest Goths
> Move on the river, up and down,
> They weep for their Alaric,
> Dead tribesman of a great renown.

> He, all too early, far from homeland,
> Was to be buried under waves and whirls,
> This, while his shoulders were surrounded
> By his so very blond and youthful curls.

And on the bank of the Busento,
The throng of Goths formed ranks around their dead.
They toiled to deviate the river
And also dug a fresh funereal bed.

They came to lower levels of the bottom
That from the waves they had just freed,
Then deep inside they sunk their hero,
In armour, riding his beloved steed.

With earth the pit they slowly covered,
And their king, to sounds of dirge,
That from the hero's tomb swift currents
Would for eternity upsurge.

Diverted for a second time through labour,
The guided river came back home.
Busento pulled into its bed the waters,
The whirlpools and the whitish foam.

And so, a choir of men was singing:
'Sleep in your glory, our brave!
No haughty Roman's greed will ever
Disturb or desecrate your grave.'

The song of praise reverberated
Above the Gothic army, strong and free.
Take it with you, waves of Busento,
Take it with you from sea to sea!

An earlier version of von Platen's poem dates back to 1820.[21] In those post-Napoleonic years, the trend towards nation-building had spread to the then disunited Germans,[22] and it is not surprising that they were looking to the past for inspiration in their nation-building efforts. The same had applied to the Italians in the first half of the nineteenth century. Both Italians and Germans achieved national unity in that century, almost simultaneously.[23] The Germans could plausibly look back at the barbarians of fifth-century

Europe as the great progenitors of their race, mighty warriors who had come, seen and conquered.

Nevertheless, Himmler was aware that despite the poem's Romantic appeal, none of the amateur treasure hunters had discovered Alaric's tomb. Reviewing the remaining evidence, he would probably have discovered with astonishment the lines written by the famous French novelist Alexandre Dumas in his book about Calabria.

In the autumn of 1835, shortly after a violent earthquake, Dumas arrived in Cosenza. He observed that the Busento's riverbed was completely dry, probably as a result of the earthquake, and was surprised to see a large number of locals engaged in excavations on the authority of 'Jarmadès' (almost certainly Jordanes), the classical author who describes the rich burial of Alaric. 'Alaric fever' had assumed epidemic proportions. Dumas noted that every time the riverbed dries, the locals resume their digging. He lightheartedly commented that in spite of repeated disappointments, the local scholars who venerate antiquity survive unharmed, and that the only valuable item ever found was a little deer made of gold, discovered at the end of the eighteenth century.[24]

In 1897, the Cosentine novelist Nicola Misasi wrote that his learned brother-in-law Francesco de Bonis, a lawyer, asserted in an original monograph that Alaric had been buried in the 'narrow valley near the gas meter'. Misasi also noted that at the beginning of the nineteenth century, the municipality of Cosenza carried out excavations near the confluence of the Busento and Crati, and that these were discontinued after many days of work when it was learned that in the year of Alaric's death, the confluence might have been located at the level of the Piazza San Domenico.[25]

Was Misasi refering to Capecelatro's unsuccessful digs or was there another excavation at the beginning of the nineteenth century?

EARLY TWENTIETH-CENTURY SEARCHES

There was still more evidence to consider. The English essayist, novelist and critic George Gissing published his travel notes in 1901, under the title *Notes of a Ramble in Southern Italy*, two years before his death at the age of 46. Gissing's most popular novels, *The Nether World* and *New Grub Street*, reverberate with his admiration for the classics, the privations of his own life and the particular blend of idealism and pessimism that filled him.

Gissing's other works, including his *Notes of a Ramble in Southern Italy*, reflect his personality and talent as well.[26]

He had had a longstanding interest in Alaric, and that was one of the reasons that brought him to Cosenza:

When night had fallen I walked a little about the scarce-lighted streets and came to an open place, dark and solitary and silent, where I could hear the voices of the two streams as they mingled below the hill. . . . I had come here to think about Alaric, and with my own eyes to behold the place of his burial. Ever since the first boyish reading of Gibbon, my imagination had loved to play upon that scene of Alaric's death. Thinking to conquer Sicily, the Visigoth marched as far as to the Capital of the Bruttii, those mountain tribes which Rome herself never really subdued: at Cosentia he fell sick and died. . . . Now, tradition has it that Alaric was buried close to the confluence of the Busento and the Crati. If so, he lay in full view of the town. But the Goths are said to have slain all their prisoners who took part in the work, to ensure secrecy. Are we to suppose that Cosentia was depopulated? On any other supposition the story must be incorrect, and Alaric's tomb would have to be sought at least half a mile away, where the Busento is hidden in its deep valley. . . . Do the Rivers Busento and Crati still guard the secret of that 'royal sepulchre, adorned with the splendid spoils and trophies of Rome'? It seems improbable that the grave was ever disturbed; to this day, there exists somewhere near Cosenza a treasure house more alluring than any pictured in an Arabian night.[27]

As beautiful as his writing is, Gissing errs in one respect: Alaric died in Cosentia (Cosenza) on his way back from Rhegium, today's Reggio di Calabria. Gissing observed that Alaric's burial place may not be located too close to the city and that the confluence of the Busento and Crati may not be a useful working hypothesis after all.

In 1937, Amelie Crevolin, a French pendulum dowser, claimed to have identified the precise location of Alaric's grave a few kilometres from Cosenza, along the Busento valley. The fascist authorities, with the full support of an eager public, received Mme Crevolin with great enthusiasm. Local newspapers published stirring articles and, amid unprecedented publicity, excavations began in June of that year.[28]

The head of the SS was probably overcome by a wonderful feeling of anticipation. When he received news that the French archaeological team was on the point of the possible discovery of the tomb of Alaric, he travelled in person to Cosenza accompanied by Eugen Dollman, his interpreter, later to become one of the representatives of the Third Reich in Italy. The Nazi treasure hunter arrived in Cosenza on 20 November 1937. His convertible took the excited Himmler to Vadue, just south of Cosenza.

But what the archaeologists had to say was very far from what Himmler had hoped to hear. Deeply disappointed, he remarked that there was no monument to commemorate the king of the Visigoths. Then his convertible stopped on the bridge crossing the Busento. To the bewilderment of the Italians present, Himmler suddenly stood to attention in his convertible and, staring intently at the placid waters of the old river, gave the Nazi salute to King Alaric, though the Goths had nothing to do with modern Germany.[29]

Himmler would have to return to Hitler with the disappointing news that the Führer's interest in Alaric, along with his own, had borne no fruit.[30]

After reaching a depth of around 26ft (8m), the workmen found only the remains of a human skeleton. While these events were unfolding, Fausto Tanziani put together a project for the recovery of Alaric's tomb. The Italians were not going to let the French beat them to it. After all, Alaric had sacked Rome, not some city in Gaul, and he had died in Cosenza, which was Italian, not French.

Tanziani prepared a topographical map of the confluence of the Busento and Crati and on it marked with crosses the most probable locations of the treasure, and with dotted lines the areas to investigate. The Superintendent of Monuments and Excavations for Calabria and especially the mayor of Cosenza, Tommaso Arnoni, were in favour of the project. Tanziani's hypotheses were never put to the test.[31]

Also that year, a private treasure-hunting initiative involving three respectable Cosentine professionals got under way. With the help of the omnipresent Amelie Crevolin, the local treasure-hunting trio began excavations that had to be abruptly discontinued due to the legal quibbles of engineer Aristide Armentano, the owner of the land in question.[32]

ALARIC DURING THE SECOND WORLD WAR

According to Paul Hoffmann, during the Second World War Himmler sent engineers and archaeologists to Cosenza to search for Alaric's final resting place, but they found nothing.[33] The Cosentine authors do not seem to mention the presence of this team in Cosenza during the war, and Hoffman does not give his sources. At any rate, both Hitler and Himmler must have been disappointed that Alaric's grave remained undiscovered. The failure of the treasure hunt mirrored the larger failure of the Nazi war effort.

Between 7 and 11 April 1943, Hitler and Mussolini held talks in Salzburg. They made the catastrophic choice to continue the fight against the Allies in North Africa. On 19 April, the people still alive in the Warsaw Ghetto rebelled. On 24 April, Heinrich Himmler's SS commenced a merciless campaign against the Jewish rebels there.

In May 1943, the situation of the Axis forces continued to deteriorate in the Battle of the Atlantic, North Africa and in Germany, where the Allies persisted in their devastating aerial bombardments. On the Eastern Front the situation remained grave for the Germans. Doenitz recalled his U-boats from the North Atlantic. On 12 May, Mussolini made the Italian Marshal Messe a field marshal in an attempt to motivate him to continue the resistance of the Germans and Italians around Tunis and Bizerta in North Africa, but the next day, Messe capitulated. Within a few days, the Allies had taken 250,000 prisoners. The end of the Second World War was in sight.[34]

Hitler was profoundly troubled. After his defeat in North Africa, he feared that the Allies were going to open a second front in Italy, a possible gateway into the heart of Europe. As in the time of Alaric, Italy was very important strategically. Hitler probably began to anticipate his own end. And where were the military experts he expected to bring him relief and salvation from total disaster? The names of those whom Hitler demanded and invoked to perform a miracle and do something to stop the demoralising series of German defeats were those of Field Marshal Erwin Rommel and Alaric, king of the Visigoths.[35]

Indeed, on 18 May 1943, Hitler selected Rommel to organise his troops and prepare them to take over Italy, should that country disintegrate or leave the Axis. The secrecy of this order was unprecedented. Hitler preferred not to issue a top-secret order and limited the directive to verbal instructions.

The name given to this operation was Alaric.[36] In his utter desperation, Hitler seems to have pinned at least some of his hopes on the magic that has always surrounded the name of Alaric in connection with his deeds in Italy. But Alaric would be of no help to the German cause in the Second World War.

After the failed attempt to assassinate Hitler in 1944, Rommel, who was recovering from a head injury, committed suicide on 14 October 1944, with cyanide provided to him by two generals. According to the generals, Hitler's message to Rommel was that he had two options: a humiliating public trial or suicide.[37] Hitler followed him in death not long after; the ghost of the Gothic warrior Alaric had done nothing to aid the latter-day barbarian in his new quest to destroy the civilised world.

The conventional story of Himmler's death is that on 23 May 1945, he outwitted Colonel Michael Murphy, Sergeant-Major Austin and Dr C.J.L. Wells, all of the British Second Army, and managed to break in his mouth a phial of cyanide, although only two days earlier Austin had witnessed the suicide of Hans Prützmann, a high-ranking SS leader, in the same room.

Sergeant-Major Austin interred Himmler's body two days later. He did not reveal the location of the grave so that nobody would ever find his final resting place.[38] It is known only that Himmler was buried on Lunenburg Heath.[39] Like Alaric, Himmler himself finished up in a secret grave, but it seems that not many are interested in finding it.

So ended the quest for Alaric's tomb until modern times.

FIFTEEN

Alaric's Burial: The Historical Record

If we are to seek out Alaric's hidden grave and the treasures it contains, we must first evaluate a bit better than Himmler did the evidence that has come down to us. It is necessary to delve once more into the historical record and assess the few sources we have for Alaric's burial before we can make some educated guesses about where Alaric lies and what we may find inside his tomb. Only then can we see how the most recent tomb-hunters stalked their quarry and evaluate the likelihood of their success.

Let us begin with the most familiar source, Edward Gibbon's *Decline and Fall of the Roman Empire*. Gibbon describes Alaric's funeral in poetic language:

> The ferocious character of the Barbarians was displayed in the funeral of a hero whose valour and fortune they celebrated with mournful applause. By the labour of a captive multitude, they forcibly diverted the course of the Busentinus, a small river that washes the walls of Cosentia. The royal sepulchre, adorned with the splendid spoils and trophies of Rome, was constructed in the vacant bed; the waters were then restored to their natural channel; and the secret spot, where the remains of Alaric had been deposited, was forever concealed by the inhuman massacre of the prisoners, who had been employed to execute the work.[1]

Gibbon has been criticised for the manner in which he narrated the burial of Alaric.[2] It has been noted that the basis of his account was the 'illiterate' *Getica* written by an 'ignorant person', Jordanes, who copied without restraint from the more learned Cassiodorus' lost *History of the Goths*, approximately 140 years after the death of Alaric. It has also been quipped that Cassiodorus himself was born eighty years after the event and that none of the three attended the funeral of Alaric.

The historian J.J. O'Donnell himself made a scholarly examination of Jordanes.[3] He wrote: 'Jordanes was a Christian of Germanic origin, probably a bishop, writing at Constantinople in 551 or 552 A.D. His *Romana* is an epitome of Roman history of little interest, dedicated to Pope Vigilius, then resident in Constantinople. His *Getica* is merely an abridgement of Cassiodorus' *Gothic History* (since lost to us). As the *Getica* reflects the most urgent of contemporary political events, it must have had a political purpose. Disagreement persists on several issues. A minority of scholars denies that Jordanes the bishop and Vigilius the pope were the people involved in writing and receiving the *Romana*. The exact nature and extent of Jordanes' borrowing from his sources (and consequently the precise identity of the sources he used) remain unclear. The universal assumption, however, is that Jordanes was not a particularly clever fellow. The principal evidence for this claim is his slovenly grammar, on the good classicizing principle that cleverness and good grammar are always found together'. In my many years as a clinical psychiatrist, I have come to appreciate that grammar and intelligence do not always go hand in hand. Moreover, if Jordanes were indeed a bishop, one would expect that he had at least a modicum of intelligence.

At one point in the *Getica*, Jordanes surprises the reader by stating, 'I also, Jordanes, although an unlearned man before my conversion, was secretary.'[4] So we are dealing here with a man who was able to act as secretary, although he was uneducated. This would not suggest an intellectually dull individual.

In his article, O'Donnell reviewed the preface that Jordanes had prepared for the *Romana* and noted that Jordanes hoped his works would facilitate religious conversion and the rejection of worldly interests. However, anyone who reads the *Getica* cannot overlook the passages in which Jordanes expresses his pride in the successes of the Goths and his thinly veiled contempt for the anti-German campaigns of the Emperor Justinian. The latter reigned in Jordanes' times and worked towards the resurrection of the old Roman Empire by taking back the ancient Roman lands in the West from the various Germanic tribes that occupied them.

On the other hand, O'Donnell emphasised that Jordanes related succinctly the facts without sermonising, and did not interfere with the reader's desire to make his/her own final assessment. This is certainly not the mark of a weak intellect. Cassiodorus, considered by many a very important source of Jordanes, could not read Greek.

Jordanes was proficient in Greek and wrote in Constantinople, so he might have had access to information not available to Cassiodorus, who lived and worked mostly in Italy, and wrote his *History of the Goths* for his master, Theodoric the Great.

CASSIODORUS' LOST WRITINGS

O'Donnell has also identified borrowings from Cassiodorus in the *Getica*, borrowings that are thought to include at least some Gothic oral sources. According to O'Donnell, Cassiodorus seems to have been only a written source for Jordanes. It is not known for certain whether Jordanes' source for Alaric's burial story was oral or written. In fact, we know nothing at all about Jordanes' source for the story, but I believe we have reason to suspect that Jordanes found it in Cassiodorus.

Indeed, in connection with the story of Alaric's burial, one interesting aspect of Cassiodorus' life is worth mentioning. He came into this world in 490 in Scylletium (modern Squillace) in Calabria, Italy. He passed away in 585 in his own monastery, located near his native town.[5] A remarkable thing about Scylletium is that it was only about 38 miles (60km) south-east of Cosentia. Thus, we are faced with the possibility that Cassiodorus may have had access to local stories about the burial of Alaric and may have been Jordanes' source for it.

Certainly, Cassiodorus, both as a local who lived many years in the area and as a very high-ranking government official, must have had a certain knowledge of Italian geography. A number of other fascinating possibilities present themselves if one looks at the details of the life of Cassiodorus and, as we shall see later, the deeds of Theodoric the Great, his master.

In 540, Cassiodorus retired near Scylletium where he lived for another forty-five years. He became a monk and founded a monastery named Vivarium. He authored several works, some of which were popular in the Middle Ages. It is intriguing that his history of the Goths has not survived while his other works have. It might be that the copies of Cassiodorus' *History of the Goths* were destroyed when it became clear that the Byzantines were going to defeat the Goths in Italy.

Jordanes who wrote his *Getica* while the war was still raging, was rather unwise to preserve Cassiodorus' respectful lines about Theodoric's independent rule in Italy and Spain, former Roman provinces. These passages could have irritated the Roman Emperor Justinian, who wanted to end the Gothic domination of Italy and bring Spain back into the empire, then ruled by the Visigoths. The latter had had Theodoric as a suzerain for several years.

The fact that Jordanes retained these paragraphs in his own writings has been interpreted as naïveté. But it could also have been the result of an outburst of pro-Gothic sentiment in which the Balkan Goth Jordanes decided not to delete the subversive lines. At times it is difficult to determine where national pride ends and poor judgement begins. After all, many people who suffered and died because they gave free expression to their nationalistic views are considered heroes and martyrs and not people with poor judgement.

With this in mind, I do not think we can safely assume that the conversion of Jordanes to Christianity had completely wiped out his pro-Gothic sympathies. History is full of examples of nationalistic and patriotic feelings coexisting with Christian religiosity. In the conclusion to the *Getica*, Jordanes' tone is sad but his admiration for the past achievements of the Goths is unmistakable.

According to O'Donnell, 'Poor Jordanes begins to emerge from our analysis as a more intelligent, but less important, figure than we have been accustomed to imagine him. He is not part of the great political schemes of his day (and neither was Cassiodorus at this time for that matter), but he is an independent and more or less responsible historian, working almost exclusively with written sources and handling them creditably. His grammar is poor, his judgment imperfect, but his independence at least emerges intact.'[6]

We can, however, assume with a reasonable degree of confidence that whatever imperfections Jordanes' work and person may have exhibited, their nature and degree do not give us any compelling grounds to conclude that his account of Alaric's burial should be abandoned as a gross fabrication or falsehood. That Alaric died and was buried in the area of Cosenza and that he was interred with treasures remains an interesting working hypothesis.

JORDANES OF CROTONE

In August 551, our controversial Pope Vigilius (537–55) published a text that had attached to it the names of a number of Italian bishops.

Vigilius produced this text while seeking sanctuary in the palace church of Sts Peter and Paul in Constantinople. One of the bishops named was Jordanes Crotonensis, Bishop of Crotona (now Crotone in Calabria, Italy).

Crotone is, as the crow flies, 50 miles (80km) south-east of Cosenza on the Ionian Sea and 37 miles (60km) north-east from Squillace, where Cassiodorus lived after his retirement in his own monastery of Vivarium; the monastery no longer exists.

It is thought likely that our Jordanes penned his *Getica* in Constantinople in 551 because his work mentions almost no current or subsequent Italian events and shows familiarity with imperial issues specific to the Constantinople of that time. It has been suggested that if our Jordanes is the Italian bishop Jordanes of Crotone, then the Vigilius to whom Jordanes sent the brief history of Rome entitled *Romana* with a dedication, together with the *Getica*, was our fickle Pope Vigilius. This seems to be the opinion of the majority of scholars.

Some time before leaving Italy, Jordanes went twice through the twelve volumes of Cassiodorus' history of the Goths while visiting the place of the retired statesman near today's Squillace, which was not far from his presumed episcopal residence in Crotone. When asked to write the *Getica* while in Constantinople, he probably had only his recollections of what he had read in Cassiodorus' history of the Goths and other sources to rely on. It would seem that Jordanes was in the entourage of Pope Vigilius when invited to write his history of the Goths.[7]

The works sent by Jordanes to Vigilius were aimed at facilitating religious conversion in the receiver paired with renunciation of all secular interests, which Vigilius, as pope, should have achieved long before that. However, in the light of Vigilius' deeds and his incredible eagerness to pursue secular goals, including while in Constantinople, when Bishop Jordanes of Crotone was presumably in his entourage, Pope Vigilius was far from having achieved a genuine conversion at that juncture. Jordanes may have been acutely aware of the profound worldliness of Vigilius.

Moreover, if Jordanes and Pope Vigilius spent a significant amount of time together in the sanctuary of one church or another, then they may have developed a close personal relationship which would have been more compatible with the ostensibly inappropriately familiar way in which Jordanes addressed Pope Vigilius in the dedication to the *Romana*.

If our Jordanes was the Italian bishop Jordanes of Crotone, that would mean that the author of the *Getica* himself spent a part of his life in southern Italy, where he may have had access to local Gothic traditions regarding Alaric's burial.

KING DECEBALUS' TREASURE

There are still other objections made to Jordanes' brief report of Alaric's burial, objections that must be examined before going in search of Alaric's grave.

Lanciani[8] asked himself whether Jordanes' account reflected the actual funeral customs of the Goths or whether it was inspired by the narrative of the treasure of the Dacian king Decebalus, a story that I had come across myself in the Romanian region of Transylvania. Remnants of this treasure were reportedly discovered by Romanian fishermen in the River Sargetia/Istrig (today's Strei) during the sixteenth century. The Romanians found 40,000 coins not far from Sântamaria Orlea, a town near Hațeg, Transylvania. Apparently, Cardinal Giorgio Martinuzzi (fl. 1551), chancellor of Transylvania, kept many coins for his personal collection. At a later date, general Giovanni Castaldo dispatched some 10,000 coins to the imperial collection in Vienna.[9]

The historical validity of the tale of Alaric's burial has been questioned. It has been suggested that Jordanes' account is a legend originating in the lands of the Lower Danube and the Black Sea, where the Visigoths were in contact with the local Scythian population. Among others, Cassius Dio's account of the 'death and burial of the Dacian king Decebalus' has been mentioned in support of this opinion.[10]

Cassius Dio, a Roman historian (?b. 155),[11] who chronicled Rome's last wars with the Dacians in the early second century AD in his *Roman History*, related how Emperor Trajan defeated the Dacians and what happened to the Dacian king Decebalus and his treasure.

Dio described the burial of part of Decebalus' treasures in a riverbed, the concealment in caves of the remainder, the killing of the captives who had buried and hidden his treasures, the suicide of Decebalus, and how the Romans found his treasure with the help of the traitor Bicilis – but Dio emphatically did *not* describe the burial of Decebalus with treasures in a riverbed.[12]

Thus, the two accounts are fundamentally different. Moreover, a relief on Trajan's Column in Rome, which was built in the years immediately following the end of the Dacian wars and thus provides information of great historical value, shows Roman soldiers escorting the sons of Decebalus into captivity and other Roman soldiers carrying Decebalus' head on a plate within a Roman encampment.[13] There is no account relating the burial of the remains of Decebalus after the Roman soldiers severed the head from his dead body and sent it off to Rome.[14] Nor is there any reason to think that the Romans would have buried the headless corpse of Decebalus with his treasures.

In addition, there is contemporary historical evidence, well preserved in reliefs on Trajan's Column, which shows that the Romans did discover the treasure of Decebalus. Indeed, one relief shows Roman soldiers leading horses laden with baskets filled with precious items.[15]

Accordingly, it is far from certain that Jordanes' rendition of Alaric's burial is a reworking of the story of Decebalus' riches. Simply burying a treasure, as opposed to burying a treasure in the grave of a heroic king cherished by his followers, are two fundamentally different activities, which involve different purposes, emotional reactions, religious implications, types of conduct and significance.

It remains conceivable that Alaric died and was buried with treasures somewhere near Cosenza according to the traditions of the Germanic elites. While the riverbed burial remains of some interest, as we shall see, it is not the only type of burial that deserves attention when looking for the final resting place of Alaric.

ATTILA THE HUN'S RIVERBED BURIAL

There is something else we need to consider. It has been noted that the story of Alaric's burial is too similar to that of Attila's burial, as related by Jordanes in the same history of the Goths, to be entirely coincidental. This would suggest that Jordanes merely copied down what he knew of Attila's funeral to fill in the missing details of Alaric's.[16]

This is a serious objection, but one that is at odds with the facts. In the case of Attila, while Jordanes does mention that he was buried with riches and that the gravediggers were killed, which is hardly surprising when one takes into account the problem posed by grave robbers, he says not one word about a *river* burial:

[Attila's] body was placed in the midst of a plain and lay in state in a silken tent as a sight for men's admiration. The best horsemen of the entire tribe of the Huns rode around in circles, after the manner of circus games, in the place to which he had been brought and told of his deeds in a funeral dirge. . . . When they had mourned him with such lamentations, a *strava*, as they call it, was celebrated over his tomb with great revelling. They gave way in turn to the extremes of feeling and displayed funereal grief alternating with joy. Then in the secrecy of night they buried his body in the earth. They bound his coffins, the first with gold, the second with silver and the third with the strength of iron, showing by such means that these three things suited the mightiest of kings: iron because he subdued the nations, gold and silver because he received the honours of both empires. They also added the arms of foemen won in the fight, trappings of rare worth, sparkling with various gems, and ornaments of all sorts whereby princely state is maintained. And that so great riches might be kept from human curiosity, they slew those appointed to the work – a dreadful pay for their labour; and thus sudden death was the lot of those who buried him as well as of him who was buried.[17]

The story of Attila's burial under a river, still in circulation today, is in fact a modern interpolation. The late Hungarian archaeologist István Bóna noted that Hungarian researchers have shown that the story that Attila was buried under the River Tisza was first mentioned by the Romantic Hungarian poet Sándor Petőfi, who lived in the first half of the nineteenth century, and it began circulating among Hungarians and internationally only later.

Hungarian scholars believe that, inspired by Jordanes' story of Alaric's burial, people began attributing the river burial to Attila during the period of extensive work on the River Tisza prior to the revolution of 1848–9. In short, it is the other way around; that is, the story circulating of Attila's burial in the riverbed of Tisza is an imitation of Jordanes' description of Alaric's funeral. All that the ancient sources knew about Attila's burial was that his remains had been interred during the night and in great secrecy.[18]

THE MAGNITUDE OF ALARIC'S TREASURE

Nowhere did Jordanes mention the exact weight and nature of the treasures buried with Alaric. But that did not stop the modern-day newspaper

La Repubblica from reporting that the Visigothic king could be at rest accompanied by nearly 25 tons of gold and 150 tons of silver.[19] Such vast quantities of precious metals would be more credible if they were intended as a representative estimate of the total amount plundered by the Visigoths.

When Alaric withdrew to Tuscany before the sack of Rome, the citizens of the city had agreed to give him 2.3 metric tons (5,000lb) of gold, 13.6 metric tons (30,000lb) of silver, 4,000 silken robes, 3,000 scarlet fleeces and 3,000lb of pepper, the last a commodity highly valued in those days for its ability to conceal the unpleasant taste of decayed meat. Zosimus reported these figures in his *New History*.[20] It would have been quite a task for the Visigoths to bury the amounts of gold and silver suggested by *La Repubblica*, and burying such quantities would probably have produced consternation among Alaric's followers, who would have concluded that even love for one's heroic king has its limits. Therefore, it is likely that only some of the Roman treasure found its way into Alaric's grave.

The treasure lay safe because Alaric's gravediggers were slaughtered. There was a similar killing of the gravediggers by the Huns to keep secret the location of Attila's tomb, and there is no evidence suggesting that the Visigoths of Alaric had fewer reasons than the Huns to be concerned about grave robbers.

It has been observed that in Europe, archaeologists have not found the remains of captives who had been used to dig the graves of dead rulers and then massacred.[21] However, one would not expect to find remains of dead people if their bodies had been thrown into the flowing waters to worship the river god, as the Franks did at the river Ticinum/Ticino.[22] The ritual of Alaric's interment remains a mystery. Even so, this textual analysis has told us much about what Alaric's burial was *not*. Jordanes' account was not simply a copy of Decebalus' burial, or Attila's. It was not a figment of Jordanes' imagination.

But we are still no closer to finding Alaric's grave. To do so we must discover some positive evidence for what and where Alaric's burial truly was. To do that, we must travel to the very site of Alaric's burial and seek out the mysteries it holds. One man claims to know where that burial place is.

SIXTEEN

Alaric's Many Burial Sites

We know that for a long time Alaric was believed to lie buried beneath the Busento near the city of Cosenza. Besides the city of Cosenza, others have claimed Alaric for themselves. Though there are several possible sites and most proposed burial places lie along the Busento or not that far from it, there is one Italian who thinks that a river from another region of Italy hides Alaric's tomb.

WHICH RIVER WAS IT?

Angelo Raffaele Amato has a theory that contradicts the ancient reports of Alaric's burial. According to him, the River Bussento (note the different spelling) in the National Park of Cilento in today's Campania would be the stream associated with the burial of Alaric. This river ends in the Gulf of Policastro, situated south of the Gulf of Salerno. The latter is south of the Gulf of Naples. The mouth of this river is located west of the modern city of Policastro Bussentino, known as Buxentum in Roman times.

Those readers who are not Italians may not be aware of how serious the battle can be between Italian cities or regions competing to claim association with the same important historical or archaeological site. At issue here is the tourism and business that come with the universal recognition of a particular city, town, village or area as the location of some famous historical or archaeological discovery, or as the area with the highest perceived potential to be the host of such a discovery.

This is a very old type of rivalry in Italy. For instance, during the Middle Ages Perugia and Assisi were frequently at war or competing in one way or another. After St Francis of Assisi died in 1226, the citizens of the town hid his remains for fear that Perugia, their hostile neighbour, might try to steal them, with the purpose of diverting to itself the economic boom that is always experienced by a place of pilgrimage.

Returning to the River Bussento in the park of Cilento, we must acknowledge that Amato has a very interesting hypothesis. Indeed, the *Barrington Historical Atlas of the Greek and Roman World*, unanimously recognised as the best tool of its type currently available, includes in the key to the map of Bruttii a river named Buxentum in Latin and Pyxous in Greek. However, this atlas does not mention any Buxentum or Buxentus or Busentus river near Consentia (Cosenza).[1]

Amato pointed out the observations of another Italian, Angelo Guzo, that the Bussento in Cilento is the only mountain river of southern Italy that follows a subterranean course for a part of its route and displays impressive limestone sinks and ravines, known as karstic phenomena. Indeed, the Bussento flows underground for 2½ miles (4km) out of its total length of 23 miles (37km), and flows through geological formations that seem ideal spots for finding a secret grave. This Bussento in Cilento is not a very long river, but the Busento of Jordanes, the river that joins the Crati in Cosenza, is even shorter (11.4 miles or 18.4km).[2] During the height of summer, the riverbed of the Busento near Cosenza can be almost completely dry, but at other seasons, water levels are higher.

Amato, whose hypothesis was presented on the website of a hotel in the Cilento National Park, makes no secret of the fact that his purpose is to 'eradicate from the root the erroneous and senseless belief that the tomb of Alaric had been excavated in the river Busento, in the vicinity of Cosenza, and to recover traces of the passage of the Visigoths in the valleys of the river Bussento, in order to facilitate the search for the tomb of Alaric and his fabulous treasure'.[3]

BUSSENTO, BUSENTO, BUXENTUM

However, there are important facts strongly suggesting that the river basin to explore for the grave of Alaric is that of the Busento near Cosenza or another river near Cosenza erroneously identified as the Busento, and not the Bussento in Cilento. Indeed, based on sources that may have included Cassiodorus, Jordanes clearly indicated the Busento near Cosenza as the area concealing the famous tomb, after noting that Bruttii was the setting:

Then turning from its course the river Busentus near the city of Cosentia – for this stream flows with its wholesome waters from the foot of a

mountain near that city – they led a band of captives into the midst of its
bed to dig out a place for his grave.[4]

Now, we know that the Busento near Cosenza is a short river that has
only local importance. The Bussento in Cilento is situated approximately
75 miles (120km) further north from Cosenza, has a winding course and is
twice as long as the Busento of Cosenza. Theoretically, a mix-up between
the two rivers might be possible, in spite of the considerable distance
between them.

However, Jordanes did not mention only Bruttii and Busento, but added
that the river he was talking about, the Busentus (Busento), was located
near Cosenza. His brief introduction to Bruttii (Chapter Six) and his
mention that the river of interest was the Busento near Cosenza, suggest
that Jordanes or his source possessed a good knowledge of Bruttii
geography. This brings to mind the learned Cassiodorus, a local who lived
many years in the area and held important positions in the administration
of Ostrogothic Italy, including at Lucania et Bruttii.

Indeed, in approximately 501, Theodoric the Great appointed
Cassiodorus' father governor of Lucania et Bruttii, his native province, as a
reward for his loyalty.[5] The Cassiodorus of interest to us, the son of the one
discussed above, was appointed *consiliarius* (adviser) to his father while still
very young, when his father was the governor of Lucania et Bruttii, which
contained both the Busento near today's Cosenza and the Bussento in today's
Cilento. Cassiodorus' letters illustrate his intimate knowledge of Bruttii.[6]

It is quite conceivable that Jordanes faithfully followed Cassiodorus and
indicated that the river of Alaric's burial was the Busento near Cosenza.
The description given by Jordanes fits very well with the rather short and
straight stream of the Busento as it flows near Cosenza, as the traveller will
realise if he takes a walk along its shores. Moreover, the description left by
Jordanes does not bring to mind the Bussento in Cilento, a winding river
flowing among the most spectacular karstic formations in southern Italy.
Indeed, there is no mention of such limestone marvels in Jordanes'
presentation of Busento. Furthermore, if Jordanes lived in Crotone, he
might well have had the opportunity to travel to Cosenza and see the
Busento with his own eyes.

Philostorgius briefly mentioned that Alaric died in Campania, as
indicated earlier. The *Barrington Atlas* map-by-map directory does not

include any other river with a name similar to Busento or Bussento for the Roman province of Latium-Campania.[7] The same atlas directory features a river named Casuentus (today's Basento) that ends in the Gulf of Tarentum (today's Taranto) just south of Metapontum (today's Metaponto), located on the roof of the arch of the foot of Italy, but this river was part of another Roman district neighbouring Bruttii (Tarentum). Nowadays, the Bussento of Cilento is part of the Italian province of Campania.

What is clear, however, is that the hypotheses we have discussed do not shed much light on the real location of Alaric's tomb. As we saw earlier, many people – both local and foreign – have tried and failed to find Alaric's tomb in the three centuries in which it has been actively sought. From the eighteenth-century treasure hunters through the Victorian Romantics to the Nazis, many have tried and failed to find Alaric's grave. Only at the end of the twentieth century would anyone seem to begin to draw near again and close in on Alaric's tomb.

SEVENTEEN

In Search of Alaric's Treasure

Far from the totalitarian nightmare depicted in George Orwell's famous novel, the year 1984 brought a turning point in history. In the former USSR, Yuri Andropov, successor to Leonid Brezhnev, died and was replaced by the old and sickly looking Konstantin Chernenko. He would die one year later and be replaced by Mikhail Gorbachev, a man who made history with his reformist policies at home and *rapprochement* in his country's relations with the United States.

There were other memorable events in 1984. On 18 February Roman Catholicism ceased to be Italy's state religion, as a result of an agreement brokered between the Italian government and the Vatican and signed by Italy's first socialist prime minister, Bettino Craxi, and Cardinal Agostino Casaroli. This crucial event, signalling the end of an era in the history of Christianity, has passed largely unnoticed.

Pope John Paul II said goodbye to the last link, albeit a symbolic one, with political power in Italy (Roman Catholicism continues to be the state religion in many other countries) in February 1984 in Rome. That same year the name of Alaric – the symbol of the fall of the Roman Empire in the West, and the Germanic leader who gave the popes the opportunity to enter secular politics in 409 – came again to the attention of Europe and the world. One is left with the nagging feeling that something has come full circle.

Still in 1984, during Craxi's first stint as prime minister (sentenced in absentia on charges of corruption, Craxi died in 2000 in Tunisia, the motherland of the ninth-century Muslim violators of the tombs of St Peter and St Paul), the construction of the Mosque of Rome began in the very bishopric of the pope, about 3 miles (5km) north-east of St Peter's tomb.[1] Saudi Arabia, which is home to the tomb of the Prophet Mohammed and to the Muslims that manage the Mosque of Rome, does not permit Christians to build churches on its territory.[2, 3]

After the end of the Second World War, there had been a few attempts to find the royal grave of Alaric, such as that of Adolfo Greco and Giuseppe Belfiore. Then, in 1968, Vincenzo Astorino announced that Alaric's rich burial place might be under the floor of the little church of St Pancratius (San Pancrazio), which stands on the banks of the Busento. He based his hypothesis on observations made by the sixteenth-century Cosentine astrologer Rutilio Benincasa. But these were isolated cases of Alaric fever. A new, full-blown epidemic would only start in 1984, with the Vadue discovery.

In that year, it was announced that vestiges of constructions dating back to the fifth century and located along the stream called the Caronte near Vadue might have formed part of the ancient tomb of Alaric. Vadue is situated a few kilometres south of Cosenza, which Himmler himself visited in 1937. The Caronte is a tributary of the north-flowing Busento and merges with the latter at a point some 1,640ft (500m) from where another stream, the Iassa, also joins the Busento. Almost as had happened in 1937, the people of Cosenza were again swept up in a wave of exhilarating anticipation and wanted to believe that, this time, it was the real thing and Cosenza and its surroundings were destined to become the focus of a huge tourism boom.[4]

With lightning speed, on Monday 2 April 1984, the international press spread the news that, at last, the tomb of Alaric had been found. The grave measured around 8ft (2½m) high, 19½ft (6m) long and 10ft (3m) wide. The German tabloids announced the discovery with large-type headlines on their front pages. The local police in Cosenza cordoned off the area where the grave had been found. The excitement was palpable, at least for a time. The traditional newspapers were much more cautious.

The professional archaeologists invited to examine the site were rather sceptical. As we have seen, since the first systematic excavations under the leadership of Ettore Capecelatro in the eighteenth century, looking for Alaric's treasure has been a popular pastime in the Cosenza area and everyone, from regional leaders to the Nazi elite, has come in search of the barbarian king's hoard. None had found it so far, and the archaeologists did not think it had been found now. The experts determined that this grave dated back only to the eighth or ninth century AD, to the disappointment of many.[5] Other sources indicate that, in the opinion of the experts, the vestiges were of reinforcements built to protect a rocky wall in the 1800s.[6]

A gigantic sigh of disappointment travelled back and forth across the Alps. But the spread of Alaric fever was impossible to stop from then on.

WHAT IS BURIED IN ALARIC'S TOMB?

On 25 February 1986 Alan Hamilton published an article in *The Times* about the world's still-unfound archaeological treasures. The article mentioned that Colin Renfrew, Disney Professor of Archaeology at Cambridge University, had no doubts about the future of his subject. Hamilton's article also discussed the opinions of Paul Bahn, a freelance archaeologist and writer from Hull in Britain, about the prospects of archaeology. In addition, Hamilton presented a list of the discoveries which contemporary archaeologists hope to make. When discussing Italy, the article mentioned Alaric's tomb and the amazing treasure buried with the dead king: 'He may have by his side the great seven-branch candlestick from Solomon's temple in Jerusalem, carried off by the Romans and subsequently seized by the Goths.'[7]

For generations, Jews everywhere have hoped that perhaps the famous great Menorah will be retrieved one day, although some of them are quite sceptical about this and believe that the Menorah was probably melted down into bullion a long time ago. There is, however, the tantalising possibility that this great religious piece remains whole and concealed with the great Visigothic king.

BUT IS THE TEMPLE TREASURE REALLY THERE?

Of course, the Goths might not have buried the Menorah with Alaric. Perhaps they thought it too valuable to bury, or not valuable enough. Some people believe the Goths kept the Menorah with them. They believe that the booty left in the hands of the Goths after Alaric's burial remained intact long after he was laid to rest.

On 18 January 1996, the *Jerusalem Post* made it known that Shimon Shetreet, the Israeli Religious Affairs Minister, had announced that Pope John Paul II was likely to visit Jerusalem in 1997 as a religious pilgrim and promoter of peace.

Shetreet also reported that he had personally asked the pope to help Israel find the gold Menorah from the Jerusalem Temple that was carried to

Rome by the victorious Titus in AD 70. Shetreet made the surprising statement that recent research at the University of Florence had suggested that the precious item might be found among the treasures concealed in the catacombs of the Vatican. This story died out very fast. The Italian research that Shetreet mentioned does not seem readily available to the public.

Other anecdotal titbits in circulation place the Menorah in the Tiber or under the Arch of Titus. The fact is that the whereabouts of the Menorah remain a mystery, but there are some intriguing clues in the writings of ancient authors.

Procopius described a major battle between the Franks, whom he called Germans, and the Visigoths, who at that time inhabited south-western Gaul in the area of Toulouse. King Clovis led the Franks. Alaric II (484–507), probable great-grandson of Alaric I, conqueror of Rome, and son-in-law of Theodoric the Great, was king of the Visigothic realm of Toulouse.[8] Though Procopius places the battle near Carcasiana (now Carcassonne), in fact, the confrontation took place at Vouillé near Poitiers in 507.[9]

Procopius related that the Franks, who did not fear the might of Theodoric the Great, began marching on the Visigothic lands. As expected, Alaric II requested urgent help from his father-in-law. Under pressure from his impatient people, Alaric II agreed to engage his army in pitched battle before Ostrogothic aid arrived. At Vouillé near Poitiers, and not near Carcasiana, the Visigoths suffered a disastrous defeat and Alaric II was killed in combat, reportedly by Clovis.

In the wake of their victory, the Franks occupied a large part of Gaul. According to Procopius, they energetically besieged Carcasiana, as they had learned that the royal Visigothic riches, seized by Alaric I during the sack of Rome in 410, were in that city. Procopius explicitly noted that the riches of Solomon, king of the Hebrews, looted by the Romans in AD 70, were in Carcasiana.

The Visigoths elected Giselic, an illegitimate son of Alaric II, as king, because Amalaric, the legitimate heir, was still a minor.

Finally, the Ostrogothic army arrived and the Franks broke off the siege of Carcasiana, but held on to the territory west of the River Rhône. Theodoric the Great installed his grandson Amalaric as king of the lands still under Visigothic control, with himself as regent.

Procopius then related that Theodoric the Great 'took all the money that lay in the city of Carcasiana' and returned to Ravenna, his capital in Italy.[10]

The account by Procopius seems to indicate that the Franks failed to capture the treasure of Solomon believed to be stored in Carcassonne. It is not clear whether Theodoric's troops entered Carcassonne immediately after the Franks left, or if there was a brief interlude during which the Visigoths may have had enough time to carry off or hide the treasure of Solomon. Of note is the fact that Procopius wrote that Theodoric had taken all the money he found in Carcassonne, but did not specify that Theodoric had taken possession of the Visigothic royal treasure and the riches of Solomon.

Looking at a map of today's France, it is easy to see that all the towns mentioned by Gregory of Tours still exist. Thus, we can trace the movements of the Franks in their war with the Visigothic kingdom of Toulouse. After the battle of Vouillé, Clovis moved south and then veered south-west to Bordeaux, where he remained for the winter. He then marched south-east to Toulouse, the capital of the Visigothic kingdom and, according to Gregory of Tours, captured all the treasure of the late Alaric II, i.e. the Visigothic treasure.

If we re-examine the map of modern France, we notice that, compared to the cities mentioned earlier, Carcassonne is very far south. Thus, Carcassonne may have been the site of one of the final desperate acts of resistance put up by the Visigoths following their disastrous defeat at Vouillé. In other words, there may have been a Frankish siege of Carcassonne in the final stages of the war, although the decisive battle had taken place much further to the north, at Vouillé, and not in the vicinity of Carcassonne. In addition, it is perfectly possible that Theodoric the Ostrogoth, who marched on southern France from Italy, arrived too late to take part in the crucial battle of Vouillé, but in time to rescue the Visigoths defending Carcassonne. Interestingly, Gregory of Tours did not mention the failure of the Franks to take Carcassonne. His account of the Frankish–Visigothic war of 507 seems to imply that Clovis removed the entire treasure of Alaric II from Toulouse.

THE ENIGMA OF PROCOPIUS

In another volume of his *History of the Wars*, Procopius seems to contradict his own account that the Visigoths had the riches of Solomon in their possession.

Procopius, a lawyer, had accompanied General Belisarius as legal adviser and secretary in the expedition against the African Vandals in 533 and therefore had been in a very good position to collect information regarding the treasures captured by Belisarius' soldiers.[11]

Procopius related that Belisarius had been given a triumph like those reserved for victorious emperors and generals in the olden times of Roman glory. The Byzantine historian narrated that Belisarius had headed a procession throughout the city and had exhibited the booty and prisoners of war in the heart of Constantinople, so thousands of people must have seen them.

The Vandalic royal treasure was among the riches exhibited and it included 'the treasure of the Jews, which Titus, the son of Vespasian, together with certain others, had brought to Rome after the capture of Jerusalem'. Then Procopius narrated that a Jew, who had noticed the sacred objects of the Jerusalem Temple, commented to someone close to the emperor that they belonged to where King Solomon had placed them and that those who had them in their palaces, i.e. the Romans and the Vandals, saw their rule end at the hands of enemy armies. When he learned of the Jew's ominous remarks, Justinian was reported to have become apprehensive about having Solomon's treasure in Constantinople and sent it to the 'sanctuaries of the Christians in Jerusalem'. It is not clear which Christian sanctuaries Procopius meant.[12]

The contradiction between Procopius' two accounts of the fate of the Temple treasure has long puzzled historians. It would be extremely difficult to assume that Procopius made up the story of the Temple riches being captured from the Vandals and displayed in the middle of Constantinople, as many of his readers would have witnessed the triumph of Belisarius for themselves.

MODERN VIEWS ON THE FATE OF THE TEMPLE TREASURE

Gregorovius narrates that although the Temple of Peace was damaged by the fire of Commodus in 192, the authorities had enough time to transfer the Jerusalem Temple treasure to an unidentified location, where it was kept for some considerable time. He believed that part of the Jewish ritual furnishings ended up in the hands of Alaric in 410, but that the sacred objects left behind by the Visigoths were carried by Gaiseric to Carthage, as reported by Procopius.[13]

Modern-day historians have also shown an interest in this famous treasure. Gatto suggests that part of the Temple treasure captured from the

Vandals may have ended up in the hands of the Arabs who conquered Jerusalem in 638. Eventually, it fell into the hands of the Crusaders who placed it in one of the Christian churches of Jerusalem. After the Crusades, very little was found of the treasure sent by Justinian to Jerusalem, so it was proposed that the treasure had fallen into Arab hands or those of the Crusaders, or even that the treasure itself was merely the stuff of legend.

Given the testimony of Procopius, who had himself participated in Belisarius' African campaign in 533 and who reports that the Jewish treasure was publicly displayed in Constantinople the next year, probably means that the treasure was real. In this context, the events surrounding the Persian invasion of Jerusalem in 614 may be one avenue of research that could fruitfully be explored.[14]

We have seen how, during the reign of Theodoric the Great, Zacharias of Mytilene penned an intriguing portrayal of Rome in the early years of the sixth century.[15] We noted then that Zacharias specifically mentioned '25 bronze statues of Abraham, Sarah, and Hagar, and of the kings of the house of David, which Vespasian the king brought up when he sacked Jerusalem, and the gates of Jerusalem and other bronze objects'.[16]

Josephus Flavius tells us that there was a total of ten external gates to the Temple of Jerusalem that were destroyed by the Romans in AD 70: four on the north side, four on the south side, and two on the east side. Nine of these gates were covered in gold and silver. Each gate had two doors some 49ft (15m) high and about 25ft (7.5m) wide. The jambs of the doors and the lintels were also covered in gold and silver.

The tenth external gate, which stood on the east side on the Temple's long axis and faced the grand interior gate leading to the Holy House itself, was made of Corinthian brass. This much larger and more beautiful gate was some 82ft (25m) high and 66ft (20m) wide. Its panels of gold and silver were much heavier than those decorating the other gates and, as a result, this gate surpassed the others in splendour. The Temple courts were built on terraces connected by steps. For instance, the worshippers had to climb twelve steps to reach the level of the Holy House. The latter's westernmost room, the Holy of Holies, was the most sacred area of the Temple.

Amazingly, the interior gateway leading to the Holy House exceeded the dimensions of the beautiful eastern Corinthian gate. This progressive increase in size overwhelmed the advancing worshipper. The gate leading to the Holy House was about 115ft (35m) high and 41ft (12½m) wide. It had no doors because it symbolised the total visibility of heaven and was entirely overlaid with gold, as was the wall around it. Through this magnificent gate adorned with golden vines and clusters of golden grapes reaching to the height of a man, the worshippers could see the front of the Holy House which was around 148ft (45m) in height, 82ft (25m) in length and 33ft (10m) in width. The façade of the Holy House was completely covered in gold and, when illuminated by the rays of the rising sun, shone with extraordinary splendour.[17]

Gregorovius also noted the statues and the gates listed by Zacharias as treasures housed in Rome. According to Gregorovius, a medieval Roman tradition claimed that the Basilica of St John in Lateran still sheltered 'the Sacred Ark of the Covenant, the Tables of the Law, the Golden Candlesticks, the Tabernacle, and the priestly vestments of Aaron'.[18]

According to Wolfram, the royal Visigothic treasure in Toulouse included 'the riches of Rome and Jerusalem'[19] and a large fraction of this Visigothic royal treasure did not fall into the hands of the victorious Franks.[20]

In support of his opinion, Wolfram cited a review article published by Dietrich Claude. This contribution to the history of the royal treasures of the early Middle Ages contains an important piece of evidence which forms the basis for Wolfram's view. Claude presented the details of Procopius' contradictory accounts on the fate of the Jerusalem treasure, and then expressed his opinion that it was more probable that Alaric I had captured it in 410. In support of his thesis, Claude relied on the reports of an Arab historian, Ben Qutaiba, which indicate that when the Arabs took Toledo in 711, they had found a golden table identified as the table of Solomon.

Ancient Christians and Muslims seemed interested in stressing their possession of parts of the Jerusalem Temple treasure, as if this would have bestowed upon them at least some of the prestige of the much older Judaism. However, Claude did comment that the solution to the puzzling controversy left to posterity by Procopius was still undecided.[21] The legendary table of King Solomon was among the presents sent by the Caliph Haroun Al-Raschid to the king of Serendib through Sindbad the Sailor.[22]

As we have seen, there are historians who have opted for the Alaric I–Alaric II (Visigothic) hypothesis. However, there are others who have opted for the Gaiseric–Belisarius (Vandal–Byzantine) hypothesis.[23]

A footnote in H.B. Dewing's translation of Procopius' *History of the Wars* proposes a very simple solution to this enigma.[24] According to this source, the Visigothic royal treasure captured in Rome by Alaric I in 410 and believed by the Franks to be inside the city of Carcasiana, did include the treasure of the Jerusalem Temple seized by the Romans of Titus in AD 70. This footnote assumes that in 410 Alaric I seized only a part of the Jewish treasure stored in Rome, and what was left of it was taken by the Vandals of Gaiseric in 455 when they sacked the eternal city themselves; then Gaiseric carried to North Africa this second part of the Jewish treasure, which in the end fell into the hands of General Belisarius seventy-eight years later. As mentioned earlier, this explanation was already put forward by Gregorovius in the second half of the nineteenth century.[25] This very old and captivating mystery is still unresolved.

However, it seems most likely that at least part of Alaric's treasure would have been buried with him, so to seek the Visigothic king's treasure we must seek out Alaric himself. For several Italians, Alaric has already been found.

EIGHTEEN

Closing in on Alaric's Grave

The year 1989 went down in history as one of dramatic changes that affected the lives of billions of people. Who can forget the heroic Chinese students demonstrating for democracy in Tiananmen Square, or the Romanian Revolution, which began in the city of Timişoara, the first European Communist Bloc uprising that the world was able to follow step by step on their television screens? This revolution toppled the dictator Nicolae Ceauşescu, an uneducated, cunning and ruthless Romanian peasant who was the darling of American presidents and even Queen Elizabeth II, and who caused such immense indignity and suffering to his people. Alaric himself had been born in what is now Romania in the Danube Delta 1,600 years earlier.

Only a matter of weeks before Romania's revolution, the Berlin Wall had fallen. Alaric's distant descendants had seized the opportunity given to them by the presence of Mikhail Gorbachev at the helm of the Soviet Union. Probably based on the events of the previous weeks, the German people had anticipated that the engines of the Soviet tanks would remain silent and the East German border guards would no longer open fire, so they began crossing the accursed Berlin Wall, initially in small, scattered groups, then as an unstoppable human flood. And the engines of the Soviet tanks did remain silent, and the East German Communist border guards did not fire a shot. The Cold War and the European Communist Bloc were dead.

And Alaric, who seems very keen to be around whenever the world is shaken by momentous events, was back in the news again.

THE DISCOVERY OF A LIFETIME

According to Fioriglio, in 1986 Vincenzo Rizzo, a research geologist at CNR (Consiglio Nazionale delle Ricerche – the National Council for

Research) had chosen to ignore the words of Jordanes and the almost 1,600-year-old tradition, and had proposed the hypothesis that Alaric's tomb was located in a tumulus (dome-like mound) situated on the right-hand bank of the River Crati in the locality of Cozzo Torre, part of the town of Bisignano, which is about 16 miles (25km) north of Cosenza. Rizzo was cooperating with CNR's Gruppo Italiano di Geomorfologia (the Italian Group of Geomorphology) and had the support of its president, Mario Panizza. The publicity was intense, perhaps fuelled by the hope of a tourism boom in the area. In June 1993 there was even an international convention dedicated to the archaeology of tumuli, with the participation of Bulgarian, Greek and Italian archaeologists. To date, no excavations have been performed at this site.[1]

Our review of Gothic burials (see Chapter One) did not identify the tumulus as a grave type used by the Goths before the crossing of the Danube in 376. Examining the interment practice of the Visigoths in Spain, there seems to be no mention of tumulus burials there either.[2]

Still in 1986, the Swedish amateur archaeologist Eric Furugard claimed that, in his reading of Jordanes, the latter actually refers to the little valley of Piedimonte, a precise spot with a little creek that flows near Busento. According to Furugard, Jordanes also related that the tomb was covered with a pile of earth that resembled a small hill, and that he identified the little hill in August 1986. Jordanes' text does not seem to include anything that would allow such a precise identification of a little creek flowing by the Busento, not to mention the fact that Jordanes does not seem to say anything about a mound piled on top of the tomb. The presence of such a mound would be difficult to reconcile with the location of the tomb in the middle of the riverbed of Busento indicated by Jordanes. No excavations were carried out at the site brought to attention by Furugard.

In 1989, other amateur archaeologists singled out a tumulus in Piè di Monte (Domanico) and actually dug it up, but not very methodically. They found nothing. Thus, in three years, there had been three claims that different tumulus-like mounds might hide the tomb of Alaric.

But some amateur archaeologists find sites that capture the public imagination more than others. Indeed, in 1989, according to the Italian magazine *Panorama*, the brothers Natale and Francesco Bosco, and their brother-in-law Massimo Nalio, all from the city of Cosenza, Calabria, found a cross of impressive dimensions, carved on a large rock[3] that was situated on a private property in Mendicino, a town south of Cosenza and slightly west of the famous River Busento.

Panorama also reported that the rocky outcrop is located in a place called Rigardi, a name that, according to the amateur archaeologists from Cosenza, is of Germanic origin and might be translated as 'look at or observe with respect'. They noted that in front of the rock with the cross, at some distance on the other side of a little stream, in fact the confluence of the streams Alimena and Caronte, there was another rocky outcrop containing two caves. In one they found something that looked like an altar. The three men – a supermarket employee, a bank employee and an insurance clerk – reportedly believe that the tomb of Alaric may be under the sand visible inside the cave. They observed that there were large quantities of sand in the area of the rocky outcrop and that the ground of the cave containing the altar looked as though it had been excavated, and then filled with sand taken from the bed of the nearby stream.[4]

It was reported that the second cave also contained sand. According to the Italian newspaper *La Repubblica*,[5] in its issue of 14 May 2001, the amateur archaeologists thought that the appearance of this second cave suggested that it had been used somehow in the process of digging the grave.

The accounts of the Bosco brothers and Massimo Nalio seem to suggest the possibility that Alaric was placed in a grave near a river and was then covered with sand dug up from the bed of that river or from its banks, which might have led people to believe that he was buried under a river. Such a belief might have been the basis for the story of Alaric's burial as we know it from Jordanes.

In the opinion of the amateur archaeologists from Cosenza, all these features, as well as the presence of the large cross on the rock located on the other side of the stream, make the site a strong candidate for professional archaeological excavation. However, the Servizio Geologico Nazionale has not confirmed that the sand in the cave came from the nearby little river.[6]

In 1996, it was suggested that the tomb of Alaric might be in a cave located under a pseudo-Roman nympheum, an area that included a pleasing arrangement of a fountain, statues and flowers, dating back to the 1700s. This cave is situated in the vicinity of Carolei near the stream called Iassa. Investigations at the site drew a blank.

Examining the cross discovered by the Bosco brothers and the terrain facing it, Tonino Cicala, a Cosentine scholar, formulated his own hypothesis in 1998. According to Cicala, if the Visigoths buried Alaric under the bed of the Caronte (in the past called Vasientu), the cross should have indicated to the diggers the exact location of the tomb. On one hand, the cross on the rocky outcrop was a Christian symbol; on the other, it functioned as a topographical device indicating the exact location of the grave. Roughly, the cross seems to point in the direction of the Caronte stream. Just above the Caronte there was an ancient road and there are many caves, most of which have yet to be explored. One of these caves might have opened under the riverbed. Cicala noted that the cross stands on a place called Regardu (finish, limit). In Cicala's interpretation, this would mean that the cross aims from a point, Regardu, at a target represented by the confluence of the stream Alimena (*ad limes*) with the Caronte (Vasientu). Cicala's hypothesis has yet to be tested, but he believes that De Felici's short story *The Hermit of Vasientu* backs it up. He cites additional supporting evidence provided by certain Germanic names in the area, possible traces of the Goths who were left behind to guard Alaric's tomb and treasure.[7]

However, Domenico Canino, another Cosentine scholar, has very different things to say about this much talked-about spot. In his opinion, published in 1999, the area abounds in Byzantine vestiges, while no remains from the late imperial-barbarian period have been found. He does not think that the cross on the rocky spur is a Christian sacred symbol, only some sort of marker.[8]

Again in 1999, the Bosco brothers expressed their view that Alaric's grave was in the two caves located near the Caronte opposite the cross, visible from afar. According to them, the Visigoths had beliefs based on a form of nature worship, especially of rocks, water and trees. In the brothers' interpretation, the cross incised on the rock is not a Christian symbol, but a representation of the sun.[9]

We know now that Jordanes did not locate the burial of Alaric at the confluence of two streams, but because of that old tradition, that is the kind of setting Italian treasure hunters have sought out in the past. The new site brought to the attention of the public by the Bosco brothers is also found at the confluence of two streams, but not of the Busento and Crati, as the tradition has maintained for centuries, but at the confluence of the stream Caronte (possibly called Acheron[10] in antiquity), a tributary of the Busento, and of the Canalicchio, seemingly also called Alimena.

Fioriglio believes that the burial took place somewhere along the urban portion of the river, not far from the legendary confluence of the Busento and Crati. He also states that the riverbed was wider at the time of the burial and probably included an area subsequently built upon.[11] This would mean that some Cosentine buildings might stand on top of a fabulous treasure.

To reach the area of interest to the Bosco brothers, one has to go south up the Busento, past the bridge of Carolei, where there is a Roman viaduct on the Caronte, and where the local old folk believe lies a treasure hidden by brigands. It has been speculated that while sailing in the direction of Sicily, the Visigoths made a stop in Amantea (the Clampetia[12] of antiquity), having been driven to seek the shelter of land by a tempest at sea, and then marched up into the mountains to reach Cosenza, the capital of Bruttii. Supposedly, this is how they arrived at the spot the Bosco brothers favour, which would have been a location less visible to the people of Cosenza.

There are problems with this hypothesis. Jordanes related that Alaric died after the Visigoths' unsuccessful attempt to cross the Straits of Messina, and most writers, including Wolfram, an authority on Gothic history, accept his account, which would preclude a Visigothic maritime expedition sailing south by the western shore of Italy.[13] The Visigoths were less likely to opt for a maritime trip when they had free access to the reliable Roman roads leading all the way to Rhegium. Thus, the Via Latina led directly from Rome to Capua and Nola, which they managed to take and plunder. A short detour south from Via Latina could take the Visigoths to Naples, which they failed to conquer.

South of the three cities mentioned above – at Nuceria Alfaterna (today's Nocera) – the Via Appia and Via Latina converged.[14] The resulting road split in two again just south of Salernum (today's Salerno). One of these two roads kept close to the coast of the Tyrrhenian Sea. The second one ran inland and further east, under the name of Via Poppilia. Cosentia (today's Cosenza) is situated on Via Poppilia.

Interestingly, Via Poppilia and the road that followed the Tyrrhenian coast joined again near Terina[15] (today's S. Eufemia Vetere[16]). The road thus formed continued under the name of Via Popilia, the most important

route in Lucania et Bruttii, all the way to Rhegium. The total distance from
Capua to Reggio di Calabria was 321 Roman miles (295 English miles or
475km).

It seems more likely that the Visigoths marched on these dependable
Roman roads than that they took the risks associated with the open sea.

A GRAVE MARKER?

But, as we have seen, the amateur archaeologists who claimed to have
found Alaric's tomb also reported the discovery of a large cross. Cicala
seems to believe it really is a Christian cross. Did the Visigoths use the cross
at that very early stage of their Christianity? We do know that their
imperial captive, Galla Placidia, possessed a silver cross, decorated with an
enamel portrait of an aristocratic woman and two children. This cross is
now in the possession of the Christian Civic Museum of Brescia, Italy.[17]
Does this mean that her captors also used the Christian cross? It is known
that the Visigoths used pendant and processional Christian crosses[18] in the
seventh century while they were living in and ruling Spain, but those expert
in Visigothic history such as Schwarcz have not specified whether the
Visigoths were marking with Christian crosses the burial places of their
dead at the beginning of the fifth century.[19]

Cicala's cross, aiming at the presumed location of the grave of Alaric, is
reminiscent of Dan Brown's pointing angels in his *Angels and Demons*.
While in Dan Brown's thriller the pointing angels served a precise role in
the plot, in the real world of the Germanic tribesmen interring their king
with treasures, the main concern would have been how to make the tomb
inaccessible and completely secret, not to leave clues for posterity as to its
whereabouts. Why would they give anybody even the slightest chance to
desecrate and plunder the grave of their beloved king?

The presence of the cross at the site publicised by the Bosco brothers, if
the cross was indeed carved around the time of the burial, and assuming
that there was a burial somewhere there associated with the cross, would
indicate that the burial was not a secret one. There remains the possibility
that the burial place was secret for a certain period, but later it became
known to other people, perhaps Goths themselves, who might have left the
altar in the cave, if it is truly a Gothic altar, and carved the cross in the
rocky outcrop discovered by the amateur archaeologists from Cosenza.

However, some think that what appears to be a cross is merely the result of naturally occurring cracks.[20]

In this context, it is interesting to mention here a strange decree issued by Theodoric the Great. Dietrich Claude concluded that gold was important for the more durable and powerful Germanic kingdoms of the Franks, Visigoths, Vandals and Lombards, as well as for the short-lived kingdoms of the Gepids and Spanish Suevians. Almost all of these Germanic kings had royal treasures.[21]

Theodoric was no exception. His hunger for gold is well documented. Burns tells us that he kept a private account called the *patrimonium*, a Latin word meaning inheritance or inherited estate. The *patrimonium* gobbled up imperial lands and absorbed additional revenue sources, such as taxes from remote regions of the kingdom, inheritances, donations, and seized possessions. Some of the officials who were responsible for it were Goths.[22] During the reign of Amalasuntha, Theodoric's daughter, the royal treasure of the Ostrogoths amounted to around 40,000lb (18,000kg) of gold.[23]

Theodoric the Great, through his trusted adviser Cassiodorus, the Roman who wrote many of his decrees and letters, issued an order that forbade the Goths under his rule to practise the pre-Christian tradition of interring valuables with their dead, a custom that contravened Christian teachings about the afterlife and was economically irrational.[24] This tradition was probably practised by the Visigoths as well, in their realm in Gaul. The most unusual part of the decree was Theodoric's order that his Gothic officials (*saiones*) retrieve the precious metals from the graves of the Goths.

Did Theodoric the Great learn from his Spanish Visigothic subjects and/or relatives (see Appendix One, p. 201) the location of Alaric's grave? And if so, did his *saiones* find it, with or without additional help from Cassiodorus? And if they found it, did they unearth the treasures of Alaric, under the pretext of the royal decree discussed above, and leave an altar and a cross at the site? We do not have an answer to these questions.

But when they buried Alaric I with treasures, the members of the Balthi clan probably did not think that they were ever going to return to Italy or that they were going to be related, after three generations, to another Goth who was going to be the king of Italy.

The idea that the Visigoths left behind a number of their people to guard the tomb of Alaric cannot be reconciled with the movements of the

Visigoths in the following years, the secret nature of the burial, and the potential hostility of the Roman authorities and population towards any small groups of Goths remaining in Cosenza.

Other scenarios might also be plausible in this context, such as the obvious: Theodoric the Great might have retained the treasure of Alaric I for himself, had he found it. His sycophantic scribes did not record such desecration of Alaric's tomb. While this certainly does not rule it out, it seems a bit too much even for someone with the reputation of Theodoric the Great.

One local tradition about the fate of the treasure of Alaric claims that the Arabs, who were in the area for a while in the Middle Ages, found it. According to another, a rich local family owning land on the shores of the Busento dug up the treasure a long time ago. Finally, one legend still in circulation has it that some German officers found it using a humble metal detector during their retreat in 1943.[25]

CONTROVERSY AT ALARIC'S SUPPOSED GRAVE

Whatever the case, the amateurs working in Cosenza seemed sure they had finally discovered the last resting place of Alaric, and were determined to prove that the grave they had found was that of the barbarian king. They were sure their discovery was the find of a lifetime. But according to *La Repubblica*, Natale Bosco lamented that the officials from Reggio Calabria's Archaeological Superintendent's Office had dismissed these findings as unimportant. *La Repubblica* went on to report that the amateur archaeologists also complained that the Archaeological Superintendent's Office had 'occupied' the terrain in question for four months without conducting a proper investigation of the site.

In addition, the same newspaper reported that the Superintendent from Rome, S. La Regina, delegated as inspector representing the Ministry, allegedly acknowledged the archaeological interest of the site and indicated that if there was a sponsor, the excavations could go ahead. The Bosco brothers submitted an application for a concession, but by the time *La Repubblica* had come across the story and published it its outcome was not known.

Eventually, *La Repubblica* noted, they took the matter to a judge, requesting the appointment of an expert to provide a final ruling on the situation. The Italian newspaper also reported that in the meantime, Mario Serio, Director General of the Ministry of Cultural Properties, had requested an assessment of the matter from Elena Latanzi, the Superintendent of Archaeology for Calabria.[26]

In 2002, *Panorama*[27] indicated that, following the reports made by the amateur archaeologists, various experts had visited the Mendicino site, including Giuseppe Roma from the Department of Archaeology and Art History of the University of Calabria. He purportedly determined that there was nothing of interest on the site found by the three amateur archaeologists. This would not be unusual. Professional archaeologists everywhere are frequently forced to conclude that the hopes of their amateur counterparts are unfounded.

But there was an unexpected twist to this story, according to *Panorama*. Soon afterwards, the Bosco brothers found out that Luigi Cirillo, a colleague of Professor Roma and a historian specialising in early Christianity, bought the lot next to the site in question. According to *Panorama*, the brothers commenced a legal battle with the Office of the Superintendent for Archaeology, determined to achieve the initiation of archaeological excavations and, in case the results confirmed their theory, have their claim to the discovery officially recognised.

The matter ended up before a tribunal in Catanzaro. It was anticipated that an expert would give a verdict. *Panorama* observed that following the administrative elections of 26 May 2002, Professor Roma became a member of the Centrist–leftist council of the city of Cosenza and was appointed cultural councillor in charge of initiatives aimed at putting to work the myth of Alaric for the benefit of the community. As to the Mendicino site, *Panorama* indicated that Professor Roma maintained his position that there was nothing of interest there, and that the truly great archaeological event in Calabria was the discovery of some Lombard fortifications.

On 30 August 2002, the Belgian newspaper *Le Soir* announced that the Italian justice system had delegated an archaeologist to excavate the cave which, the three amateur archaeologists from Cosenza believe, is a treasure trove and the final resting place of the German who symbolises the fall of the Roman Empire. They hope that this excavation will finally prove the legends that surround Alaric and resolve for posterity the uncertainties of his life, death and burial.

Many people remain interested in this treasure story and Alaric's deeds because they yearn to witness greatness or at least its remains, and to come in contact, albeit indirectly, with crucial moments in history in order to understand them. Travelling in time in this way can provide a short-lived but thrilling illusion of immortality.

Nevertheless, the world must continue to wait and wonder whether his tomb has really been found and whether someone has, at last, come face to face with Alaric.

Epilogue

Past things shed light on future ones; the world was always of a kind; what is and will be was at some other time; the same things come back, but under different names and colors; not everybody recognizes them, but only he who is wise and considers them diligently.

Francesco Guicciardini, quoted in Luigi Barzini, *The Italians*, p. ix

Among the many things written about Alaric's death and burial, there are some that are more likely than others. These would include the fact that Alaric died unexpectedly near Cosenza before the end of the year 410 and was buried with treasures in the region of Cosenza, in keeping with the well-documented tradition of the Gothic elites. Gold and treasures played a major role in the early Germans' beliefs about the afterlife. They felt it was important to place gold in graves, as they thought that the precious metal could be of help in the next world, and not only during this life as a means to preserve wealth, achieve splendour, and mark one's position in the social pecking order. The fact that gold did not rust was probably an effective symbol of immortality for the early Germans. These beliefs may have contributed to their well-known gold lust, in which they clearly persisted in the early stages of Gothic Christianity.

Less certain was Alaric's burial under the Busento riverbed; there are historians and archaeologists who have expressed doubts about its veracity. Some have said that it would have been difficult for the Visigoths to divert the Busento. However, considering that the Busento is far from being a large river, it would have been possible to divert it using a sufficient number of captives. At any rate, it would have been easier to divert the Busento than the Tisza, as the nineteenth-century Hungarian tradition claims the Huns did to bury Attila. But then there is the problem of riverbed erosion, apparently a significant issue with the Busento and other local rivers in the area of Cosenza. Similarly, the killing of the gravediggers is unproven;

archaeologists tell us that mass killings of this type at the burial of tribal chiefs have not been documented in Europe. However, if the bodies of those sacrificed were thrown into the flowing waters to appease the river god, then one would not expect to find the remains of the gravediggers.

But we need not lock ourselves into the fixed, stubborn belief that Alaric was buried under a river. As the amateur Italian archaeologists have suggested, the tomb of Alaric may be somewhere in the basin of the River Busento near Cosenza, or perhaps in the basin of another local river mistakenly identified as the Busento, and not necessarily under a river. Right now the world must still await the excavation of the latest site marked as Alaric's grave to see if the Visigothic king has at last been found.

As I write, in 2006, the dig has not yet happened, and so long as Alaric's grave remains hidden, the mystery will continue. And so long as the mystery persists, future generations will continue to be drawn to the life of Alaric and the epic story of the cataclysmic fall of Rome that still echoes down the centuries as a warning of what could happen whenever civilisation retreats before barbarism.

APPENDIX ONE

Visigothic Kings

Alaric I (395–410)
Athaulf (410–15); buried Alaric I near Cosentia (Cosenza)
Valia (415–18)

KINGDOM OF TOULOUSE (SOUTHERN FRANCE)

Theoderid (418–51), son-in-law or son of Alaric I
Thorismund (451–3), grandson of Alaric I
Theodoric II (453–66), grandson of Alaric I
Euric (466–84), grandson of Alaric I (murdered his own brother, Theodoric II)
Alaric II (484–507), great-grandson of Alaric I; killed by Clovis in combat; his treasure was in danger of being captured by the Franks, but what happened to it remains unclear
Theodoric the Great (511–26), Ostrogothic king of Italy and father-in-law of Alaric II; also regent of the Visigoths after the death of Alaric II
Amalaric (526–31), son of Alaric II and grandson of Theodoric the Great; killed by Franks in Barcelona while trying to rescue his treasures
Theudis (531–48), former sword-bearer to Theodoric the Great

KINGDOM OF TOLEDO (SPAIN)

Leovigild, first king of the realm of Toledo (568–9)
Reccared, converted his Spanish Visigoths from Arianism to Catholicism (589); Spain thus Catholic to this day
The Arabs, vanquished the Visigoths and found amazing treasures (711)

APPENDIX TWO

A Chronology of Rome from 846[1]

846	Siege and sack by Muslim Arabs
896	Siege and conquest by German Holy Roman Emperor Arnulf of Carinthia
932	Siege by Germanic Burgundian Hugh of Provence (Vienne), king of Italy
936	Siege by Germanic Burgundian Hugh of Provence (Vienne), king of Italy
941	Siege by Germanic Burgundian Hugh of Provence (Vienne), king of Italy
963–6	Siege and sack by German Holy Roman Emperor Otto I
998	Siege by German Holy Roman Emperor Otto III
1081–4	Siege by German Holy Roman Emperor Henry IV
1084	Sack by Normans of Robert Guiscard
1167	Siege by German Holy Roman Emperor Frederick I 'Barbarossa' (Red Beard)
1241	Siege by German Holy Roman Emperor Frederick II
1312	Conquest by German Holy Roman Emperor Henry VI
1328	Conquest by German Holy Roman Emperor Ludwig (Louis) of Bavaria
1405	Siege by Ladislas (Ladislav) of Anjou, king of Naples and Hungary
1408	Siege and occupation by Ladislas (Ladislav) of Anjou, king of Naples and Hungary
1411	Siege by Ladislas (Ladislav) of Anjou, king of Naples and Hungary
1412	Siege and sack by Ladislas (Ladislav) of Anjou, king of Naples and Hungary
1417	Conquest by the *condottiere* (mercenary leader) Braccio Fortebraccio da Montone

1433–4	Siege by the *condottiere* Braccio Fortebraccio da Montone
1527	Siege, conquest and sack by troops of the Holy Roman Emperor Charles V
1798	French occupation
1809–14	French occupation
1849	Siege and occupation by the French
1870	Siege and occupation by the Italians
1943	Siege and occupation by the Germans

Notes

Introduction

1. Herwig Wolfram, *History of the Goths*, Berkeley, CA, 1990, pp. 158–60.
2. Jordanes, *The Origin and Deeds of the Goths*, trans. Charles C. Mierow, chap. 30, sections 157 and 158.
3. Alan Hamilton, 'Spectrum: Past with a rich future/The world's archaeological treasures yet to be uncovered', *The Times*, 25 February 1986.
4. www.goldsucher.de

Chapter One

1. *Claudian*, trans. Maurice Platnauer, Cambridge, MA, 1998. Vol. 2, II.XXVII.105.
2. Apollonius Rhodius, *Argonautica*, ed. and trans. R.C. Seaton, 303. Cambridge, MA, 1912.
3. Wolfram, *History of the Goths*, pp. 30–3.
4. Peter Heather, *The Goths*, Oxford, 2002, p. 99.
5. *Ibid.*, pp. 25–30.
6. *Ibid.*, p. 31.
7. 'Gothic language'. *Encyclopædia Britannica*. Retrieved 23 August 2003, from Encyclopædia Britannica Premium Service. www.britannica.com/eb/article?eu=38242
8. Tacitus, *La Germanie*, trans. Danielle De Clercq, Brussels, 2003, BK 27. 1.
9. Heather, *The Goths*, pp. 18–23.
10. *Ibid.*, p. 66.
11. *Ibid.*, p. 70.
12. Ammianus Marcellinus, *The Later Roman Empire (A.D. 354–378)*, selected and trans. Walter Hamilton, London, 2004. Book 16, 12.50.
13. Wolfram, *History of the Goths*, pp. 42–56.
14. Ammianus, *The Later Roman Empire*, Book 31, 7.7–7.14.
15. Andreas Schwarcz, 'Cult and religion among the Tervingi and the Visigoths and their conversion to Christianity', in P. Heather (ed.), *The Visigoths*, San Marino, 1999, pp. 448–50.
16. Wolfram, *History of the Goths*, p. 52.
17. Schwarcz, 'Cult and religion', p. 453.
18. *Ibid.*, pp. 454–5.
19. Eamon Duffy, *Saints and Sinners. A History of the Popes*, n.p., 1997, p. 46.

20. Gayla Visalli (ed.), *After Jesus. The Triumph of Christianity*, Pleasantville and Montreal, 1992, pp. 213–33.
21. Schwarcz, 'Cult and religion', p. 463.
22. 'Arius' in *Larousse Dictionary of World History*, Paris, 1995, p. 55.
23. Visalli (ed.), *After Jesus*, p. 220.
24. Tacitus, *La Germanie*, IX.1.
25. Jordanes, *The Origin and Deeds of the Goths*, V.41.
26. Schwarcz, 'Cult and religion', p. 450.
27. Paulus Orosius, *The Seven Books of History against the Pagans*, trans. Roy J. Deferrari, Washington, DC, 1981, VII, 37.
28. *Ibid.*
29. Procopius, *History of the Wars*, Volumes III (Books V–V.15), IV (Books VI.16–VII.35), and V (Books VII.36–VIII), trans. H.B. Dewing, Cambridge, MA, 2000, VI, 25.9.
30. Schwarcz, 'Cult and religion', p. 455.
31. *Ibid.*, pp. 448–55.
32. Peter Heather, 'The Creation of the Visigoths', in *The Visigoths*, ed. Peter Heather, San Marino, 1999, pp. 46–55.
33. Heather, *The Goths*, p. 147.

Chapter Two

1. Filippo Coarelli, *Roma*, Milan, 1994, pp. 25–35 and 366.
2. Claudio Rendina, *La grande guida dei monumenti di Roma*, Rome, 2002, p. 462.
3. Bertrand Lançon, *Rome in Late Antiquity*, New York, 2001, pp. 5–7.
4. Coarelli, *Roma*, pp. 25–35 and 366.
5. *Ibid.*
6. Ludovico Gatto, *Storia di Roma nel Medioevo*, Rome, 2003, p. 48.
7. Lançon, *Rome in Late Antiquity*, p. 45.
8. Andrew Wallace-Hadrill, *Ammianus Marcellinus. The Late Roman Empire*, introduction and notes, London, 1986, pp. 23–4.
9. Matthew Bunson, *A Dictionary of the Roman Empire*, New York, 1991, p. 345.
10. Lançon, *Rome in Late Antiquity*, pp. 76–80.
11. Francesco Scagnetti and Giuseppe Grande, *Colour Map of Imperial Rome*, Rome, 2005.
12. Lançon, *Rome in Late Antiquity*, pp. 76–80.
13. *Ibid.*, pp. 12–13.
14. Gatto, *Storia di Roma nel Medioevo*, p. 48.
15. Lançon, *Rome in Late Antiquity*, pp. 120–1.
16. Gatto, *Storia di Roma nel Medioevo*, pp. 120–1.
17. Coarelli, *Roma*, pp. 20–4.
18. Gatto, *Storia di Roma nel Medioevo*, p. 31–2.
19. Lançon, *Rome in Late Antiquity*, pp. 15–16.
20. Richard Krautheimer, *Rome: Profile of a City, 312–1308*, pp. 13–16.
21. Lançon, *Rome in Late Antiquity*, pp. 21–2.

22. C. Bernardi Salvetti, *S. Maria degli Angeli alle Terme e Antonio Lo Duca* Rome, 1965, p. 81.
23. Kenneth W. Harl, *Coinage in the Roman Economy, 300 B.C. to A.D. 700*, Baltimore and London, 1996, p. 274.
24. Wolfram, *History of the Goths*, pp. 43–56.
25. Claudio Rendina, *Storia insolita di Roma*, Rome, 2002, p. 144.
26. J.B. Bury, *History of the Later Roman Empire*, London, 1923, Vol. I, pp. 46–55.
27. J.W.H.G. Liebeschuetz, *The Decline and Fall of the Roman City*, Oxford, 2001, p. 10.
28. Bury, *History*, Vol. 1, pp. 45–5.
29. Gatto, *Storia di Roma nel Medioevo*, pp. 19–20.
30. *Ibid.*, p. 20.
31. Eusebius, *Church History*, Book VIII, IV, 3–4.
32. Bernardi Salvetti, *S. Maria degli Angeli*, pp. 57–8.
33. Lactantius, *On the Death of the Persecutors*, Chap. 19.
34. *Ibid.*, Chap. 18.
35. *Ibid.*, Chap. 24.
36. *Ibid.*, Chap. 20.
37. *Ibid.*, Chap. 24.
38. Gatto, *Storia di Roma nel Medioevo*, p. 21.
39. I.P. Pressly, *York*, London, n.d., p. 7.
40. Lactantius, *On the Death of the Persecutors*, Chap. 25.
41. *Ibid.*, Chap. 26.
42. Gatto, *Storia di Roma nel Medioevo*, pp. 21–2.
43. *Ibid.*, p. 22.
44. Lactantius, *On the Death of the Persecutors*, Chap. 34.
45. Eusebius, *Life of Constantine*, Book 1, Chap. 37 and 38.
46. Lactantius, *On the Death of the Persecutors*, Chap. 44.
47. *Ibid.*
48. Bunson, *Dictionary of the Roman Empire*, pp. 277–8.
49. Gatto, *Storia di Roma nel Medioevo*, p. 23.
50. Coarelli, *Roma*, pp. 180–4.
51. Gatto, *Storia di Roma nel Medioevo*, p. 22.
52. Eusebius, *Life of Constantine*, Book 1, Chaps 28–32.
53. Gatto, *Storia di Roma nel Medioevo*, pp. 22–3.
54. *Ibid.*, pp. 23–4.
55. *Ibid.*, p. 66.
56. Bunson, *Dictionary of the Roman Empire*, pp. 279–80.
57. Lançon, *Rome in Late Antiquity*, pp. 90–1.
58. Linda Jones Hall, 'Cicero's *instinctu divino* and Constantine's *instinctu divinitatis*: The evidence on the Arch of Constantine for the Senatorial view of the "Vision" of Constantine'. *Journal of Early Christian Studies* 6 (4) winter 1998, pp. 647–71.
59. Rodolfo Lanciani, *Pagan and Christian Rome*, Boston and New York, 1892, Chap. 1, pp. 18–20.

60. Visalli (ed.), *After Jesus*, p. 212.
61. Lançon, *Rome in Late Antiquity*, p. 88.
62. Coarelli, *Roma*, pp. 182–3.
63. *Ibid.*, pp. 180–4.
64. *Ibid.*
65. Gatto, *Storia di Roma nel Medioevo*, p. 24.
66. Lançon, *Rome in Late Antiquity*, p. 21.
67. Raymond Davis (ed.), *Liber Pontificalis* (The Book of Pontiffs), revd edn, trans. with an introduction by Raymond Davis, Liverpool, 2000, p. xxviii.
68. *Ibid.*, pp. 21–2.
69. *Ibid.*, p.xi.
70. *Ibid.*, p. xxviii.
71. *Ibid.*
72. *Ibid.*, pp. xxx–xxxi and pp. 14–28.
73. Lançon, *Rome in Late Antiquity*, p. 27.
74. Rendina, *La grande*, p. 366.
75. Eusebius, *Life of Constantine*, Book 4, Chap. 62.
76. Margherita Cecchelli, 'I luoghi di Pietro e Paolo', in Letizia Pani Ermini (ed.), *Christiana Loca*, Rome, 2000, p. 90.
77. Visalli (ed.), *After Jesus*, pp. 234–5.
78. Peter Brown, *The Cult of the Saints*, Chicago, 1982, pp. 5–10.
79. Eusebius, *Life of Constantine*, Book 4, Chap. 61.
80. Rendina, *Storia*, p. 181.
81. Lanciani, *Pagan and Christian Rome*, pp. 131–45.
82. John Fleming, Hugh Honour and Nikolaus Pevsner, *The Penguin Dictionary of Architecture*, London, 1991, p. 370.
83. Lanciani, *Pagan and Christian Rome*, pp. 131–45.
84. Davis (ed.), *Liber Pontificalis*, pp. xxxi–xxxii and 19–20.
85. *Ibid.*, pp. xxxii and 19–21.
86. Rendina, *La grande*, pp. 502–6.
87. Gatto, *Storia di Roma nel Medioevo*, p. 27.
88. Visalli (ed.), *After Jesus*, pp. 221–2.
89. *Ibid.*, pp. 227–32.
90. *Ibid.*, p. 233.
91. Edward Gibbon, *The Decline and Fall of the Roman Empire*, with notes by Revd H.H. Milman, London, 1845, Vol. 3, Chap. 31, Part 2.
92. *Ibid.*
93. Robert Twigger, 'Inflation: the value of the pound 1750–1998', Economics policy and statistics section. House of Commons Library. Research paper 99/20. 23 February 1999. www.parliament.uk/commons/lib/research/rp99/rp99-020.pdf, pp. 8–20.
94. Lawrence H. Officer and Samuel Williamson, 'Computing "Real Value" over time with a conversion from British pounds to US dollars, or vice versa', Economic History Services, September 2005. www.eh.net.hmit/exchange/.

95. Coarelli, *Roma*, pp. 43–199.
96. Bunson, *Dictionary of the Roman Empire*, p. 194.
97. Lançon, *Rome in Late Antiquity*, p. 4.
98. Coarelli, *Roma*, p. 365.
99. Rendina, *La grande*, p. 159.
100. Ferdinand Gregorovius, *History of the City of Rome in the Middle Ages*, Vol. 1 (AD 400–568), New York, 2000, p. 40.
101. Samuel Ball-Plattner and Thomas Ashby, *A Topographical Dictionary of Ancient Rome*, London, 1929, pp. 297–302.
102. Lançon, *Rome in Late Antiquity*, p. 21.
103. Coarelli, *Roma*, p. 44.
104. *Ibid.*, pp. 44–111.
105. *Ibid.*, pp. 51–3.
106. Lançon, *Rome in Late Antiquity*, pp. 87–91.
107. *Ibid.*
108. Coarelli, *Roma*, p. 73.
109. Gatto, *Storia di Roma nel Medioevo*, pp. 51–2.
110. *Ibid.*
111. Lançon, *Rome in Late Antiquity*, pp. 48–50.
112. Aldo Mazzolai, *Alarico: Nell'inerte Impero*, Florence, 1996, p. 130.
113. Ball-Platner and Ashby, *Topographical Dictionary*, p. 72–6.
114. Gregorovius, *History*, Vol. 1, pp. 40–4.
115. Lançon, *Rome in Late Antiquity*, p. 18.
116. Coarelli, *Roma*, p. 145.
117. Ammianus, *The Later Roman Empire*, Book 16, Chap. 10.
118. Coarelli, *Roma*, p. 145.

Chapter Three

1. Claudio Rendina (ed.), *La Grande Enciclopedia di Roma*, Rome, 2000, p. 1041.
2. Rendina, *Storia*, p. 144.
3. Lançon, *Rome in Late Antiquity*, p. 7.
4. Coarelli, *Roma*, p. 25.
5. Lançon, *Rome in Late Antiquity*, pp. 11–12.
6. Rendina, *La grande guida*, p. 569.
7. Coarelli, *Roma*, pp. 302–10.
8. Gregorovius, *History*, Vol. 1, p. 27.
9. Coarelli, *Roma*, pp. 36–41.
10. Sextus Julius Frontinus, *The Aqueducts of Rome*, I, 4.
11. Coarelli, *Roma*, pp. 39–40.
12. *Ibid.*, pp. 36–7.
13. Gatto, *Storia di Roma nel Medioevo*, pp. 119–21.
14. Ammianus, *The Later Roman Empire*, Book 14, Chap. 6, 19 and Book 28, Chap. 4.

15. Lançon, *Rome in Late Antiquity*, pp. 82–3.
16. *Ibid.*, p. 82.
17. Gatto, *Storia di Roma nel Medioevo*, pp. 51–2.
18. Lançon, *Rome in Late Antiquity*, p. 81.
19. Gatto, *Storia di Roma nel Medioevo*, pp. 51–2.
20. Lançon, *Rome in Late Antiquity*, pp. 52–6.
21. *Ibid.*, p. 81.
22. *Ibid.*
23. *Ibid.*
24. *Ibid.*, pp. 83–4.
25. *Ibid.*
26. Orosius, *Seven Books of History*, VII, 37.
27. Bunson, *Dictionary of the Roman Empire*, p. 48.
28. Wallace-Hadrill, *Ammianus*, pp. 21 and 39 (Introductory note).
29. Duffy, *Saints and Sinners*, p. 24.
30. Rendina, *La grande guida*, p. 424.
31. Duffy, *Saints and Sinners*, p. 23.
32. *Ibid.*
33. *Ibid.*, p. 25.
34. Rendina, *Storia*, p. 160.
35. Ammianus, *The Later Roman Empire*, Book 27, Chap. 3.
36. Davis, *Liber Pontificalis*, p. xxxvii.
37. Duffy, *Saints and Sinners*, p. 29.
38. Gatto, *Storia di Roma nel Medioevo*, p. 38.
39. Duffy, *Saints and Sinners*, pp. 30–1.
40. Ranuccio Bianchi Bandinelli, *Roma*, Vol. 2, 2005, p. 367.
41. Coarelli, *Roma*, p. 73.
42. Duffy, *Saints and Sinners*, p. 25.
43. *Ibid.*
44. Visalli, *After Jesus*, p. 247.
45. Duffy, *Saints and Sinners*, pp. 24–31.
46. Gatto, *Storia di Roma nel Medioevo*, pp. 29–31.
47. *Ibid.*, p. 37.
48. Duffy, *Saints and Sinners*, p. 31.
49. Lançon, *Rome in Late Antiquity*, p. 88.
50. *Ibid.*, p. 92.
51. Wallace-Hadrill, *Ammianus*, pp. 18–19.
52. Visalli, *After Jesus*, p. 247.
53. Gatto, *Storia di Roma nel Medioevo*, pp. 38–43.
54. Lançon, *Rome in Late Antiquity*, p. 21.
55. Gatto, *Storia di Roma nel Medioevo*, pp. 43–6.
56. Gregorovius, *History*, Vol. 1, pp. 144–6.
57. Wallace-Hadrill, *Ammianus*, p. 450, note 10.

58. *Ibid.*, pp. 18–19 and 29.

59. Gatto, *Storia di Roma nel Medioevo*, pp. 61–3.

60. Claudian, *Panegyric on the Sixth Consulship of the Emperor Honorius*, trans. Maurice Platnauer, Cambridge, MA, 1998, II. XXVII. ll.540–660.

61. Gregorovius, *History*, Vol. 1, pp. 117–22.

62. Gatto, *Storia di Roma nel Medioevo*, pp. 61–3.

63. Gregorovius, *History*, Vol. 1, pp. 117–22.

64. Barnish, *Cassiodorus*, p. 93, explanatory note in brackets.

65. Gregorovius, *History*, Vol. 1, pp. 117–22.

Chapter Four

1. Procopius, *History of the Wars*, III.ii. 2–5.

2. Heather, *The Goths*, p. 48.

3. Simon MacDowall and Angus McBride, *Germanic Warrior. AD 236–568*, Oxford, 2003, plate 1.

4. Wolfram, *History of the Goths*, pp. 119–20.

5. *Ibid.*, pp. 70–2.

6. Alexander Demandt, 'So lange wird Germanien schon besiegt', *Frankfurter Allgemeine Zeitung*, 9 July 2003, No. 156, p. 8.

7. MacDowall and McBride, *Germanic Warrior*, pp. 57–8.

8. *Ibid.*, pp. 56–7.

9. Wolfram, *History of the Goths*, pp. 119–20.

10. *Ibid.*, p. 117.

11. *Ibid.*, p. 123.

12. *Ibid.*, p. 119.

13. *Ibid.*, p. 120.

14. *Ibid.*, p. 407, note 218.

15. Heather, 'The Creation of the Visigoths' in his *The Goths*, p. 79.

16. Wolfram, *History of the Goths*, p. 144.

17. *Ibid.*, p. 127.

18. *Claudian*, trans. Platnauer, Vol. 2, XXVI.610.

19. Wolfram, *History of the Goths*, pp. 131–4.

20. Mazzolai, *Alarico*, front cover.

21. John Whitney Hall (ed.), *History of the World*, North Dighton, 2002, p. 191.

22. Procopius, *History of the Wars*, III.ii.2–5.

23. Wolfram, *History of the Goths*, p. 136.

24. *Ibid.*, p. 137.

25. *Ibid.*, pp. 136–7.

26. *Ibid.*, p. 138.

27. J.B. Bury, *The Invasion of Europe by the Barbarians*, New York and London, 2002, pp. 68–9.

28. *Ibid.*, pp. 64–5.

29. Wolfram, *History of the Goths*, pp. 139–46.
30. Heather, *The Goths*, pp. 138–46.
31. Zosimus, *New History*, London, 1814, Book 5.
32. Heather, 'The Creation', pp. 43–92.
33. Wolfram, *History of the Goths*, p. 24.
34. *Ibid.*, p. 141.
35. *Ibid.*
36. Bury, *History*, p. 112.
37. Zosimus, *New History*, Book 5.
38. Bury, *The Invasion*, pp. 69–70.
39. Wolfram, *History of the Goths*, pp. 141–2.
40. *Ibid.*, p. 142.
41. *Ibid.*, p. 142–3.
42. *Ibid.*, p. 148–9.
43. *Ibid.*, pp. 149–50.
44. Heather, *The Goths*, p. 146.
45. Wolfram, *History of the Goths*, pp. 152–3.
46. *Claudian*, II.XXVI.610.
47. *Ibid.*, II.XXVIII.125.
48. Wolfram, *History of the Goths*, pp. 152–3.
49. Bury, *The Invasion*, p. 83.
50. Heather, *The Goths*, p. 146.
51. Wolfram, *History of the Goths*, p. 153.
52. Orosius, *The Seven Books of History*, VII. 37.
53. Wolfram, *History of the Goths*, p. 153.
54. Bury, *The Invasion*, p. 83.
55. E.A. Thompson, *Romans and Barbarians. The Decline of the Western Empire*, Madison, 1982, pp. 17–19.
56. Lançon, *Rome in Late Antiquity*, p. 37.
57. Gregorovius, *History*, Vol. 1, pp. 125–6.
58. Wolfram, *History of the Goths*, p. 154.
59. Gregorovius, *History*, Vol. 1, p. 125.
60. Zosimus, *New History*, Book 5.
61. Bury, *The Invasion*, p. 86.
62. Heather, *The Goths*, p. 147.
63. Lançon, *Rome in Late Antiquity*, pp. 36–40.
64. Wolfram, *History of the Goths*, p. 154.
65. Lançon, *Rome in Late Antiquity*, p. 37.
66. *Ibid.*, pp. 12–13.
67. Coarelli, *Roma*, pp. 26–7.
68. Lançon, *Rome in Late Antiquity*, p. 37.
69. Zosimus, *New History*, Book 5.
70. *Ibid.*

71. *Ibid.*
72. *Ibid.*
73. *Ibid.*
74. *Ibid.*
75. Lançon, *Rome in Late Antiquity*, p. 37.
76. *Ibid.*, pp. 37–8.
77. Wolfram, *History of the Goths*, p. 156.
78. Lançon, *Rome in Late Antiquity*, p. 38.
79. Wolfram, *History of the Goths*, pp. 155–6.
80. Rendina, *Storia*, pp. 165–6.
81. John Paul II, Discorso del Santo Padre Giovanni Paolo II ai membri del circolo di Roma, 7 February 1981 (speech of the Holy Father John Paul II to the Members of the Club of Rome, 7 February 1981), La Santa Sede (the Holy See). www.vatican.va
82. Lançon, *Rome in Late Antiquity*, p. 38.
83. Wolfram, *History of the Goths*, pp. 156–7.
84. Lançon, *Rome in Late Antiquity*, p. 38.
85. Wolfram, *History of the Goths*, p. 157–8.
86. *Ibid.*
87. Lançon, *Rome in Late Antiquity*, p. 38.
88. Wolfram, *History of the Goths*, p. 158.
89. Zosimus, *New History*, Book 6.
90. Wolfram, *History of the Goths*, p. 158.
91. Philostorgius, *Ecclesiastical History*, Book 12, Chap. 3.

Chapter Five

1. St Jerome. Letter 127. To Principia.
2. Procopius, *History of the Wars*, III, ii. 27.
3. Coarelli, *Roma*, p. 249.
4. Gatto, *Storia di Roma nel Medioevo*, p. 59.
5. Procopius, *History of the Wars*, III. ii. 8–26.
6. Gregorovius, *History*, Vol. 1, p. 153.
7. Procopius, *History of the Wars*, III. ii. 27.
8. Rendina, *Storia*, p. 709.
9. Gatto, *Storia di Roma nel Medioevo*, p. 32.
10. *Ibid.*, pp. 59–60.
11. Mazzolai, *Alarico*, p. 96.
12. Bernardi Salvetti, *Maria degli Angeli*, p. 37.
13. Rendina, *La grande*, p. 362.
14. Gregorovius, *History*, Vol. 1, p. 320.
15. Lanciani, *Ancient Rome*, p. 324.
16. Leonard Victor Rutgers, *The Jews in Late Ancient Rome*, Leiden, Boston, Cologne, 1995, pp. xvii and 1.

17. Gregorovius, *History*, Vol. 1, pp. 154–5.
18. Lançon, *Rome in Late Antiquity*, p. 37.
19. Heather, *The Goths*, p. 147.
20. Coarelli, *Roma*, pp. 87–8.
21. Gatto, *Storia di Roma nel Medioevo*, p. 59.
22. Lançon, *Rome in Late Antiquity*, p. 39.
23. Ball Platner and Ashby, *Topographical Dictionary*, p. 75.
24. Coarelli, *Roma*, pp. 56–7.
25. Rendina, *La grande guida*, p. 307.
26. Coarelli, *Roma*, pp. 145–7.
27. *Ibid.*, pp. 145–7.
28. Matthew Krauss and Andrew S. Jacobs, *Remains of the Jews: The Holy Land and Christian Empire in Late Antiquity*, Stanford, CA, 2004. See also *Bryn Mawr Classical Review* 2005.09.03.
29. Paul Johnson, *A History of the Jews*, London, 1987, pp. 144–5.
30. Lançon, *Rome in Late Antiquity*, p. 162.
31. Krauss and Jacobs, *Remains*.
32. Orosius, *The Seven Books of History*, VII, 40.
33. Zosimus, *New History*, Book 6.
34. J.J. O'Donnell, 'The aims of Jordanes', *Historia* 31 (1982): 223–40.
35. Jordanes, *The Origin and Deeds of the Goths*, XXX, 156.
36. Orosius, *The Seven Books of History*, VII, 39.
37. Sozomenus, *Ecclesiastical History*, Book 9, Chap. 10.
38. Gibbon, *Decline and Fall*, Chaps 3, 21, 4.
39. Visalli, *After Jesus*, pp. 266–7.
40. St Jerome. Preface to Book 3 of Ezekiel.
41. Gatto, *Storia di Roma nel Medioevo*, p. 60.
42. Rendina, *La grande enciclopedia*, p. 692.
43. St Jerome. Letter 127. To Principia, pp. 12–13.
44. *Ibid.*, pp. 13–14.
45. Eric Ollivier, 'Le temps s'est arrêté à Cosenza', *Le Figaro*, 25 December 2001.
46. Rutgers, *The Jews*, pp. 73–95.
47. Harry J. Leon, *The Jews of Ancient Rome*, Peabody, 1995, p. 55.
48. Leonard V. Rutgers, Klaas van der Borg, F. M. Arie de Jong and Imogene Poole, 'Radiocarbon dating: Jewish inspiration of Christian Catacombs', *Nature* (21 July 2005).
49. Rutgers, *The Jews*, p. 1.
50. Lanciani, *Pagan and Christian Rome*, p. 324.
51. Rutgers, *The Jews*, pp. xvii and 1.
52. Lanciani, *Pagan and Christian Rome*, p. 326.
53. Mazzolai, *Alarico*, p. 97.
54. Procopius, *History of the Wars*, III. ii. 26.
55. Bury, *The Invasion*, p. 64.

56. Mazzolai, *Alarico*, p. 98.
57. Bunson, *Dictionary of the Roman Empire*, pp. 198 and 330.
58. Mazzolai, *Alarico*, p. 107.
59. Davis, *Liber Pontificalis*, pp. 16–17.
60. *Ibid.*, pp. 35–7.
61. *Ibid.*, pp. 16–18.
62. Lanciani, *Pagan and Christian Rome*, p. 150.
63. *Ibid.*
64. S.J.B. Barnish, *Cassiodorus: Variae*, Liverpool, 1992, XII.20.4
65. *Ibid.*, p. xiv.
66. Davis, *Liber Pontificalis*, pp. xxxix and 35–6.
67. Rendina, *Storia*, p. 166.
68. Mazzolai, *Alarico*, p. 97.
69. Gregorovius, *History*, Vol. 1, pp. 156 and 191.
70. Wolfram, *History of the Goths*, pp. 162–3.
71. Gibbon, *Decline and Fall*, Chaps 3, 21, 6.
72. Gatto, *Storia di Roma nel Medioevo*, p. 60.
73. St Jerome. Letter 127. To Principia.
74. Wolfram, *History of the Goths*, p. 159.
75. Gregorovius, *History*, Vol. 1, pp. 160–1.

Chapter Six

1. Wolfram, *History of the Goths*, pp. 159–61.
2. Jordanes, *The Origin and Deeds of the Goths*, XXX, 154.
3. Philostorgius, *Ecclesiastical History*, Chap. 3.
4. Alessandro Cristofori, *Gli spazi geografici della Storia Romana: l'Italia. Regio III: Lucania et Bruttii*. Courtesy of Progetto Telemaco. Università di Bologna. www.telemaco.unibo.it
5. Mazzolai, *Alarico*, p. 113.
6. *Ibid.*
7. Jordanes, *The Origin and Deeds of the Goths*, XXVI.
8. O'Donnell, 'The aims'.
9. Philostorgius, *Ecclesiastical History*, Chap. 3.
10. Procopius, *History of the Wars*, III. ii. 37.
11. Angelo Raffaele Amato, 'Il tesoro di Alarico nell Cilento'. www.cilentohotel.com
12. John Mann, *Murder, Magic and Medicine*, Oxford, 2002, p. 21.
13. Andrew Chevallier, *The Encyclopedia of medicinal plants*, Montreal, 1996, p. 158.
14. *Ibid.*, p. 66.
15. *Ibid.*, p. 192.
16. Sozomenus, *Ecclesiastical History*, IX, VI.
17. Socrates Scholasticus, *Ecclesiastical History*, II.x.x
18. Marcel Brion, *La vie d'Alaric*, Paris, 1930, p. 256.

19. Mazzolai, *Alarico*, p. 114.
20. Beniamino Fioriglio, 'La febbre di Alarico', in Tobia Cornacchioli, Luciana De Rose, Beniamino Fioriglio, Gian Piero Givigliano and Dora Ricca, *Alarico. Re dei Visigoti*, Cosenza, 2000, p. 115.
21. *Ibid.*, p. 114.
22. Brion, *La vie*, p. 263.
23. Heather, *The Goths*, p. 66.
24. Tacitus, *La Germanie*, XIV.1.
25. MacDowall and McBride, *Germanic Warrior*, p. 6.
26. Heather, The Goths, p. 65.
27. Tacitus, *La Germanie*, XIV, 3.
28. Wolfram, *History of the Goths*, pp. 272 and 379.
29. Cristian Olariu, 'Visigoths and Romans during the fourth century A.D. Assimilation, resistance, and cultural interferences', Analele Universităii Bucureşti, *istorie* 45 (1996): 32–4.
30. Schwarcz, 'Cult and Religion', p. 450.
31. Olariu, 'Visigoths and Romans', pp. 32–4.
32. Pablo C. Diaz, 'Visigothic political institutions', in Peter Heather, *The Visigoths*, San Marino, 1999, p. 328.
33. Wolfram, *History of the Goths*, p. 160.
34. Brion, *La vie*, p. 263.
35. Heather, *The Goths*, p. 70.
36. Schwarcz, 'Cult and Religion', p. 450.
37. Brion, *La vie*, pp. 264–5.
38. Schwarcz, 'Cult and Religion', p. 463.
39. Government of New Zealand. State of the environment of the Taranaki region – 2003. www.trc.govt.nz/state_of_environment
40. Giovanni Della Casa Venturelli. *Alaricus Rex Gothorum*. www.Alaricvs.com
41. István Bóna, *Les Huns*, St Germain-du-Puy, 2002, p. 74.
42. Wolfram, *History of the Goths*, pp. 161–246.
43. *Ibid.*, p. 161.
44. Bunson, *Dictionary of the Roman Empire*, p. 198.
45. Bury, *The Invasion*, pp. 98–101.
46. Wolfram, *History of the Goths*, pp. 162–3.
47. *Ibid.*
48. Bury, *The Invasion*, pp. 98–101.
49. Wolfram, *History of the Goths*, pp. 172–246.
50. Gibbon, *Decline and Fall*, III, XXXI, Part VI.
51. Gregory of Tours, *The History of the Franks*, trans. Lewis Thorpe, London, 1974, III. 10.

Chapter Seven

1. Lançon, *Rome in Late Antiquity*, pp. 16 and 39.
2. *Ibid.*, p. 39.
3. Rendina, *La grande guida*, pp. 546–7.
4. Orosius, *The Seven Books of History*, VII, 40.
5. Gatto, *Storia di Roma nel Medioevo*, pp. 63–6.
6. Gregorovius, *History*, Vol. 1, p. 195.
7. Wolfram, *History of the Goths*, pp. 163–6.
8. Lançon, *Rome in Late Antiquity*, p. 82.
9. Gregorovius, *History*, Vol. 1, pp. 176–9.
10. Bury, *History*, Vol. 1, pp. 210–11.
11. Procopius, *History of the Wars*, Books 5–6.15, Cambridge, MA and London, 2000, p. 129, fn. 2.
12. Gregorovius, *History*, Vol. 1, pp. 166–9.
13. Mazzolai, *Alarico*, p. 99.
14. Lançon, *Rome in Late Antiquity*, pp. 14–15.
15. Davis, *Liber Pontificalis*, pp. 32–4.
16. Rendina, *Storia*, p. 166.
17. Orosius, *The Seven Books of History*, Book 7, 39.
18. Davis, *Liber Pontificalis*, pp. 32–4.
19. *Ibid.*, pp. xxxviii–xxxix and 32–3.
20. Bury, *History*, Vol. 1, Chap. 2, n. 81; Twigger, *Inflation*, pp. 8–20; Officer and Williamson, 'Computing "real value"'.
21. Harl, *Coinage*, p. 283.
22. *Ibid.*, pp. 271 and 283–4.
23. Gregorovius, *History*, Vol. 1, pp. 181–2.
24. *Ibid.*, pp. 182–3.
25. Mazzolai, *Alarico*, p. 130.
26. Duffy, *Saints and Sinners*, pp. 30–1.
27. Gregorovius, *History*, Vol. 1, pp. 182–3.
28. Visalli, *After Jesus*, pp. 268–71.
29. Duffy, *Saints and Sinners*, pp. 31–2.
30. Gregorovius, *History*, Vol. 1, pp. 183–5.
31. Gatto, *Storia di Roma nel Medioevo*, p. 64.
32. Gregorovius, *History*, Vol. 1, pp. 186–7.
33. *Ibid.*, pp. 186–7.
34. Bury, *The Invasion*, pp. 117–19.
35. Bury, *History*, Vol. 1, pp. 248–9.
36. *Ibid.*, pp. 224–5.
37. *Ibid.*
38. Bury, *The Invasion*, p. 121.
39. *Ibid.*

40. Davis, *Liber Pontificalis*, pp. xxxix–xl and 36–8.
41. Gregorovius, *History*, Vol. 1, pp. 187–92.
42. Davis, *Liber Pontificalis*pp. 36–8.
43. Bury, *History*, Vol. 1, pp. 224–5 and 241–51.
44. Gatto, *Storia di Roma nel Medioevo*, p. 65.
45. Bury, *The Invasion*, pp. 127–9.
46. *Ibid.*, pp. 129–30.
47. *Ibid.*, pp. 142–3.
48. Bury, *The Invasion*, p. 131 and pp. 141–56.
49. Jordanes, *The Origin and Deeds of the Goths*, XXXV.
50. Bury, *The Invasion*, pp. 145–51.
51. Maurice Bouvier-Ajam, *Attila. Le fléau de Dieu*, Paris, 1982, pp. 308–12.
52. Bury, *The Invasion*, p. 149.
53. Bouvier-Ajam, *Attila*, pp. 313–34.
54. *Ibid.*, pp. 50–4.
55. *Ibid.*, pp. 72–4.
56. Marcello Brusegan, *Storia insolita di Venezia*, Rome, 2003, p. 24.
57. Bouvier-Ajam, *Attila*, pp. 365–8.
58. Gregorovius, *History*, Vol. 1, pp. 196–9.
59. *Ibid.*, p. 199.
60. Duffy, *Saints and Sinners*, pp. 34–6; Visalli, *After Jesus*, p. 327.
61. Gatto, *Storia di Roma nel Medioevo*, pp. 66–9.
62. Gregorovius, *History*, Vol. 1, p. 203–4.
63. Visalli, *After Jesus*, pp. 258–9.
64. Duffy, *Saints and Sinners*, pp. 35–6.
65. Bouvier-Ajam, *Attila*, pp. 373–4.
66. Rendina, *Storia*, p. 168.
67. Bouvier-Ajam, *Attila*, pp. 371–7.
68. Bury, *The Invasion*, pp. 152–3.
69. Bouvier-Ajam, *Attila*, pp. 383–4.
70. Jordanes, *The Origin and Deeds of the Goths*, XLII.
71. Bouvier-Ajam, *Attila*, pp. 400–1.
72. Bury, *The Invasion*, pp. 153–6.
73. *Ibid.*
74. Bouvier-Ajam, *Attila*, p. 48.
75. Duffy, *Saints and Sinners*, p. 34.
76. Gregorovius, *History*, Vol. 1, pp. 203–5.
77. *Ibid.*, p. 219.
78. *Ibid.*, pp. 206–10.
79. *Ibid.*, pp. 207–8.
80. *Ibid.*, pp. 209–11.
81. Lançon, *Rome in Late Antiquity*, pp. 40–1.
82. Gregorovius, *History*, Vol. 1, pp. 210–12.

83. *Ibid.*, pp. 212–22.
84. Gatto, *Storia di Roma nel Medioevo*, pp. 73–7.
85. *Ibid.*, p. 74.
86. Gregorovius, *History*, Vol. 1, p. 218
87. Procopius, *History of the Wars*, III.iii–vii.
88. Gregorovius, *History*, Vol. 1, p. 320.
89. *Ibid.*, p. 220.
90. Davis, *Liber Pontificalis*, p. 37.
91. Gatto, *Storia di Roma nel Medioevo*, p. 76.
92. Gregorovius, *History*, Vol. 1, p. 220.
93. Gatto, *Storia di Roma nel Medioevo*, pp. 73–7.
94. Gregorovius, *History*, Vol. 1, pp. 218–19.
95. *Ibid.*, pp. 221–2.
96. *Ibid.*, p. 224.
97. Gregorovius, *History*, Vol. 1, p. 222.
98. Gatto, *Storia di Roma nel Medioevo*, p. 77.

Chapter Eight

1. Bury, *The Invasion*, pp. 159–74.
2. Gregorovius, *History*, Vol. 1, pp. 223–54.
3. *Ibid.*, pp. 223–31.
4. *Ibid.*
5. Krautheimer, pp. 51–3 and 60–7.
6. Rendina, *La Grande Guida*, pp. 357–8 and 672–3.
7. Davis, *Liber Pontificalis*, p. 40.
8. Gregorovius, *History*, Vol. 1, pp. 233–9 and fn. on p. 237.
9. *Ibid.*, pp. 240–4.
10. Rendina, *La grande guida*, p. 437.
11. *Ibid.*
12. Gregorovius, *History*, Vol. 1, pp. 246–7.
13. *Ibid.*, pp. 247–8.
14. Bury, *The Invasion*, pp. 166–7.
15. Rendina, *Storia*, p. 170.
16. Walter Goffart, *Barbarians and Romans*, Princeton, NJ, 1980, p. 60.
17. Thompson, *Romans and Barbarians*, pp. 65–6.
18. Rendina, *Storia*, p. 170.
19. Thompson, *Romans and Barbarians*, p. 75.
20. Davis, *Liber Pontificalis*, pp. 42–5.
21. *Ibid.*, p. xliii.
22. Liebeschuetz, *Decline and Fall of the Roman City*, pp. 9–11.
23. *Ibid.*, pp. 342–54.
24. Rendina, *Storia*, p. 138.

25. Bury, *History*, Vol. 2, p. 401.
26. Liebeschuetz, *Decline and Fall of the Roman City*, pp. 347–8.
27. *Ibid.*, p. 349.
28. *Ibid.*, p. 342.
29. Gregorovius, *History*, Vol. 1, pp. 253–4.

Chapter Nine

1. Wolfram, *History of the Goths*, Appendix 2.
2. Thomas Burns, *A History of the Ostrogoths*, Bloomington and Indianapolis, 1991, pp. 65–6.
3. *Ibid.*
4. Bury, *The Invasion*, pp. 179–83.
5. Wolfram, *History of the Goths*, pp. 281–4.
6. *Ibid.*, Appendix 2.
7. Burns, *Ostrogoths*, pp. 67–8.
8. Zacharias of Mytilene, *The Syriac Chronicle*, Book 10, Chap. 16.
9. Burns, *Ostrogoths*, p. 68.
10. Gregorovius, *History*, Vol. 1, pp. 81 and 82 (note).
11. *Ibid.*, p. 291.
12. Burns, *Ostrogoths*, pp. 69–70.
13. Gregorovius, *History*, Vol. 1, pp. 287–90.
14. Lançon, *Rome in Late Antiquity*, pp. 95–6.
15. Davis, *Liber Pontificalis*, pp. 45–8.
16. Rendina, *Storia*, p. 178.
17. Gregorovius, *History*, Vol. 1, pp. 290–2.
18. Rendina, *Storia*, p. 178.
19. *Ibid.*
20. *Ibid.*, pp. 172–81.
21. Lançon, *Rome in Late Antiquity*, p. 119.
22. Gregorovius, *History*, Vol. 1, p. 313, note 1.
23. Lançon, *Rome in Late Antiquity*, pp. 12–13.
24. Barnish, *Cassiodorus*, p. xliii and IV.51, I.25, III.30.1.
25. Gregorovius, *History*, Vol. 1, pp. 296–302.
26. Lançon, *Rome in Late Antiquity*, p. 121.
27. Gregorovius, *History*, Vol. 1, pp. 302–12.
28. Procopius, *Anecdota or Secret History*, Chap. 9.
29. Gregorovius, *History*, Vol. 1, pp. 303–4.
30. Lançon, *Rome in Late Antiquity*, p. 22.
31. Coarelli, *Roma*, p. 191.
32. Barnish, *Cassiodorus*, V.42, and p. 93n.
33. Gregorovius, *History*, Vol. 1, p. 307.
34. *Ibid.*, pp. 307–11.

35. *Ibid.*, pp. 314–20.
36. Leon, *The Jews*, pp. 44–5 and 135.
37. Gregorovius, *History*, Vol. 2, p. 427.
38. Wolfram, *History of the Goths*, pp. 327–8.
39. Rendina, *Storia*, pp. 178–80.
40. Liebeschuetz, *Decline and Fall of the Roman City*, pp. 349–50.
41. Davis, *Liber Pontificalis*, p. 50 (54.10), p. 52 (55.7) and p. 54 (58.2).
42. *Ibid.*, p. 50 (54.10).
43. Rendina, *Storia*, p. 180.
44. Wolfram, *History of the Goths*, pp. 331–2.
45. *Ibid.*, pp. 281–3.
46. Rendina, *Storia*, pp. 180–2.
47. Davis, *Liber Pontificalis*, p. 52 (56.2).
48. Wolfram, *History of the Goths*, pp. 334–42.
49. Rendina, *Storia*, p. 180.
50. Wolfram, *History of the Goths*, pp. 336–7.
51. *Ibid.*, p. 338.
52. *Ibid.*, pp. 339–41.
53. *Ibid.*, pp. 341–2.
54. Rendina, *Storia*, p. 180.

Chapter Ten

1. Mango, *Oxford History of Byzantium*, pp. 1–2.
2. Liebeschuetz, *Decline and Fall of the Roman City*, pp. 349–51.
3. Rendina, *Storia*, pp. 182–4.
4. Lançon, *Rome in Late Antiquity*, pp. 12–13.
5. Gregorovius, *History*, Vol. 1, pp. 406–7.
6. *Ibid.*, pp. 390–1.
7. *Ibid.*, pp. 380–1.
8. Lançon, *Rome in Late Antiquity*, p. 13.
9. Gregorovius, *History*, Vol. 1, pp. 381–2 and p. 381, fn. 2.
10. *Ibid.*, pp. 400–2.
11. Duffy, *Saints and Sinners*, pp. 42–3.
12. Gregorovius, *History*, Vol. 1, pp. 398–9.
13. Duffy, *Saints and Sinners*, p. 43.
14. *Ibid.*
15. Rendina, *Storia*, pp. 182–3.
16. *Ibid.*, p. 182.
17. *Ibid.*
18. Duffy, *Saints and Sinners*, p. 43.
19. Davis, *Liber Pontificalis*, pp. 58–9.
20. Gregorovius, *History*, Vol. 1, pp. 431–5.

21. Gatto, *Storia di Roma nel Medioevo*, pp. 101–2.
22. Procopius, *History*, Vol. 3, front cover flap/jacket blurb.
23. Gatto, *Storia di Roma nel Medioevo*, pp. 101–2.
24. Duffy, *Saints and Sinners*, pp. 45–57.
25. Gregorovius, *History*, Vol. 1, p. 493.
26. Duffy, *Saints and Sinners*, p. 46.
27. Gregorovius, *History*, Vol. 1, pp. 441–3.
28. Rendina, *La grande guida*, pp. 271–2.
29. Rendina, *Storia*, pp. 182–4.
30. Coarelli, *Roma*, p. 35.
31. Gatto, *Storia di Roma nel Medioevo*, pp. 103–7.
32. Rendina, *Storia*, p. 184.
33. Wolfram, *History of the Goths*, p. 361.
34. Duffy, *Saints and Sinners*, p. 43.
35. *Ibid.*, pp. 43–4.
36. *Ibid.*, pp. 44–5.
37. Rendina, *Storia*, p. 184
38. Lançon, *Rome in Late Antiquity*, p. 121.
39. *Ibid.*, pp. 21–2.
40. *Ibid.*, pp. 14–15; Gatto, p. 120–1; Duffy, p. 46.
41. Rendina, *Storia*, pp. 184–9.
42. Gregorovius, *History*, Vol. 2, pp. 33–9; Duffy, pp. 46–7.
43. Visalli, *After Jesus*, pp. 318–20.
44. Duffy, *Saints and Sinners*, pp. 48–50.
45. *Ibid.*, pp. 54–7.
46. *Ibid.*, p. 45.
47. Lançon, *Rome in Late Antiquity*, p. 6–7.
48. Giada Lepri, *L'urbanistica di Borgo e Vaticano nel Medioevo*, Rome, 2004, pp. 16–17.
49. Lançon, *Rome in Late Antiquity*, p. 45.
50. Rendina, *Storia*, p. 184.
51. Duffy, *Saints and Sinners*, pp. 49–50.
52. *Ibid.*
53. Gregorovius, *History*, Vol. 2, pp. 32–3.
54. Duffy, *Saints and Sinners*, pp. 62–80.
55. *Ibid.*, pp. 64–5.
56. *Ibid.*, pp. 66–8.
57. Lepri, *L'urbanistica*, p. 21.
58. Rendina, *La grande guida*, p. 522.
59. Rendina, *Storia*, pp. 190–204.
60. Davis, *Liber Pontificalis*, pp. 66–7.
61. Rendina, *Storia*, p. 194.
62. Duffy, *Saints and Sinners*, pp. 60–1.
63. Davis, *Liber Pontificalis*, p. xlvi.

64. Rendina, *Storia*, p. 194.
65. Rendina, *Storia*, pp. 194–8.
66. Warren Treadgold, 'The struggle for survival (641–780)', in Cyril Mango (ed.), *The Oxford History of Byzantium*, Oxford, 2002, pp. 136–7; Rendina, *Storia*, p. 198.
67. Rendina, *Storia*, p. 198.
68. Treadgold, 'The struggle', pp. 129–31 and 138.
69. Duffy, *Saints and Sinners*, pp. 62–3.
70. *Ibid.*, pp. 63–4.
71. Rendina, *Storia*, p. 198.

Chapter Eleven

1. Rendina, *Storia*, p. 200.
2. Duffy, *Saints and Sinners*, pp. 68–9.
3. Rendina, *Storia*, p. 200.
4. Duffy, *Saints and Sinners*, p. 74.
5. Rendina, *Storia*, p. 200.
6. Duffy, *Saints and Sinners*, p. 69.
7. *Ibid.*, pp. 68–9.
8. *Ibid.*, pp. 71–2.
9. Rendina, *Storia*, p. 202.
10. *Ibid.*
11. Gregorovius, *History*, Vol. 2, pp. 304–6; Rendina, *Storia*, p. 204.
12. Rendina, *Storia*, p. 204.
13. Lepri, *L'urbanistica*, pp. 16–17.
14. Gregorovius, *History*, Vol. 2, pp. 316–18.
15. Lepri, *L'urbanistica*, p. 17.
16. Gregorovius, *History*, Vol. 2, pp. 318–20 and p. 318, fn. 2.
17. Lanciani, *Ancient Rome*, pp. 204–5.
18. Gregorovius, *History*, Vol. 2, p. 311.
19. *Ibid.*, p. 320.
20. *Ibid.*, pp. 335–9; Rendina, *Storia*, pp. 204–6.
21. Gregorovius, *History*, Vol. 2, pp. 338 and 345.
22. Duffy, *Saints and Sinners*, pp. 72–4; Rendina, *Storia*, p. 206.
23. Rendina, *Storia*, p. 206.
24. *Ibid.*, p. 208.
25. Duffy, *Saints and Sinners*, pp. 72–3.
26. Rendina, *Storia*, p. 208.
27. Gatto, *Storia di Roma nel Medioevo*, p. 124.
28. Friedrich Heer, *The Holy Roman Empire*, London, 1995, p. 13.
29. Rendina, *Storia*, p. 208.
30. Duffy, *Saints and Sinners*, pp. 73–4.
31. Coarelli, *Roma*, pp. 302–5 and 309–12.

32. Rendina, *La grande guida*, pp. 120–3.
33. Lepri, *L'urbanistica*, p. 24.
34. Gregorovius, *History*, Vol. 2, pp. 385–98.
35. *Ibid.*, pp. 410–19.
36. Rendina, *Storia*, pp. 208–10.
37. Duffy, *Saints and Sinners*, p. 75.
38. Rendina, *Storia*, p. 212.
39. Heer, *Holy Roman Empire*, pp. 9–11.
40. Rendina, *Storia*, p. 212.
41. *Ibid.*, pp. 213–14.
42. Heer, *Holy Roman Empire*, p. 11.
43. Gregorovius, *History*, Vol. 2, pp. 502–8.
44. Rendina, *Storia*, pp. 214–15.
45. Duffy, *Saints and Sinners*, p. 77.
46. Rendina, *Storia*, pp. 214–15.
47. Heer, *Holy Roman Empire*, pp. 11–13.
48. *Ibid.*, pp. 8–10.
49. *Ibid.*, pp. 1–2.
50. *Ibid.*, p. 9.
51. Rendina, *Storia*, p. 218.
52. *Ibid.*
53. *Ibid.*, pp. 218–21.
54. Heer, *Holy Roman Empire*, pp. 19–20; Hermann Kinder and Werner Hilgemann, *Penguin Atlas of World History*, Vol. 1, London, 1978, p. 125.
55. Rendina, *Storia*, p. 220.
56. Patrick J. Geary, *Furta Sacra. Theft of Relics in the Central Middle Ages*, Princeton, NJ, 1990, pp. 40–2.
57. Brusegan, p. 53; Rendina, *La grande guida*, pp. 415–16.
58. Gregorovius, *History*, Vol. 3, pp. 80–1.
59. Coarelli, *Roma*, p. 41.
60. Duffy, *Saints and Sinners*, p. 78.

Chapter Twelve

1. Letizia Pani Ermini, *Christiana Loca. Lo spazio cristiano nella Roma del primo millennio*, Rome, 2000, p. 20.
2. Rendina, *La grande guida*, p. 529.
3. Lanciani, *Pagan and Christian Rome*, pp. 135–41 and 286–7.
4. Gregorovius, *History*, Vol. 3, pp. 87–91.
5. Lorenzo Bianchi, 'Le Scholae Peregrinorum', in Pani Ermini (a cura di), *Christiana Loca. Lo spazio Cristiano nella Roma del primo millennio*, Rome, 2000, pp. 211–15.
6. Raymond Davis, *The Lives of the Ninth-century Popes (Liber Pontificalis)*, Liverpool, 1995, pp. 93–6.

7. Gregorovius, *History*, Vol. 3, p. 89.
8. Pani Ermini, *Christiana Loca*, p. 20.
9. Gatto, *Storia di Roma nel Medioevo*, p. 205.
10. Bianchi, 'Le Scholae', pp. 211–15.
11. Christine Huda Dodge, The Everything Understanding Islam Book, Bath, 2003, p. 120
12. Davis, *The Lives*, pp. 96–7 (fnn.).
13. Pani Ermini, *Christiana Loca*, p. 21.
14. Duffy, *Saints and Sinners*, pp. 5–6.
15. Gregorovius, *History*, Vol. 3, p. 89.
16. Philip K. Hitti, *The Arabs: A Short History*, Washington, DC, 1998, p. 205.
17. Federico Arborio Mella, *Gli Arabi e l'Islam*, Milan, 2000, pp. 176–9.
18. Davis, *The Lives*, pp. 93–6.
19. *Ibid.*, p. 96, fn. 92.
20. Arborio Mella, *Gli Arabi*, pp. 176–7.
21. Rendina, *Storia*, p. 222.
22. Gregorovius, *History*, Vol. 3, p. 89; Duffy, *Saints and Sinners*, p. 79; Pani Ermini, *Christiana Loca*, p. 21.
23. Paul Magdalino, 'The Medieval Empire (780–1204)', in Cyril Mango (ed.), *The Oxford History of Byzantium*, Oxford, 2002, pp. 170–1 and 184.
24. Lançon, *Rome in Late Antiquity*, p. 162.
25. Gatto, *Storia di Roma nel Medioevo*, pp. 204–5.
26. Jerome Murphy-O'Connor, *The Holy Land*, Oxford, 1998, p. 49.
27. Arborio Mella, *Gli Arabi*, pp. 199–200.

Chapter Thirteen

1. Gabriella de Falco, *Viscere di tufo. La città raccontata*, Mendicino, 1994, p. 7.
2. *Ibid.*
3. *Ibid.*, p. 8.
4. *Ibid.*
5. Cosenza, *Italy*, Touring Club of Italy, 1999, p. 171.
6. de Falco, *Viscere di tufo*, pp. 7–10.

Chapter Fourteen

1. Peter Padfield, *Himmler*, London, 2001, p. 10.
2. *Ibid.*, pp. 24–5.
3. *Ibid.*, p. 83.
4. *Ibid.*, pp. 170–4.
5. Christopher Hale, *Himmler's Crusade*, Hoboken, NJ, 2003, pp. 85–7.
6. *Ibid.*, p. 336.
7. Martin Gilbert, *The Second World War: A Complete History*, New York, 1991, pp. 128 and 438.

8. Hale, *Himmler's Crusade*, p. 336.

9. Fioriglio, 'La febbre di Alarico', pp. 122–3.

10. Tobia Cornacchioli, in Tobia Cornacchioli *et al.*, *Alarico. Re dei Visigoti*, Cosenza, 2000, p. 100.

11. *Ibid.*, pp. 97–107.

12. Fioriglio, 'La febbre di Alarico', pp. 116–17.

13. *Catholic Encyclopedia*, 1909; entry for Giordano Bruno.

14. Sabine Fröhlich, *Giordano Bruno und die Inquisition*.

15. Cornacchioli *et al.*, *Alarico*, pp. 99–100.

16. Kinder and Hilgemann, *Penguin Atlas of World History*, pp. 280–1.

17. *Ibid.*

18. Pantaleone Sergi, 'Indiana Jones Calabresi nella tomba di Alarico', *La Repubblica*, 14 May 2001.

19. Fioriglio, 'La febbre di Alarico', pp. 126–7.

20. Giossuè Carducci, 'Dalle "Ballate" di A.G. von Platen', *Scelta di poemi religiosi, morali, e patriotici*, L'Arpa del Popolo, 1855.

21. Kurt Wölfel and Jürgen Link, *August von Platen, Werke*, Vol. 1, 1982, p. 706.

22. Heer, *Holy Roman Empire*, p. 279.

23. Whitney Hall, *History of the World*, p. 380.

24. Cornacchioli *et al.*, *Alarico*, pp. 100–1.

25. *Ibid.*, pp. 102–3.

26. Benét's *Reader's Encyclopedia*, 3rd edn, 1987, p. 383.

27. George Gissing, *Notes of a Ramble in Southern Italy*, Vol. 3: *The Grave of Alaric*, London, 1901.

28. Fioriglio, 'La febbre di Alarico', p. 127.

29. *Ibid.*, p. 128.

30. Giovanni Fasanella, '*Tomba barbara o bufala calabra?*', *Panorama*, Anno XL, Nr. 35.

31. Fioriglio, 'La febbre di Alarico', p. 128.

32. *Ibid.*, pp. 127–9.

33. Paul Hofmann, 'Calabria by the sea', *New York Times*, 26 September 1999.

34. Donald Sommerville, *World War II Day by Day*, London, 1991, pp. 175–80.

35. Gilbert, *The Second World War*, p. 430.

36. *Ibid.*

37. *Ibid.*, p. 602.

38. Padfield, *Himmler*, pp. 610–11.

39. Hale, *Himmler's Crusade*, p. 371.

Chapter Fifteen

1. Gibbon, *Decline and Fall*, III, XXXI, V.

2. W.I. Thomas, 'Standpoint for the interpretation of savage society', *American Journal of Sociology* 15 (1909):145–63.

3. O'Donnell, 'The aims'.

4. Jordanes, *The Origin and Deeds of the Goths*.
5. 'Cassiodorus', *Encyclopædia Britannica*. Retrieved 11 August 2003, from Encyclopædia Britannica Premium Service. www. britannica.com/eb/article?eu=20987
6. O'Donnell, 'The aims'.
7. Henry Wace, *A Dictionary of Christian Biography and Literature to the End of the Sixth Century, with an Account of the Principal Sects and Heresies*; see entry for 'Jordanes, historian of the Goths'.
8. Rodolfo Lanciani, *Ancient Rome in the Light of Recent Discoveries*, Boston and New York, 1898, p. 291.
9. Paul Cristian Radu, 'Blestemul comorii lui Decebal', *Jurnalul Național*, 15 March 2004.
10. Wolfram, *History of the Goths*, pp. 160 and 440, n. 268.
11. Bunson, *Dictionary of the Roman Empire*, pp. 131–2.
12. Cassius Dio, *Roman History*, epitome of Book 68, 14.
13. Coarelli, *Roma*, p. 139, Fig. 109.
14. Bunson, *Dictionary of the Roman Empire*, p. 128.
15. Coarelli, *Roma*, pp. 138–9, Fig. 103.
16. Schwarcz, 'Cult and religion', pp. 463–4.
17. Jordanes, *The Origin and Deeds of the Goths*, XLIX.256–8.
18. Bóna, *Les Huns*, p. 74.
19. Sergi, '*Indiana Jones Calabresi*'.
20. Zosimus, *New History*, Book 5.
21. Bóna, *Les Huns*, pp. 74–5.
22. Procopius, *History*, VI.xxv. 6–11.

Chapter Sixteen

1. R.J.A. Talbert (ed.), *Barrington Atlas of the Greek and Roman World. Map-by-Map Directory*, Vol. 1. Princeton and Oxford, 2000, p. 699.
2. Istituto Nazionale de Economia Agraria. Programma Operativa Multiregionale. Reg (CEE) n. 2081/93-QCS 1994/99. Stato dell'Irrigazione in Calabria, p. 41.
3. Amato, '*Il tesoro di Alarico*'.
4. Jordanes, *The Origin and Deeds of the Goths*, XXX.
5. J. O'Donnell, *Cassiodorus*, Chap. 1: 'Background and some dates', 1995, pp. 2–6.
6. Barnish, *Cassiodorus Variae*, VIII.31.5, VIII.33.3–5, XII.12.
7. Talbert (ed.), *Barrington Atlas*, p. 642.

Chapter Seventeen

1. www.fondazionecraxi.org/home.htm
2. Magdi Allam, 'Troppo moderato, via il nuovo imam di Roma', *Corriere della Sera*, 16 May 2004.
3. Jeff M. Sellers, 'Flogged and Deported', *Christianity Today*, 22 April 2002.
4. Fioriglio, '*La febbre di Alarico*', pp. 129–31.

5. www.goldsucher.de
6. Fioriglio, '*La febbre di Alarico*', p. 130.
7. Hamilton, 'Spectrum'.
8. Wolfram, *History of the Goths*, Appendix 2.
9. Gregory of Tours, *History of the Franks*, II.37.
10. Procopius, *History*, V. xii. 36–45.
11. *Ibid.*, III, front flap.
12. *Ibid.*, IV. ix; Gregorovius, *History*, Vol. 1, pp. 215–17.
13. Procopius, *History*, IV.ix.
14. Peter Sarris, 'The Eastern Empire from Constantine to Heraclius', in Mango (ed.), *Oxford History of Byzantium*, p. 53.
15. Burns, *Ostrogoths*, pp. 67–8.
16. Zacharias of Mytilene, *Syriac Chronicle*, Book 10, Chap. 16.
17. Josephus Flavius, *The Jewish Wars*, Book V, Chap. 5.
18. Gregorovius, *History*, Vol. 1, p. 217.
19. Wolfram, *History of the Goths*, p. 221.
20. *Ibid.*, pp. 243–4.
21. Dietrich Claude, '*Beiträge zur Geschichte der frühmittelalterlichen Königschätze*', *Early Medieval Studies: Antikvariskt Arkiv* 54 (1973): 5–24.
22. Andrew Lang, *The Arabian Nights*, Sindbad Voyage 7.
23. Visalli, *After Jesus*, p. 292.
24. Procopius, *History*, V. xii. 36–45.
25. Gregorovius, *History*, Vol. 1, pp. 214–18.

Chapter Eighteen

1. Fioriglio, '*La febbre di Alarico*', pp. 130–1.
2. Gisela Ripoll Lopez, 'Symbolic life and signs of identity in Visigothic times', in Peter Heather (ed.), *The Visigoths*, San Marino, 1999, pp. 406–10.
3. Fasanella, *Tomba barbara*.
4. *Ibid.*
5. Sergi, '*Indiana Jones Calabresi*'.
6. Fioriglio, '*La febbre di Alarico*', p. 131.
7. *Ibid.*, pp. 131–4.
8. *Ibid.*, p. 134.
9. *Ibid.*, p. 135.
10. Talbert (ed.). *Barrington Atlas*, p. 696.
11. Fioriglio, '*La febbre di Alarico*', p. 113.
12. Talbert (ed.). *Barrington Atlas*, p. 697.
13. Wolfram, *History of the Goths*, p. 159.
14. Cristofori, *Gli spazi geografici*.
15. *Ibid.*
16. Talbert (ed.). *Barrington Atlas*, p. 701.

17. Visalli, *After Jesus*, pp. 299 and 340.

18. Ripoll Lopez, 'Symbolic life', p. 425.

19. Schwarcz, 'Cult and religion', p. 469.

20. Fioriglio, '*La febbre di Alarico*', pp. 131 and 134.

21. Claude, '*Beiträge*', pp. 5–24.

22. Burns, *Ostrogoths*, p. 171.

23. Wolfram, *History of the Goths*, p. 336.

24. *Ibid.*, pp. 14 and 228.

25. Fioriglio, '*La febbre di Alarico*', pp. 119–20.

26. Sergi, '*Indiana Jones Calabresi*'.

27. Fasanella, *Tomba barbara*.

Appendix Two

1. Rendina, *Storia*, p. 709, modified.

Bibliography

ANCIENT SOURCES

Ammianus Marcellinus, *The Later Roman Empire (A.D. 354–378)*, selected and trans. Walter Hamilton, London, 2004

Apollonius Rhodius, *Argonautica*, 303, ed. and trans. R.C. Seaton, Cambridge, MA, 1912. Courtesy www.sunsite.berkeley.edu

Barnish, S.J.B., *Cassiodorus: Variae*, trans. with notes and introduction by S.J.B. Barnish, Liverpool, 1992

Claudian, *Claudian*, trans. Maurice Platnauer, Vol. 2, Cambridge, MA, 1998

Davis, Raymond, *The Lives of the Ninth-century Popes (Liber Pontificalis)*, trans. with an introduction and commentary by Raymond Davis, Liverpool, 1995

——, *Liber Pontificalis* (The Book of Pontiffs), rev. edn, trans. with an introduction by Raymond Davis, Liverpool, 2000

Dio, Cassius, *Roman History*, trans. Earnest Cary, Cambridge, MA, 1914–27. Courtesy LacusCurtius, William P. Thayer. www.penelope.uchicago.edu/Thayer/

Eusebius, *Church History*. Courtesy www.newadvent.org

——, *Life of Constantine*. Courtesy Paul Halsall. www.fordham.edu/halsall/

Frontinus, Sextus Julius, *The Aqueducts of Rome*, Courtesy LacusCurtius, William P. Thayer. penelope.uchicago.edu/Thayer/

Gregory of Tours, *The History of the Franks*, trans. Lewis Thorpe, London, 1974

Jerome, St, *The Principal Works of St. Jerome*, ed. Philip Schaff. Courtesy Calvin College www.ccel.org

Jordanes, *The Origin and Deeds of the Goths*, trans. Charles C. Mierow. Courtesy J. Vanderspoel. www.ucalgary.ca

Josephus Flavius, *The Jewish Wars*, trans. William Whiston. Courtesy Calvin College www.ccel.org

Lactantius, *On the Death of the Persecutors*. Courtesy Calvin College www.ccel.org

Orosius, Paulus, *The Seven Books of History against the Pagans*, trans. Roy J. Deferrari. Washington, DC, 1981

Philostorgius, *Ecclesiastical History* (Epitome compiled by Photius, Patriarch of Constantinople), trans. Edward Walford. London. Henry G. Bohn, York Street, Covent Garden, 1755. Courtesy Calvin College www.ccel.org

230   *Bibliography*

Procopius, *History of the Wars*, Book 4, trans. H.B. Dewing, New York, 1916. Courtesy Paul Halsall. www.fordham.edu/halsall/

——, *History of the Wars*, Vol. 3 (Books 5–5.15), 4 (Books 6.16–7.35), and 5 (Books 7.36–8), trans. H.B. Dewing, Cambridge, MA, 2000

——, *Anecdota or Secret History*, Courtesy LacusCurtius, William P. Thayer. www.penelope.uchicago.edu/Thayer/

Socrates Scholasticus, *Ecclesiastical History*, ed. Philip Schaff. Courtesy Calvin College www.ccel.org

Sozomenus, *Ecclesiastical History*, ed. Philip Schaff. Courtesy Christian Classics Ethereal Library, Calvin College www.ccel.org

Tacitus, *La Germanie*, trans. Danielle De Clercq, Brussels, 2003. Courtesy Bibliotheca Classica Selecta, Catholic University of Louvain, Belgium. www.bcs.fltr.ucl.ac.be/Bib.html

Zacharias of Mytilene, *Syriac Chronicle*. Courtesy www.tertullian.org/fathers/

Zosimus, *New History*, London, 1814. Courtesy www.earlychristianwritings.com

MODERN SOURCES

Allam, Magdi, '*Troppo moderato, via il nuovo imam di Roma*', *Corriere della Sera*, 16 May 2004

Amato, Angelo Raffaele, 'Il tesoro di Alarico nell Cilento'. www.cilentohotel.com

Arborio Mella, Federico, *Gli Arabi e l'Islam*, Milan, 2000

Ball Platner, Samuel and Thomas Ashby, *A Topographical Dictionary of Ancient Rome*, London, 1929. William P. Thayer LacusCurtius. www.penelope.uchicago.edu/Thayer/

Barzini, L., *The Italians*, New York, 1965

Benét's *Reader's Encyclopedia*, 3rd edn, New York, 1987

Bernardi Salvetti, C.S., *Maria degli Angeli alle Terme e Antonio Lo Duca*, Rome, 1965

Bettenson, Henry and Maunder, Chris, *Documents of the Christian Church*, Oxford, 1999

Bianchi Bandinelli, Ranuccio, *Roma*, Vols 1 and 2. *Corriere della Sera*, 2005

Bianchi, Lorenzo, 'Le *scholae peregrinorum*', in Letizia Pani Ermini, a cura di, *Christiana Loca. Lo spazio Cristiano nella Roma del primo millennio*, Rome, 2000, pp. 211–15

Bóna, István, *Les Huns*, St Germain-du-Puy, 2002

Bouvier-Ajam, Maurice, *Attila. Le fléau de Dieu*, Paris, 1982

Boyle, Leonard, *St. Clement's Rome*, Rome, 1989

Brion, Marcel, *La vie d'Alaric*, Paris, 1930

Brown, Peter, *The Cult of the Saints*, Chicago, 1982

Brusegan, Marcello, *Storia insolita di Venezia*, Rome, 2003

Bunson, Mathew, *A Dictionary of the Roman Empire*, New York, 1991

Burns, Thomas, *A History of the Ostrogoths*, Bloomington and Indianapolis, 1991

Bury, J.B., *History of the Later Roman Empire*, London, 1923. William P. Thayer, LacusCurtius. www.penelope.uchicago.edu/Thayer/

——, *The Invasion of Europe by the Barbarians*, New York, London, 2000

Carducci, Giosuè, 'Dalle "Ballate" di A.G. von Platen. L'Arpa del Popolo', in *Scelta di poemi religiosi, morali, e patriotici*, 1855. Courtesy Giovanni della Casa Venturelli. www.Alaricvs.com

Catholic Encyclopedia, 1909 (online R. Knight 2005). Courtesy www.newadvent.org/cathen/

Cecchelli, Margherita, 'I luoghi di Pietro e Paolo', in Letizia Pani Ermini (ed.), *Christiana Loca*, Rome, 2000, pp. 89–97

Chevallier, Andrew, *The Encyclopedia of Medicinal Plants*, Montreal, 1996

Claude, Dietrich, '*Beiträge zur Geschichte der frühmittelalterlichen Königschätze*', *Early Medieval Studies: Antikvariskt Arkiv* 54 (1973): 5–24

Coarelli, Filippo, *Roma*, Milan, 1994 Codart www.codart.nl

Cornacchioli, Tobia, Luciana De Rose, Beniamino Fioriglio, Gian Piero Givigliano and Dora Ricca, *Alarico. Re dei Visigoti*, Cosenza, 2000

Cristofori, Alessandro, *Gli spazi geografici della Storia Romana: l'Italia. Regio III: Lucania et Bruttii*. Courtesy Progetto Telemaco. Universitá di Bologna. www.telemaco.unibo.it

de Falco, Gabriella, *Viscere di tufo. La città raccontata*, Mendicino, Cosenza, 1994

de Scudery, Georges, *Alaric ou Rome Vaincu*, The Hague, 1685

della Casa Venturelli, Giovanni, www.Alaricvs.com

Demandt, Alexander, '*So lange wird Germanien schon besiegt*', *Frankfurter Allgemeine Zeitung*, Nr. 156, S.8, 7 September 2003

Department of Archaeology of Rome, www.archeorm.arti.beniculturali.it/sma/eng/history.html

Diaz, Pablo C., 'Visigothic political institutions', in Peter Heather (ed.), *The Visigoths*, San Marino, 1999, p. 328

Duffy, Eamon, *Saints and Sinners. A History of the Popes*, Wales, 1997

Encyclopaedia Britannica, www.britannica.com

Farah, Caesar E., *Islam*, Hauppauge, NY, 1994

Fasanella, Giovanni, '*Tomba barbara o bufala calabra?*', *Panorama*, Anno XL, Nr. 35

Fioriglio, Beniamino, '*La febbre di Alarico*', in Tobia Cornacchioli, Luciana De Rose, Beniamino Fioriglio, Gian Piero Givigliano and Dora Ricca, *Alarico. Re dei Visigoti*, Cosenza, 2000, pp. 109–40

Fleming, John, Hugh Honour and Nikolaus Pevsner, *The Penguin Dictionary of Architecture*, London, 1991

Fröhlich, Sabine, *Giordano Bruno und die Inquisition*. www1.unibremen.de/~semiotik/inquisition.html

Gatto, Ludovico, *Storia di Roma nel Medioevo*, Rome, 2003

Geary, Patrick J., *Furta Sacra. Theft of Relics in the Central Middle Ages*, Princeton, NJ, 1990

Gibbon, Edward, *The Decline and Fall of the Roman Empire*, with notes by the Revd H.H. Milman, 1845. Courtesy www.cca.org

Gilbert, Martin, *The Second World War: A Complete History*, revd edn, New York, 1991

Gissing, George, *Notes of a Ramble in Southern Italy*, London, 1901. Courtesy Mitsuharu Matsuoka. www.lang.nagoya-u.ac.jp

Goffart, Walter, *Barbarians and Romans*, Princeton, NJ, 1980

Gregorovius, Ferdinand, *History of the City of Rome in the Middle Ages*, Vol. 1 (AD 400–568), New York, 2000; Vol. 2 (AD 568–800) and Vol. 3 (800–1002), New York, 2001

Hale, Christopher, *Himmler's Crusade*, Hoboken, NJ, 2003

Hall, Linda Jones, 'Cicero's "instinctu divino" and Constantine's "instinctu divinitatis": The Evidence of the Arch of Constantine for the Senatorial View of the Vision of Constantine', *Journal of Early Christian Studies* 6, no. 4 (winter 1998): 647–71

Hamilton, Alan, 'Spectrum: Past with a rich future. The world's archaeological treasures yet to be uncovered', *The Times*, 25 February 1986

Harl, Kenneth W., *Coinage in the Roman Economy, 300 B.C. to A.D. 700*, Baltimore and London, 1996

Heather, Peter, 'The Creation of the Visigoths', in P. Heather (ed.), *The Visigoths*, San Marino, 1999

——, *The Goths*, Oxford, 2002

Heer, Friedrich, *The Holy Roman Empire*, London, 1995

Hitti, Philip K., *The Arabs: A Short History*, Washington, 1998

Hofmann, Paul, 'Calabria by the sea', *New York Times*, 26 September 1999

Huda Dodge, Christine, *The Everything Understanding Islam Book*, Bristol, 2003

Istituto Nazionale de Economia Agraria, *Programma Operativa Multiregionale. Reg. (CEE) n.2081/93-QCS 1994/99. Stato dell'Irigazione in Calabria*

John Paul II, *Discorso del Santo Padre Giovanni Paolo II ai membri del Circolo di Roma*, 7 February, 1981. La Santa Sede. www.vatican.va

Johnson, Paul, *A History of the Jews*, London, 1987

Kinder, Hermann and Werner Hilgemann, *Penguin Atlas of World History*, Vol. 1, London, 1978

Krauss, Mathew and Andrew S. Jacobs, *Remains of the Jews: The Holy Land and Christian Empire in Late Antiquity*, Stanford, CA, 2004. See also *Bryn Mawr Classical Review* 3 September 2005

Krautheimer, Richard, *Rome: Profile of a City, 312–1308*, New Jersey, 1983

Lanciani, Rodolfo. *Ancient Rome in the Light of Recent Discoveries*, Boston and New York, 1898. Courtesy William P. Thayer, LacusCurtius. www.penelope.uchicago.edu/Thayer/

——, *Pagan and Christian Rome*, Boston and New York, 1892. Courtesy William P. Thayer, LacusCurtius. www.penelope.uchicago.edu/Thayer/

Lançon, Bertrand, *Rome in Late Antiquity*, New York, 2001

Lang, Andrew, *The Arabian Nights*, selected and ed. Andrew Lang. Courtesy The Free Library lang.thefreelibrary.com/Arabian-Nights

Leon, Harry J., *The Jews of Ancient Rome*, Peabody, 1995

Lepri, Giada, *L'urbanistica di Borgo e Vaticano nel Medioevo*, Rome, 2004

Liebeschuetz, J.W.H.G., *The Decline and Fall of the Roman City*, Oxford, 2001

MacDowal, Simon and Angus McBride, *Germanic Warrior. AD 236–568*, Oxford, 2003

Magdalino, Paul, 'The medieval empire (780–1204)', in Cyril Mango (ed.), *The Oxford History of Byzantium*, Oxford, 2002, pp. 169–208

Mango, Cyril (ed.), *The Oxford History of Byzantium*, Oxford, 2002

Mann, John, *Murder, Magic and Medicine*, Oxford, 2000

Mazzolai, Aldo, *Alarico: Nell'inerte Impero*, Florence, 1996

Murphy-O'Connor, Jerome, *The Holy Land*, Oxford, 1998

New Zealand Government www.trc.govt.nz

O'Donnell, J. James, 'The Aims of Jordanes', *Historia* 31 (1982): 223–40. Courtesy J. James O'Donnell. ccat.sas.upenn.edu

——, *Cassiodorus*. Courtesy J. James O'Donnell. E-text, 1995. ccat.sas.upenn.edu

Officer, Lawrence H. and Williamson, Samuel, *Computing 'real value' over time with a conversion from British pounds to US dollars, or vice versa*. Economic History Services, September 2005. www.eh.net.hmit/exchange/; www.measuringworth.com

Olariu, Cristian, 'Visigoths and Romans during the fourth-century A.D. assimilation, resistance, and cultural interferences', Analele Universităţii Bucureşti, *istorie*, 45 (1996): 31–6

Ollivier, Eric, '*Le temp s'est arrêtté à Cosenza*', *Le Figaro*, 25 December 2001

Padfield, Peter, *Himmler: Reichs Führer-SS*, London, 2001

Pani Ermini, Letizia, a cura di, *Christiana Loca. Lo spazio Cristiano nella Roma del primo millennio*, Rome, 2000

Pressly, I.P., *York*, London, Bombay, Toronto

Radu, Paul Cristian, '*Blestemul comorii lui Decebal*', *Jurnalul Naţional*, 15 March 2004

Rendina, Claudio (a cura di), *La grande enciclopedia di Roma*, Rome, 2000

——, *Storia insolita di Roma*, Rome, 2002

——, *La grande guida dei monumenti di Roma*, Rome, 2002

Ripoll Lopez, Gisela, 'Symbolic life and signs of identity in Visigothic times', in Peter Heather (ed.), *The Visigoths*, San Marino, 1999

Rutgers, Leonard Victor, *The Jews in Late Ancient Rome*, Leiden, Boston and Cologne, 1995

——, Klaas, van der Borg, Arie F.M. de Jong, Imogene Poole, 'Radiocarbon dating: Jewish inspiration of Christian Catacombs', *Nature*, 21 July 2005

Sarris, Peter, 'The Eastern Empire from Constantine to Heraclius', in Cyril Mango (ed.), *The Oxford History of Byzantium*, Oxford, 2002, pp. 19–70

Scagnetti, Francesco and Giuseppe Grande, Roman Antiquities Research Unit. Colour map of Imperial Rome, Rome, 2005

Schwarcz, Andreas, 'Cult and religion among the Tervingi and the Visigoths and their conversion to Christianity', in Peter Heather (ed.), *The Visigoths*, San Marino, 1999

Sellers, Jeff M., 'Flogged and Deported', *Christianity Today*, 22 April 2002. www.christianitytoday.com

Sergi, Pantaleone, 'Indiana Jones Calabresi nella tomba di Alarico', *La Repubblica*, 14 May 2001

Sommerville, Donald, *World War II Day by Day*, London, 1991

Soprintendenza Archeologica di Roma. www.archeorm.arti.beneculturali.it/sar2000/default.asp

Talbert, R.J.A. (ed.), *Barrington Atlas of the Greek and Roman World. Map-by-Map*

Directory, Vols 1 and 2. Princeton, NJ and Oxford, 2000

Thomas, W.I., 'Standpoint for the interpretation of savage society', *American Journal of Sociology* 15 (1909): 145–63. Courtesy Lloyd Gordon Ward and Robert Throop of Brock University, St Catharines, Canada. www.brocku.ca

Thompson, E.A., *Romans and Barbarians. The Decline of the Western Empire*, Madison, WI, 1982

Touring Club of Italy, *Italy*, Milan, 1999

Treadgold, Warren, 'The struggle for survival (641–780)', in Cyril Mango (ed.), *The Oxford History of Byzantium*, Oxford, 2002, pp. 129–52

Twigger, Robert, *Inflation: the value of the pound 1750–1998*. Economics policy and statistics section. House of Commons Library. Research paper 99/20, 23 February 1999. www.parliament.uk/commons/

Visalli, Gayla (ed.), *After Jesus. The Triumph of Christianity*, Pleasantville and Montreal, 1992

Wace, Henry, *A Dictionary of Christian Biography and Literature to the Sixth Century A.D., with an Account of the Principal Sects and Heresies*. Courtesy Calvin College www.ccel.org

Wallace-Hadrill, Andrew, *Ammianus Marcellinus. The Late Roman Empire*, introduction and notes, London, 1986

Whitney Hall, John (ed.), *History of the World*, North Dighton, 2002

Wölfel, Kurt, and Jürgen Link, *August Graf von Platen*, Munich, 1982. Courtesy www.lyrikwelt.de

Wolfram, Herwig, *History of the Goths*, Berkeley, Los Angeles and London, 1990

www.fondazionecraxi.org/biografia10.htm

www.goldsucher.de

Index

Note: major entries are in chronological order, where appropriate. Italic page numbers refer to maps.